Antiquing Weekends

52 EXCURSIONS ACROSS AMERICA

GLADYS MONTGOMERY

UNIVERSE

PHOTOGRAPHY CREDITS

The publisher would like to thank the following for permission to reproduce their photographs. All are courtesy of the inns, antiques dealers, and shows identified in captions, and of the photographers listed below.

Front cover: Photo Terry Donnelly/Getty Images, The Old Mill Shop, Osceola, WI.

Gavin Ashworth: 55. Frank Barnett Photography/Portland, OR: 99 (bottom), 168, 169, 170. Kurt Brokhausen: 122. Bruce Buck: 13 (left), 56. Tony Gravett: 49. John Jernigan: 97, 98. Paul Johnson Photography: 42, 43, 45. Jan Lee/Backyard Photography: 135. John M. Lewis Photography: 76. Jumping Rocks Photographic Services: 23, 81, 82. Karl Loveless: 124, 125. Gladys Montgomery: 3, 6 (top and middle left), 10, 36, 50, 101 (bottom), 119, 134. Peter Paige: 44, 46 (right). Corey Parton: 94. Randall Perry: 40, 41. Rare Brick: 6 (bottom), 70, 109, 160, 165, 166, 167, 214. Roger G. Reuillard, Art Specialties Maine: 19, 199. David Richmond: 103, 104. Hubert Schreibl: 24, 209. D. E. Smith Photography: 129, 130. Kevin Sprague: 34, 51, 194. Billy Struhs: 68, 89, 90, 91. Phuwadol Thamathitikhun: 142, 144, 206, 210. Robert Tinney: 106. Timothy White: 46 (left). Scott K. Wilson Photography: 29. Roy Wright: 6 (middle right), 57, 175. Rusty Yates: 32.

Circle details, courtesy of: Channel Road Inn Bed and Breakfast: 158. Chinaberry Hill: 17, 173, 193. Governor's House Inn: 68, 91. The Griswold Inn: 44. Historic Indian & World Tribal Arts Santa Fe: 151. Homestead Inn: 42. Houstonia Bed & Breakfast: 125. The Inn at Irving Place: 175. Inn at Occidental: 70, 109, 160, 166, 167, 214. Lion and the Rose Victorian Bed & Breakfast: 99, 170. Longwood Country Inn: 93. Photos by Gladys Montgomery: 21 (courtesy Elise Abrams Antiques); 35, 37, 136, 184 (courtesy Susan Silver Antiques); 38 (courtesy Berkshire Home & Antiques); 54, 61 (courtesy of Judd & Peg Gregory Antiques); 79, 105 (courtesy Judy Pascal); 85, 189, 213 (courtesy Painted Porch Antiques); 99, 164 (courtesy Brewster's Antiques); 128 (courtesy Blossom); 144 (courtesy Copake Auction). Norumbega Inn: 199. Roseland Plantation: 206, 210. Settler's Crossing: 74. Shaker Village of Pleasant Hill: 114. Stonover Farm Bed and Breakfast: 51, 194. Swann House Historic Dupont Circle Inn: 82. Wilburton Inn: 209.

Back cover: top, left: courtesy Garthoeffner Gallery and the Heart of Country Antiques Show; top, middle: Frank Barnett Photography/Portland, OR, courtesy The Lion and the Rose Victorian Bed & Breakfast; top, right: Billy Struhs, courtesy Governor's House Inn; bottom: Timothy White, courtesy The Griswold Inn. Circle detail: Gladys Montgomery, courtesy Susan Silver Antiques.

First published in the United States of America in 2006
by UNIVERSE PUBLISHING
A Division of Rizzoli International Publications, Inc.
300 Park Avenue South
New York, NY 10010
www.rizzoliusa.com

Project Editor: Sandra Gilbert
Designer: Victoria Pohlmann

ISBN-10: 0-7893-1372-3
ISBN-13: 978-0-7893-1372-0

Library of Congress Catalog Control Number: 2005935035
2006 2007 2008 2009 2010/10 9 8 7 6 5 4 3 2 1

Printed in the United States of America

OPPOSITE: A DISPLAY EVOKING 18TH-CENTURY LIFE INCLUDES CHINESE EXPORT PORCELAIN AND A PERIOD PORTRAIT AT PRAIRIE PEDDLER ANTIQUES IN ALTON, ILLINOIS.

Contents

CLOCKWISE FROM TOP: DISPLAY ROOM AT SUSAN SILVER ANTIQUES, SHEFFIELD, MASSACHUSETTS; THE SITTING ROOM OF THE INN AT IRVINGTON PLACE, NEW YORK CITY; GUEST ROOM AND ANTIQUE GLASSWARE AT THE INN AT OCCIDENTAL, SONOMA COUNTY, CALIFORNIA; AND EXTERIOR OF FREDERICK HATFIELD ANTIQUES, SHEFFIELD, MASSACHUSETTS.

Introduction

For the inveterate antiquer, or those of us who want a new diversion from weekend chores and errands, few things are more liberating or satisfying than to explore new or favorite territory, visit antiques shops, shows, or flea markets, and return home with something terrific. Antiquing enriches the experience of traveling, and it provides a reason to travel. One reason for this is that antiques dealers tend to live in places with beautiful scenery, historic architecture, good restaurants, and a wealth of cultural and outdoor activities.

This country offers countless antiquing opportunities. For a 230-year-old nation, we have a lot of objects, both homegrown and imported—from $8.5 million 18th-century Newport tea tables to $2,500 19th-century Chinese cupboards and $20 Depression glass compotes—enough to satisfy every level and sort of taste. Many states boast an "antiques capital," many tourist destinations at least one multi-dealer mall, and many a rural route claims its share of roadside sales, stretching up to 450 miles in length. In some areas of the country, you'll find mostly period pieces from the time when residential areas burgeoned. But you can also find New England antiques in Ohio, Florida, Texas, and California, and vice versa, because Americans have collected widely, and, when they have moved, they have taken their possessions with them.

Antiques dealers and show managers often talk about how the Internet has changed their businesses. People, especially those under 40, are not out there like they used to be. That's a shame, because for anyone who is attracted to antiques, online shopping is no substitute for being in a room full of wonderful objects.

Like travel, antiquing feeds one's curiosity. Once you begin looking at them and for them, objects are captivating, not just for their visual appeal, but for their stories and history. Shopping and talking with antiques dealers and collectors is one of the best ways to learn about what you're buying, but it also is a great experience in and of itself. Most collectors and dealers are doing what they do because some object once captured their imagination. The best dealers love what they sell, and it shows.

Although, strictly speaking, an antique is defined as an object that is 100 or more years old, this book also lists venues that carry mid-20th century pieces. It covers shops run by some of the country's pre-eminent individual dealers, along with antiques mega-malls, flea markets, and a few auctions. And it includes a show calendar provided by *The Magazine* ANTIQUES. Some dealers display their wares in multi-dealer shops and malls, and some only do shows. The truth is, you never know where something fabulous will turn up. An expert on Southern furniture describes his delight—and surprise—at finding a c.1875 Philadelphia pier table and hall tree (now in the Louisiana State University Museum of Art in Baton Rouge) in a Washington, Louisiana, antiques mall. True antiquers are rarely snobs about where they shop.

The antiquing destinations in this book include large cities and tiny towns and number many more than 52 (one for every weekend of the year). For instance, in the chapter on The World's Longest Yard Sale, you'll find listings for antiques shops in Louisville and Lexington, Kentucky, Chattanooga, Tennessee, and Birmingham, Alabama. Also mentioned are museums with decorative arts and antiques-related collections, historical museums, house museums with period furnishings, outdoor activities, and other diversions.

The best thing you can do as an antiquer is to educate yourself. Read about the objects that interest you, whether they're American, European or Asian, Pilgrim Century or ancient. Pick up a copy of Albert Sack's *Good, Better, Best, Superior, Masterpiece*,

IN TEXAS HILL COUNTRY, GUEST ACCOMMODATIONS AT SETTLER'S CROSSING ARE IN SEVEN RESTORED ANTIQUE BUILDINGS WITH 18TH- AND 19TH-CENTURY FURNISHINGS.

the Keno brothers' *Hidden Treasures,* or a book about a particular category of antiques, like textiles, glass, or ceramics. Watch *Find!* or *Antiques Roadshow,* subscribe to *The Magazine* ANTIQUES, *Antiques & Fine Art, Antiques and the Arts Weekly, Maine Antique Digest,* or a regional antiquing publication. Study pieces in stores and museums, at antiques shows, and at auction previews. If you're interested in furniture, learn to "read" it. Generally speaking, a piece in original condition will be valued more highly than a repaired or refinished piece. And, since the 100-year criteria defining what pieces are antique now covers turn-of-the-century items, important distinctions are when a piece was made and whether it was mass-produced or not. Style, type of wood, and construction details like pegs, tenons, dovetails, hand-hewn wood in drawers, hardware, finishes,

FINE COLONIAL REVIVAL WOODWORK GRACES A CABINET AT CHINABERRY HILL INN IN TACOMA, WASHINGTON.

and repairs speak volumes about when, where, and how something was made. There's no better way to develop a sense of relative value or to understand what you're buying. It's not always easy to spot a fake.

It is also important to understand how an object increases in value and price according to how many times it changes hands and who's touched it. First, the matter of provenance: A Chippendale chair with a well-documented history of ownership by George Washington might bring ten times the price of a comparable chair, merely because of its provenance. Second, the matter of mark-up: this occurs every time an object changes hands. A "picker" (who scours the countryside for antiques and sells them to dealers) might purchase an early-19th-century painted table for $200 at a small-town estate sale, and sell it to a dealer who prices it at $900 at a show. If a city dealer with an upscale clientele then acquires the table, he or she might sell it for $5,000 or more. One of the thrills of antiquing is discovering a special object at an undervalued price.

Many shows, including those in major cities, include a preview party the evening before the show opens, a social occasion that allows early buying. At smaller and outdoor shows, dealers may be buying from one another while unpacking their trucks, so it often pays to be an early bird at these shows. Conversely, bargains can sometimes be negotiated at the end of a show. Usually, the admission for early buying is higher than for the normal run of a show. Shipping is widely available, but you may want to factor this cost into your budget. At outdoor shows, dress for the weather and for walking, and bring cash and a checkbook. Not all dealers at shows process credit cards. Auctions can also yield amazing finds, and the best advice is to examine pieces carefully at the preview and set your spending limit. At shows and in antiques shops, it's all right to ask, "What's your best price on this?"

When using this book, please keep in mind that show dates and venues change, and it's best to check these before making travel plans. Shop hours change, sometimes seasonally, and many dealers prefer to open by appointment (or chance), so it's wise to call ahead. There are enough listings in this book to get you started, but most destinations contain many more shops than space allowed us to list. Before you go, you can check on the Internet. When you're out antiquing, local dealer recommendations will lead you to additional shops.

One lifetime can contain only so many objects. Choose the ones that really speak to you—and the best you can afford—and enjoy the thrill of the hunt.

AN EMPIRE BUREAU IN GREY PAINT IS TOPPED WITH FARMHOUSE
ACCESSORIES AT SHELTON ANTIQUES IN ALTON, ILLINOIS.

New England

Down East Maine

I n Maine, the term "Down East" refers to the state's northern coast, from Bangor east to Lubec, the easternmost town in the U.S. It encompasses yachting harbors, Campobello Island (Franklin Delano Roosevelt's summer retreat), Acadia National Park, and Cadillac Mountain, the first place in the U.S. to glimpse the sunrise. Summer is short here, and weekends are precious. A great way to spend one is antiquing in the Deer Isle and Blue Hill area.

This area doesn't have a large number of shops, but what is there is choice, and the scenery is beautiful, with boulder-strewn fields, acres of blueberries, pine forests, tidal flats, intimate coves, and ocean views. The nation's longest-running summer antiques show is held in Blue Hill on the first weekend in August; sponsored by the George Stevens Academy, it attracts some of Maine's top dealers. On the third Sunday

AT OAKLAND HOUSE SEASIDE INN ON EGGEMOGGIN REACH, ONE ACCOMMODATION IS SHORE OAKS, A 1907 ARTS & CRAFTS MAINE COTTAGE. A ROOM UNDER THE EAVES SHOWCASES MISSION FURNITURE AND ACCESSORIES, AND COMES WITH A BONUS—THE SOUND OF WAVES LAPPING ON THE ROCKY SHORE.

EAGULL GALLERY IN STONINGTON IS THE ONLY ANTIQUES STORE IN TOWN, AND WORTH THE TRIP FOR ITS WELL-CHOSEN AMERICAN AND WEST INDIAN FURNITURE, DECORATIVE ACCESSORIES, AND ART, AND FOR A VIEW OF ONE OF THE PRETTIEST HARBORS IN MAINE.

in July, at the Blue Hill Fairgrounds, the Downeast Antiques Fair features over 70 dealers from as far away as Florida; the same show runs again on a Tuesday and Wednesday in mid-August. As for antiques shops, Blue Hill has several; a few dot the road to Deer Isle Village, and there are some in Stonington, Sargentville, Brooklin, and other towns. On the coast nearby, Ellsworth's Big Chicken Barn and shops in Searsport offer additional antiquing opportunities.

Competing with antiques for attention are restaurants and lobster pounds, art and photographic galleries, artisan potters and weavers, the Haystack Mountain School of Crafts, the Woodenboat School, Nervous Nellie's Jams and Jellies, and the museum home of Jonathan Fisher, the redoubtable folk artist who was Blue Hill's first pastor. In Stonington, visitors cruise on a schooner or lobster boat, or hop the ferry to Isle au Haut. Arts venues include the old Stonington Opera House, with theater, music and dance performances, and the Kneisel Hall Music Festival. The Penobscot Marine Museum in Searsport is worth a visit.

For an in-town lodging, visitors often choose the Blue Hill Inn or Stonington's Inn on the Harbor, and with advance planning one can stay at a bed and breakfast at Isle au Haut's lighthouse. But the quintessential summer lodging in Maine is the "cottage" on the rocky shoreline, the kind of place that has been in the same family for generations. Oakland House, in Brooksville, is that kind of place.

Oakland House was opened in 1889 by an enterprising sea captain who hung a sign that still welcomes guests today. Accommodations include 14 rustic cottages, a mansard-roofed hotel with wraparound porches, and Shore Oaks, a 1907 Craftsman cottage with authentic Arts & Crafts furnishings. There's New England cuisine with vegetables fresh from the hotel's gardens, a library with volumes spanning 100 years, a lobster cookout every Thursday on the beach, and the original 1889 tubs with five faucets, which provided salt and fresh water for the spa baths popular then. An office contains a fax and Internet service, but the sound of gulls, seals, and bell buoys substitutes for telephones and television. With swimming, a dock and moorings, hikes, and a breathtaking view of Eggemoggin Reach and the Pumpkin Island lighthouse from old-fashioned rocking chairs on the porch, guests face only one gnawing question: How many antiques stores does one need to visit in a weekend, anyway?

BEFORE YOU GO, visit
www.visitmaine.com/seasonal/fall/attract_trail_east.php
www.maineantiques.org
www.maineantiquedigest.com

FAVORITE LODGING:
Oakland House Seaside Inn
435 Herrick Road
Brooksville, ME 04617
207-359-8521; 800-359-7352
ww.oaklandhouse.com

THIS REVERSE PAINTING ON GLASS ON A C.1840 MANTEL CLOCK ECHOES A MOTIF SEEN IN PERIOD THEOREM PAINTINGS.

Vermont's Champlain Valley & Quebec's Eastern Townships

I t's a tossup whether Vermont's northwestern corner is better for antiquing than Quebec's Eastern Townships. Fortunately, as these two areas are just a short distance apart, it's possible to explore them both over a long weekend or two. Vermont's Lake Champlain Valley and Quebec's Eastern Townships—called Cantons d'Est in French and known for their French-inflected New England ambiance—are gorgeous places, with breathtaking lake and mountain scenery, picturesque rural towns, and roads dotted with old one-room schoolhouses. Some of the area's other delights include local cheeses and wines, and the maple syrup and maple sugar candy produced from the sap of the sugar maples, which, in autumn, splash the Quebec and Vermont landscape with red, orange, and gold. In winter, at Quebec's Bromont Ski Resort, *tire sur la neige*, a taffylike popsicle, is made from warm maple syrup and snow. Is Quebec's maple syrup better than Vermont's? That's another tossup.

DELICATELY PATTERNED WALLPAPER, A COTTAGE-STYLE DRESSER, AND A KING-SIZE FOUR-POSTER BED MIX HAPPILY IN THE NANTUCKET ROOM OF BURLINGTON'S WILLARD STREET INN, AN IMPRESSIVE 1880S BRICK MANSION WITH A VIEW OF LAKE CHAMPLAIN.

THE FRONT DOOR OF THE WILLARD STREET INN, A QUEEN ANNE/
GEORGIAN REVIVAL MANSION, OPENS TO A STRIKING CHERRY-PANELED
FOYER AND GRAND STAIRCASE. A MARBLE-FLOORED SOLARIUM IS AMONG
THE ORIGINAL FEATURES GUESTS ENJOY TODAY.

Antiques stores in the Lake Champlain Valley and southern Quebec have a wonderful array of country and vintage furnishings, with some formal pieces, many farmhouse finds, and country pieces with time-worn painted surfaces. You will also see early-20th-century pieces, including Arts & Crafts and Colonial Revival, along with some wonderful china, glassware, and textiles. It's interesting to note the stylistic differences between 19th-century New England and Canadian country furniture; the latter is often French-influenced, chunkier, a bit more rustic, and with wonderful color.

On the U.S. side of the border, shops are scattered throughout northeastern Vermont. Burlington, Vermont's largest city, has about six antiques shops, and within 40 miles are shops on the Lake Champlain islands and in the towns of Colchester, Winooski, Essex Junction, Shelburne, New Haven, Basin Harbor, Ferrisburgh, Charlotte, Middlebury, Vergennes, and St. Albans. In Quebec's Eastern Townships, there's antiquing in North Hatley, Knowlton (Lac Brome), and Eastman; you'll also find a shop or two in Magog and Sutton, which are just five miles from the U.S. border. For big-city antiquing in Canada, head for Montreal or for the Rue Saint-Paul in the Old Port area of Quebec City. In mid-October, Eastman, Quebec, holds an annual Friday/Saturday/Sunday antiques show, which draws 30 dealers.

On the shore of Lake Champlain, Burlington, settled in 1773, is an old industrial town with an active nightlife, particularly in the Church Street Marketplace, with its boutiques, nightclubs, and restaurants. Burlington's waterfront park is ideal for a sunset picnic and recreation, and serves as a point of departure for lake cruises. Southeast of Burlington, in Waterbury, a visit to Ben & Jerry's ice cream factory gives new meaning to the phrase "destination dining."

Museums in northwestern Vermont include the Robert Hull Fleming Museum, with fine art and anthropological items, and the Ethan Allen Homestead, a restored

1787 farmhouse that was home to Vermont's founder and Revolutionary War hero, Ethan Allen; both are in Burlington. The Rokeby Museum, once the home of Quaker pioneers and a stop on the Underground Railroad, is in Ferrisburgh. In Middlebury are the Henry Sheldon Museum of Vermont History, poet Robert Frost's home, and the Middlebury College Museum of Art, with its collections of Cypriot pottery, 19th-century European and American sculpture, and contemporary prints. You can taste Vermont wines at Boyden Valley, sample local cheeses, or explore a maze in a cornfield (www.vermontcornmaze.com).

In Shelburne, the Shelburne Museum is a must-see for lovers of Americana. With over 150,000 objects spanning four centuries, its outstanding collections include 25 19th-century structures (including a covered bridge, a round barn, a lighthouse, and the restored 220-foot steamboat *Ticonderoga*, a National Historic Landmark), folk and decorative arts, tools, toys, textiles, and works by Monet, Manet, Cassatt, Degas, Andrew Wyeth, Thomas Cole, Winslow Homer, and Grandma Moses.

Quebec's Eastern Townships cover a 1,900-square-mile area, and are a favorite summer and weekend destination for Montreal residents. North Hatley, situated at the outlet of Lake Massawippi, was founded in 1776 by British loyalists from the American colonies, and it became the summer haven of choice for Southern aristocrats after the Civil War. Today, it's a delightful village, with pre-1900 farmhouses and Victorian cottages, a pretty lakefront, and clusters of antiques shops, art galleries, and stores selling British imports, from Yorkshire teas to Aran sweaters. Knowlton is also known as Lac Brome, while North Hatley is still an Anglophile's haven, having refused to change its name to Hatley Nord. Museums in this area include the Brome County Museum and the c.1854 Knowlton Academy in downtown Knowlton. In the Eastern Townships, you can follow the Dunham Valley wine route, tour an old copper mine at the Mines Capelton, or visit two Benedictine abbeys—Saint Benedict and Saint-Benoit-du-Lac—where Gregorian chants are sung at vespers and you may sample cheeses and cider made by the monks.

The lakes and mountains of northwestern Vermont and the Eastern Townships offer numerous outdoor activities, and several towns have lovely lakefronts studded with parks and restaurants. Art galleries are many, and performing arts offerings include theater, concerts, and festivals. In Alburg, Vermont, there is the Lake Champlain Bluegrass Festival; in North Hatley, the Piggery is Quebec's longest-running summer theater. This area is a paradise for skiers and snowboarders: Stowe is just 36 miles east of Burlington. The Eastern Townships encompass four ski areas: high-tech Orford, Owl's Head, the idyllic Mont Sutton Bromont (where slopes are open on alternate Saturdays until 3 a.m. and offer a view of the Montreal skyline). Skiing closest to the city of Montreal is at Mont Tremblant.

This part of Vermont and the Eastern Townships boast several historic inns where decor includes antique furnishings. Good choices in North Hatley include Auberge Hatley, a 1903 mansion with 23 antiques-decorated rooms, Tapioca Bed and Breakfast, and Manoir Hovey, a c.1900 mansion built to resemble George Washington's Mount Vernon, with 40 antiques-furnished rooms, a private beach, and golf. Other options are Auberge le St.-Amour, a turn-of-the-century mansion, now an eight-room inn, in Sutton, and the 1874 Lakeview Inn in Knowlton. Several inns contain gourmet restaurants.

In northwestern Vermont, some favorite inns among antiquers are the Swift House Inn in Middlebury, the North Hero House in North Hero, the Queen Anne-style Heart of Village Inn and the farmhouse Willow Pond Inn in Shelburne, and the Queen Anne Lang House on Main Street in Burlington. One of the nicest is Burlington's Willard Street Inn, built in the late 1880s, a luxurious brick Queen Anne mansion with stunning original woodwork and lighting, coffered ceilings, period wallpaper and furnishings, a solarium overlooking English gardens, and 14 individually appointed guest rooms, each with a private bath. There, you can enjoy a pleasant stroll to Lake Champlain or Marketplace restaurants, sip tea in the parlor, play a game of bocci ball or croquet on the lawn, or make your friends jealous with weekend antiquing updates through the inn's wireless Internet access.

BEFORE YOU GO, visit
www.vtliving.com/antiques/burl.shtml
www.easterntownships.org
www.northhatley.net

FAVORITE LODGING:
The Willard Street Inn
349 South Willard Street
Burlington, VT 05401
800-577-8712
www.willardstreetinn.com

Mid-Coast Maine

E specially in summer and in autumn, few places in the U.S. can compete with Maine as an ideal place to spend a weekend or vacation. Its rocky shoreline and breathtaking ocean views, pine forests, perennial gardens and fields of lupine, temperatures rising to the 80s by day and dipping to the 40s at night, salt- and pine-scented air, fresh seafood, and down-to-earth character have attracted visitors for over a century. Many agree with the state slogan: This is "The Way Life Should Be."

Along Maine's mid-coast, from Portland to Rockland, and in communities a short distance inland, the Maine Antiques Dealers Association lists over 180 dealers. Its brochure, with names and locations, is available locally; its website (www.maine antiques.org) is searchable by locale and specialty. In addition, this area has myriad summer weekend flea markets, annual shows, and high-quality auctions. *The Maine Antique Digest* (www.maineantiquedigest .com), one of the country's most respected antiquing publications, offers extensive information on dealers, shows, and auctions in the state and beyond. Portland and nearby Scarborough, Cape Elizabeth, Falmouth, and Yarmouth each have a number of dealers.

North of Portland, Route 1 meanders up the coast through a number of antiquing havens, including Bath, Newcastle, Thomaston, Camden, Lincolnville, and Rockland. In Wiscasset there's sometimes a traffic jam during summer—not a problem for antiquers stopping to explore the town's 15 shops for country furniture and folk and decorative arts.

The Maine Antiques Dealers Association sponsors two high-quality annual shows in this area: a midweek coastal show in

BUILT IN 1886, THE NORUMBEGA INN, OVERLOOKING PENOBSCOT BAY, BOASTS ORNATE WOODWORK AND STAINED-GLASS WINDOWS, SUCH AS THE ONE IN ITS LIBRARY ROOM.

A BOOTH AT THE MAINE ANTIQUES FESTIVAL HELD IN UNION HINTS AT THE WONDERFUL OBJECTS TO BE FOUND AT THIS ANNUAL AUGUST SHOW.

Damariscotta in late August and a Thursday–Friday show in Portland in mid-September. These bring together about 70 member dealers from Maine and elsewhere. The accent is on Americana, with refined and country furniture and accessories, folk art, ceramics, and glass. The show opens on Thursday at 10 a.m., and with a policy of no early buying, shoppers begin lining up at about 8 a.m. Though usually held in Portland, the show's location is subject to change; it's best to check the Association's website.

Another show the antiquing cognoscenti don't like to miss is the annual outdoor/indoor Maine Antiques Festival held on a weekend in mid-August at the fairgrounds in Union, a short jog inland. "The Union Show," as it's known, features over 200 dealers from the New England, South, Mid-Atlantic, and Midwest regions, a well as Texas and Canada. It's prime shopping territory for rustic and "high country" furniture, European and Asian pieces, paintings, vintage pull-toys, cottage bedroom sets, hooked rugs and textiles, art pottery, china and silver, jewelry, folk art, and more.

If your idea of "the way life should be" involves seafood caught the day you eat it, tennis, golf, sailing, canoeing, kayaking, fishing, horseback riding, or hiking, then Maine is a good place to be. Recreational opportunities include windjammer, whale watching and other cruises out of Portland, Camden, and Rockland. There's also music, summer theater, and museums including the Maine Maritime Museum and its 1886 Donnell House in Bath; Historic New England's Nickels-Sortwell House and Castle Tucker in Wiscasset; and the Farnsworth Museum in Rockland, with its collection of landscapes and seascapes, featuring many by members of the Wyeth family. Portland holds its Old Port Festival the first Sunday in June, and Rockland's Lobster Festival, which takes place the first weekend in August, is as colorful as those scarlet crustaceans, even if you're disinclined to eat them. Another option is to drive an hour or so inland to explore antiques shops in Augusta, Hallowell, and Gardiner, or to take a ferry to one of the islands in Penobscot Bay.

Portland's historic house museums include the McClellan-Sweat House, part of the Portland Art Museum; the Wadsworth-Longfellow House, home of the Maine Historical Society; Victoria Mansion, a stunning Italianate villa with 90% of its original features intact; and the 18th-century Georgian-style Tate House. Portland also has a Museum of African Tribal Art. The city's historic Old Port is a six-block area of antique buildings and cobblestone lanes between Commercial and Congress streets.

For mid-coast lodgings, some top choices in Portland are the c.1830 Percy Inn, a brick row house in the West End Historic District at Longfellow Square; the c.1869 Inn on Carlton, on the Western Promenade; and the c.1836 Pomegranate Inn, also in the historic Western Promenade neighborhood. In Wiscasset, Marston House bed and breakfast, in a carriage house adjacent to a country antiques store, is distinguished by its fresh country styling, and two cozy, romantic guest rooms with fireplaces but *sans* TV and other distractions. Just north of the village of Camden, on Route 1, one of Maine's poshest bed and breakfasts, the Norumbega, stands on a hill overlooking Penobscot Bay. Built in 1886 in the style of a European castle, it is richly detailed with opulent golden oak paneling and carved woodwork, stained-glass windows, and many fireplaces. With comfortable period and upholstered furniture, its traditional interiors, wonderful breakfasts, and cocktail hour evoke the elegant confidence of old money. Given the wealth of antiquing opportunities along Maine's mid-coast, almost anyone might wish they had more of that.

BEFORE YOU GO, visit
www.maineantiques.org
www.maineantiquefest.com
www.maineantiquedigest.com

FAVORITE LODGINGS:

Marston House
Main Street
Wiscasset, ME 04578
207-882-6010
www.marstonhouse.com

Norumbega Inn
63 High Street
Camden, ME 04843
207-236-4646
www.norumbegainn.com

Southern Vermont: Manchester & Dorset

The image of picturesque New England—white clapboard buildings with dark shutters arrayed around a village green, tree-lined streets, pristine church steeples against the sky—is typical of so many small Vermont towns. With its crisp air, proud mountains, bucolic scenery, and sugar maples that are a riot of red, orange, and gold in autumn, Vermont is visually stunning and historically evocative. Maybe that's why it's home to some of New England's outstanding antiques dealers, with wonderful 18th- and 19th-century formal and country American furniture, folk art, and decorative accessories, including quilts, hooked rugs, and other textiles.

A drive around southern Vermont will take you through many of those quintessentially New England towns. Within 50 miles of Manchester are more than 75 dealers, tucked away in the Dorsets, Arlington, Bennington, Danby, Wallingford, Wilmington, Chester, Londonderry, Williamsville, Townshend, and Newfane, with many along and off of Routes 7 and 30. The Vermont Antiques Dealers' Association's website (www.vermontada.com) and brochure, available locally, contain lists of shops and dealers. Though the accent here tends to be on American and fine country furniture, you'll also find tramp art and similar rustic items, European and Scandinavian pieces, cottage furnishings, and sporting items. If you're making an extended trip here or want other options in the area, good antiquing also can be found across the border in Glens Falls, Saratoga Springs, and other New York towns; in the Berkshires area of Massachusetts 75 miles to the south; and in southwest New Hampshire; or you can continue north on Route 7 to Burlington, Vermont, and Quebec's Eastern Townships.

On the last weekend of September, the Vermont Antiques Dealers' Association Show, a Saturday/Sunday event held indoors at Hunter Park Pavilion in Manchester Center, draws about 75 exhibitors with top-quality country and folk art pieces, and more formal high country furniture; its preview party is on Thursday evening. The Hildene Antiques Show is usually held on the Sunday of that same weekend with 70 exhibitors, who display items with a New England country sensibility on the front lawn of the Hildene Mansion in Manchester Village.

This area also has numerous smaller shows. In early July, a one-day Saturday show that alternates location between Dorset and Hildene draws 130 dealers. Then on the

THE PORCH AT THE FOUR COLUMNS INN OFFERS A QUINTESSENTIAL VERMONT
VIEW OF NEWFANE'S CLASSIC VILLAGE GREEN AND STEEPLED WHITE CHURCH.

last weekend in July, the Saturday/Sunday Green Mountain Antiques Show gathers 55 dealers in Woodstock. Newfane holds its annual Saturday show in mid-February. Bennington's Stoneware Collectors' Friday/Saturday Show is in late April; Manchester's Friday/Saturday Fly Fishing and Sporting Antiques and Collectibles show is the last weekend in June. In autumn, Weston's Friday/Saturday/Sunday show is held the last weekend in September; the Bromley Mountain Saturday/Sunday show is the first weekend in October at its base lodge in Peru; Manchester's annual show is the first Sunday in October; and Ludlow's two shows (one at the Okemo Mountain Resort, the other one at the high school) are held the first Saturday of October, with previews Friday night. Other shows have previews on the evening preceding the start of the show.

Southern Vermont's two largest outdoor flea markets are in Wilmington (a Saturday/Sunday event from the last weekend in May through mid-October) and in Newfane (on Sundays, May through October). Local auctions and estate sales are also a great way to find things. One good bet is Hersom Estate Sales, based in Dorset; collectors typically line up before sunrise.

Founded in 1761, Manchester was an early industrial town where water-powered mills finished marble quarried in Dover, 45 miles to the northwest. In the mid-19th century, southern Vermont became a popular summer destination. Among those who vacationed here were Mary Todd Lincoln and her sons, who planned to return in 1865 with President Lincoln, a trip never taken because of his assassination. In 1905, Robert

IN MANCHESTER, THE WILBURTON INN, A TUDOR-STYLE MANSION WITH COFFERED CEILINGS, OPULENT PANELING, AND ANTIQUES-FILLED GUEST ROOMS, IS A FAVORITE PLACE TO STAY DURING THE DORSET, HILDENE, AND VERMONT DEALERS' ASSOCIATION SHOWS.

Todd Lincoln returned to the place he loved as a child, and built Hildene, a magnificent Georgian-style mansion. Set on 500 acres with extensive meadows and formal gardens planted in 1907, and furnished with antiques, it is a museum and venue for many events, including a garden show and a classic and antique car show, both held in June.

The Green Mountains begin at the Massachusetts border and continue through Vermont to the Canadian border. The mountains' Long Trail, established between 1910 and 1930, is the oldest long-distance trail in the U.S. There's hiking all along this "footpath in the wilderness." Vermont offers some of the best downhill skiing in the East, trout fishing in the spring, and numerous other outdoor sports. There are arts and crafts festivals, art exhibits, county fairs, Revolutionary War and Civil War encampments and reenactments, and a full calendar of music and other performing arts offerings. Known for the dairy farms that dot its verdant landscape, Vermont is a leading cheese maker; its many boutique cheeses and the ever-reliable cheddar made in Grafton are perfect to enjoy on a picnic or on the front porch of the area's wood-floored, tin-ceiling country stores, while admiring distant mountain peaks. In this area, a good meal and a quaint inn are never far away.

The Bennington Museum contains the largest public collection of Grandma Moses paintings and memorabilia; military and historical artifacts such as the Bennington Flag, thought to be the oldest Stars and Stripes in existence; early tools, dolls, and toys; 19th- and 20th-century American glass; American art; and 18th- and 19th-century American furniture; and an outstanding collection of Bennington pottery.

Historic sites include the 1865 Park-McCullough House, a 35-room Victorian mansion in North Bennington; the Vermont Covered Bridge Museum in Bennington; the Bennington Center for the Arts with wildlife art, and Native American and Navajo rugs; the Wayside Country Store in Arlington; Robert Frost's Stone House Museum in Shaftsbury; Adam's Old Stone Grist Mill Museum in Bellow's Falls; the Estey Organ Museum in Brattleboro; the Brattleboro Museum and Art Center, housed in the 1849 railroad depot; the Farrar-Mansur House and the Old Mill Museum in Weston; and Weston's historic 1838 Church on the Hill, which hosts evening concerts in summer.

Two favorite places to stay are the Four Columns Inn in Newfane and the Wilburton Inn in Manchester Village. The Four Columns Inn is a glorious Greek Revival mansion on a tranquil village green, next door to a white-steepled church and overlooking fields, streams, and ponds, at the foot of a 150-acre private mountain. Its elegant interiors mix vibrant colors and lively fabrics with antique and period-appropriate furnishings, and its luxury amenities include gas fireplaces, private baths, spa tubs, sitting areas, TVs and DVD players, an award-winning restaurant, and an elegant breakfast buffet. The Wilburton Inn, once part of Hildene, is a stately turn-of-the-century brick Tudor mansion, situated on the crest of a cliff overlooking Battenkill Valley, the focal point of a 20-acre property that contains tennis courts, a swimming pool, and perennial and sculpture gardens. The 35 rooms in the mansion and other buildings are beautifully appointed with period and antique furnishings, and feature private baths and fireplaces. At breakfast, the dining room table is set with gleaming silver, crystal, and fresh flowers from the inn's gardens. Whether you choose the fantasy of a glamorous mansion or that of a classical white-clapboard house on a village green, you're unlikely to be disappointed with the accommodations or the antiquing in this part of Vermont.

BEFORE YOU GO, visit
www.travel-vermont.com
www.vermontlife.com
www.manchestervermont.com
www.antiquing.com
www.vermontada.com
www.hildene.org

FAVORITE LODGINGS:

The Four Columns Inn
On the Green
Newfane, VT 05345
800-787-6633
www.fourcolumnsinn.com

The Wilburton Inn
River Road (off Historic Route 7A)
Manchester Village, VT 05254
802-362-2500; 800-648-4944
www.wilburton.com

New Hampshire Antiques Week

By one informed estimate, during the nine-day period in early August that marks New Hampshire Antiques Week, an average of a million dollars a day might change hands. Most of it is spent on fine Americana, particularly New England antiques. This is a week that collectors don't want to miss.

The centerpiece, the New Hampshire Antiques Show, a high-caliber event sponsored annually for nigh on 50 years by the New Hampshire Antiques Dealers Association (NHADA), features some 65 dealers with objects of exceptional quality, ranging from formal furniture and fine decorative accessories to country primitives and folk art. Held in Manchester and running Thursday through Saturday in early August, this is the region's finest show. Adding to the excitement is a cluster of additional shows that tailgate on this one. The weekend before the NHADA show is the annual Manchester auction of American furniture and folk art, paintings, and decorative accessories by Ronald Bourgeault's Northeast Auctions; based in Portsmouth, New Hampshire, it is one of the region's best auction houses.

JEWETT-BERDAN'S BOOTH AT THE NEW HAMPSHIRE ANTIQUES DEALERS ASSOCIATION SHOW, THE CENTERPIECE OF ANTIQUES WEEK, DISPLAYS SOME OF THE FINE, EARLY NEW ENGLAND OBJECTS FOR WHICH THIS SHOW IS KNOWN.

Other shows in Manchester during Antiques Week are the Riverside Antiques Show, with over 60 dealers from 20 states exhibiting 18th- to early-20th-century country and formal furniture and decorative accessories on Tuesday, Wednesday, and Thursday; and the Granite State Antiquarian Book and Ephemera Fair, with about 60 dealers displaying books and paper items on Friday and Saturday. About 30 miles away, at the fairgrounds in Deerfield, one satellite event is the Americana Celebration Antique Show, which runs on Tuesday, and draws some 135 exhibitors with 18th- and 19th-century furniture and decorative arts. In Bedford, six miles from Manchester, are four shows: the Start of Manchester Antiques Show, an indoor Tuesday/Wednesday show with Americana, country, primitive, and folk art, which includes appraisals, lectures, and book signings; the Mid-Week in Manchester Antiques Show, with more than 100 exhibitors, on Wednesday and Thursday; the Granite State Antiques Show, held on Thursday and Friday; and the Bedford Pickers Market Antiques Show, featuring over 100 dealers, on Friday.

The small city of Manchester has some great antiques dealers, and one advantage of antiquing in New Hampshire is that there's no sales tax. Manchester, the state's chief manufacturing center, first settled in 1722, became home to many French Canadians and at one time boasted more cotton mills than any place in the country. Its Currier Museum of Art is known for its collections of European and American paintings, as well as decorative arts, early photography, and sculpture. The Currier's holdings include the Zimmerman House (1950), the only New England residence designed by Frank Lloyd Wright, who also created its freestanding furniture, textiles, gardens, and mailbox. Other museums include the Historical Society's Millyard Museum and the Marconi Museum of Radio Communications. With 900 acres of parks and the Lake Massabesic watershed, recreational opportunities abound.

New Hampshire has many charming bed and breakfasts and inns. Some nearby are the Ash Street Inn in Manchester, the Bedford Village Inn in Bedford, and Stepping Stones B&B located 23 miles from Manchester in Wilton Center.

BEFORE YOU GO, visit
www.newhampshire.com
www.nhada.org

FAVORITE LODGINGS:

Ash Street Inn
118 Ash Street
Manchester, NH 03104
603-668-9908
www.ashstreetinn.com

Bedford Village Inn
Olde Bedford Way
Bedford, NH 03110
603-472-2001; 800-852-1166
www.bedfordvillageinn.com

Three Corners:
Cape Ann, Massachusetts;
Coastal New Hampshire;
& Southern Maine

The area where a tiny lick of New Hampshire separates Massachusetts from Maine is not only scenic and historically rich, but also full of antiques stores. It's only about 60 miles from Essex, Massachusetts, located on the Commonwealth's "other cape," Cape Ann, north through Portsmouth, New Hampshire, to Wells, in southern coastal Maine. There's antiquing in Massachusetts on Routes 133 and 1A and on Route 1 from New Hampshire up into Maine.

On Cape Ann, Essex, known as an "antiques capital," has nearly 20 shops. Merchandise ranges from high-style Continental furniture to country painted ladderbacks and New England redware, and from gilded chandeliers and inlaid chairs to exotic Moroccan tables and garden benches, and the quality is good. Nearby, Newburyport has ten dealers, several of whom specialize in high-quality early American furniture. In Rowley, Todd Farm Antique Shops has a Sunday-morning flea market with 240 vendors from New England and New York; they set up by 5 a.m., so early birds get the best finds. At Topsfield Fairgrounds, a Saturday-to-Sunday indoor-outdoor show held on the last weekend in June usually attracts about 200 dealers with antique and vintage furniture, including primitives and decorative items, old advertising ephemera and posters, and jewelry. In some years, an additional show is held on the fourth weekend of August.

In coastal New Hampshire, group shops in Hampton, Hampton Bays, and North Hampton present an eclectic mix of items, from country antiques to vintage linens and milk glass. In Portsmouth, in a thriving boutique- and café-filled historic district, you'll find a few shops with fine American antiques and vintage eye-catchers for creative interiors. Detours inland to Stratham or Exeter, for instance, are likely to yield results. Inland, Route 4, west of Portsmouth, running through the town of Northwood, is known as New Hampshire's "Antique Alley." Lined with more than ten shops, this stretch of road is legendary for good finds.

GEORGIAN-STYLE FURNISHINGS, TAPESTRIES, ARTWORK, AND POLISHED WOOD FLOORS CREATE PERIOD AMBIANCE AT THE THREE CHIMNEYS INN, OVERLOOKING THE OYSTER RIVER IN DURHAM. THE INN COMPRISES A 1795 CARRIAGE HOUSE AND A C.1650 HOMESTEAD, ONE OF NEW HAMPSHIRE'S OLDEST SURVIVING STRUCTURES.

In southern Maine, York has one of the best antique co-ops in New England, located on Route 1 and a prime source for New England country furnishings and Americana. Wells also has a number of fine dealers.

Other attractions include the fresh seafood served at many restaurants, including Woodman's in Essex, which claims to have invented fried clams. Essex has an excellent shipbuilding museum. It is also the location of a must-see: one of the most inspired collections of folk art in the U.S.—the home of Nina Fletcher Little, now a museum owned by Historic New England, a preservation organization that operates house museums in every New England state except Vermont. These include three properties in nearby Newbury. In Ipswich, Massachusetts, the Whipple House is a rare example of First Period architecture and period interiors, and in Newburyport, the Cushing House Museum's exhibits include a fine collection of sea captains' portraits.

Portsmouth, New Hampshire, is a treasure-trove of 18th-century architecture and museums with period interiors: the collection of houses at Strawbery Banke, John Paul Jones's home, the 1664 Jackson House, the Rundlet-May House, the 1784 Governor John Langdon House with its McKim, Mead, and White addition, and the early-18th-century Warner House Museum (which may be New England's finest Georgian mansion), are just a few of them. Performing arts venues, active in summer, include the Music Hall of Portsmouth and the Seacoast Repertory Theater.

Southern Maine's historic house museums with period interiors include Historic New England's Hamilton House and Sarah Orne Jewett House, both in South Berwick, and Sayward-Wheeler House in York Harbor. Local treasures also include Kennebunk's Taylor-Barry House. In York, museums include the Old Gaol, the John Hancock Warehouse and Wharf, the Emerson-Wilcox House, and the Elizabeth Perkins House.

Many accommodations are available along this route. On Cape Ann, in Ipswich, is the Inn at Castle Hill, overlooking the glorious Crane's Beach. A favorite inn in southern New Hampshire and a bit off the beaten path is the Three Chimneys Inn in Durham. Listed on the National Register of Historic Places, it incorporates a c.1650 homestead, which is one of New Hampshire's oldest surviving structures, and a 1795 carriage house, both with original architectural details. Its 23 guest rooms are elegantly appointed with Georgian-style furniture, antique artwork, tapestries, and Oriental rugs, plus modern comforts and amenities, including soaking tubs, Jacuzzis, and a restaurant.

In Kennebunkport, Maine, an antiquers' favorite is the Captain Lord Mansion, a stunning Federal mansion complete with cupola, built during the War of 1812. Its antique and reproduction furnishings include canopy beds and Centennial Chippendale pieces. Among its considerable charms are Jacuzzis, gas fireplaces, and a warm gathering room, where cheese, crackers, and fruit are available throughout the day. When antiquing in this area, where another shop awaits just down the road, that could be a very long day, or a very long weekend, indeed.

BEFORE YOU GO, visit
www.travelnewengland.com
www.seacoastnh.com
www.northofboston.org
www.bornsteinshows.com
www.toddfarm.com
www.nhada.org
www.antiquealley.com
www.mada.org

FAVORITE LODGINGS:

The Captain Lord Mansion	**Three Chimneys Inn**
Pleasant Street	17 Newmarket Road
Kennebunkport, ME 04046	Durham, NH 03824
800-522-3141	603-868-7800; 888-399-9777
www.captainlord.com	www.threechimneysinn.com

Brimfield, Massachusetts & Connecticut's Quiet Corner

A mong outdoor antiques shows, Brimfield, held in May, July, and September, is the mother lode. It extends for a mile along Route 20 in central Massachusetts, a mile packed with 4,000 dealers who come from all over the country to exhibit their wares in 22 separate fields. If you can start your visit on Tuesday, when the first fields open, and stay through Sunday, when bargains can be significant, it gets even better. Brimfield has virtually everything under the sun: furniture, glass, china, paintings, architectural elements, doorknobs, hinges, garden ornaments, old LPs, lamps, textiles, silver, jewelry, *objets d'art* and *objets de junque*, chotchkes, and reproductions. Rain or shine, cold or blistering hot, shoppers clog the paths and poke through booths. It's the rare person who walks away empty-handed.

The fields at Brimfield present an incredible variety, but dealers tend to return to the same fields; there are some top-notch textile dealers in May's, prime Americana in Hertan's, and quality carpets and decorative items in Sturtevant's North. Opening times vary. Dealers typically take cash or personal checks; some accept credit cards. Some will ship purchases; otherwise, there's an UPS/FedEx booth in Brimfield Acres North, and Norm's Trucking in Hertan's Field. Porters can help carry large items to the shippers or to buyers' cars. Food is available, parking is not free, some fields charge for admission, and people are asked not to bring pets.

On the Monday before Brimfield is the Vintage Textile Show at the Host Hotel in Sturbridge. At the same venue on Thursday, Nan Gurley's Sturbridge show, featuring over 40 dealers indoors, is a good way to beat bad weather and find quality items.

The town of Sturbridge, east of Brimfield, has a few antiques shops, and Old Sturbridge Village, an outstanding museum. An early-19th-century "town," where houses are furnished to the period, the museum's programs include working crafts people and farmers, and its store stocks excellent antiques-related books. Some 65 miles northeast lie Groton and West Townsend, known among New England cognoscenti as great sources for tall clocks, as well as early and country pieces; Skinner Auctions (www.skinnerinc.com), in Bolton, is worth checking for the superb items it offers.

Just across the state border, northeastern Connecticut's "Quiet Corner" is a calm counterpoint to Brimfield's intensity. Its bed and breakfast inns are often the lodging

THE SPRIGHTLY RED-YELLOW-GREEN COLOR SCHEME AND FOUR-POSTER BED IN THIS GUEST ROOM AT THE FRIENDSHIP VALLEY INN, A FEDERAL FARMHOUSE IN CONNECTICUT'S QUIET CORNER, OFFER THE PERFECT ANTIDOTE TO THE 4,000-DEALER EXTRAVAGANZA THAT IS BRIMFIELD, JUST A SHORT DRIVE AWAY.

of choice for Brimfield visitors, and the route allows guests to avoid Route 20 traffic to the show. But there's also good antiquing here. Putnam's brick downtown area has about a dozen shops. Several specialize in 18th-, 19th-, and 20th-century American, French and English antiques, and several are multi-dealer shops with antiques, vintage items, and collectibles. At the Antiques Marketplace, for instance, the more than 200 dealers offer furniture, including Mission-style, lamps, decorative items, clocks, fine china, and jewelry. You'll also find shops in Pomfret, Coventry, Canterbury, Tolland, Torrington, and Woodstock, and one of New England's oldest and best architectural salvage suppliers is in Brooklyn. In early April, nearly 50 dealers convene in Danielson to present quality, affordable items at the annual Country Antiques in Connecticut's Quiet Corner Show.

The Quiet Corner's attractions include Historic New England's Roseland Cottage, a Carpenter Gothic museum house in Woodstock; the Connecticut Wine Trail; Sharpe Hill Vineyard in Pomfret, with a recreated early-19th-century tavern restaurant and barn housing its award-winning winery; Nathan Hale Homestead and Caprilands Herb Farm in Coventry; the Windham Textile & History Museum in Willimantic; a Highlands Festival in Scotland; the Trail Wood Audubon sanctuary in Hampton; Creamery Brook Bison buffalo farm in Brooklyn (reservations necessary); and the Prudence Crandall Museum house with period rooms in Canterbury.

If coming for Brimfield, reserve early for lodging. A good bed and breakfast in town is the Yankee Cricket; three miles away in Wales, Massachusetts, is the 1846 Cora Needham House. Connecticut's Quiet Corner inns include the Federal period Friendship Valley Inn in Brooklyn, and, in Woodstock, the Inn at Woodstock Hill and the c.1714 Elias Child House.

BEFORE YOU GO, visit
www.brimfield.com
www.brimfieldexchange.com
www.brimfieldfleamarkets.com
www.vintagefashionandtextileshow.com
www.tourism.state.ct.us
www.ctquietcorner.org
www.putnamantiques.com

FAVORITE LODGINGS:

Friendship Valley Inn
60 Pomfret Road
Brooklyn, CT 06234
860-779-9696
www.friendshipvalleyinn.com

The Yankee Cricket
106 Five Bridge Road
Brimfield, MA 01010
www.yankeecricket.com

The Berkshires

T he mountains of western Massachusetts define a small but distinct region that reaches from northwestern Connecticut to southern Vermont and westward into New York. The Berkshires, as this area is called, is one of New England's best antiquing destinations, and one of the least complicated to navigate. Shops line Route 7 from Great Barrington south into and beyond Sheffield, with additional shops in Egremont, Pittsfield, Williamstown, and other communities. The Berkshire Art and Antique Dealers Association lists 55 members, and there are many other shops and auctions that are not members. This area has mostly individual dealer shops, each with its own specialty, such as fine china, dining room furnishings, wicker, or estate jewelry. The quality is excellent, and the prices can be, too.

The Berkshires is also convenient to other nearby antiquing venues. Route 7 South leads to Connecticut's Litchfield Hills. Route 7 North continues up through Vermont. Thirty miles west of Great Barrington is Hudson, New York. And Brimfield is about 65 miles to the east. All are recommended.

At Stonover Farm, a shingle-style bed and breakfast near Tanglewood in Lenox, Massachusetts, a mantel detail and comfortable upholstered furnishings recall the Colonial Revival's culture of ease. A pond, acres of meadows, a carriage house, and a gallery showcasing contemporary artists await after a day's antiquing.

English settlers first came to this area in the 1730s, establishing missions to bring Christianity to the Native Americans, and the Berkshires has been a summer destination for New Yorkers and Bostonians since the mid-19th century when the area's first train tracks were laid. The region's mountain landscapes, quality of light, and proximity to New York and Boston attracted artists and writers, including Herman Melville, George Inness, Daniel Chester French, and Edith Wharton. House museums featuring period decor include Melville's and French's homes, as well as The Mount, the estate of Edith Wharton, whose first published work was *The Decoration of Houses*. Other house museums in the region include several 18th-century buildings: Mission House, the Colonel John Ashley House, and Bidwell Manse. The Merwin House in Stockbridge, owned by Historic New England, presents generations of furnishings acquired by that family, while Naumkeag represents life in an upper-class "cottage" of the early 20th century. Three museums are devoted to the Shakers, who had a large presence in this area: Hancock Shaker Village; Mount Lebanon Shaker Museum in New Lebanon, New York; and the outstanding and little-known Shaker Museum and Library in Old Chatham, New York. The c.1830 Old Sturbridge Village museum is about an hour to the east, near Brimfield. Historic Deerfield, with its fine antiquarian collections and museum houses, is about an hour to the northeast, in Deerfield.

The Berkshires' summer cultural season includes the Boston Symphony at Tanglewood, Jacob's Pillow Dance Festival, the Williamstown Theater Festival, and many other venues and theater companies. Some cultural attractions, like the Mahaiwe Performing Arts Center in Great Barrington, run all year long. The area also has fine art museums, including the Norman Rockwell Museum in Stockbridge; the Sterling & Francine Clark Art Institute in Williamstown, with its outstanding collections of 19th-century European and American painting, sculpture, English silver, early photography, and decorative art from the Renaissance to the early 20th century; and MASSMoCA, a contemporary art museum in North Adams. With the Appalachian Trail and the Audubon Society's Pleasant Valley wildlife preserve, lakes, and mountains, the Berkshires offers hiking, bicycling, and skiing.

One of the charms of this area is the distinct personality of its towns: Williamstown, a college town; Lenox, a white-clapboarded New England classic; and Great Barrington, with its 19th-century brick storefronts. Each is full of shops and restaurants. Other communities are smaller, with quaint inns, at least one fine restaurant, and taverns. Historic accommodations are plentiful, and there are some very elaborate ones: mansions on grand estates include Wheatleigh, Blantyre, and Canyon Ranch, rated one of the nation's best spas. Antiquers often favor the 1773 Red Lion Inn, with a lovely porch overlooking Main Street in Stockbridge (a scene immortalized by Norman Rockwell). Gedney Farm in New Marlborough is an 18th-century country inn with simple period-appropriate furnishings and its own spa. The Williamsville Inn,

ONE OF THE SHOPS THAT MAKES THE BERKSHIRES OF WESTERN MASSACHUSETTS A PRIME ANTIQUING DESTINATION IS PAINTED PORCH ANTIQUES ON ROUTE 7 IN SHEFFIELD. IT OFFERS FRENCH AND CANADIAN COUNTRY FURNISHINGS AND ACCESSORIES SUCH AS CUPBOARDS, TABLES, BLANKET CHESTS, AND OIL JARS.

with New England-style furnishings and a culinary school, is in West Stockbridge. For the experience of staying in a classic Berkshires Shingle-style "cottage," it would be difficult to surpass the c.1890 Stonover Farm Bed and Breakfast in Lenox, situated on ten country acres close to Tanglewood. It recalls the culture of ease enjoyed in the Berkshires at the turn of the century. Stonover's interiors, furnished with a refreshing mix of classic furniture and contemporary art by artists represented by the inn's gallery, are equipped with every amenity one could wish for, including Internet access. Each of these inns features private baths, fireplaces, comfortable gathering spots, hearty breakfasts, and proximity to antiquing.

BEFORE YOU GO, visit
www.berkshires.org
www.berkshireantiquesandart.com

FAVORITE LODGING:
Stonover Farm Bed and Breakfast
169 Under Mountain Road
Lenox, MA 01240
413-637-9100
www.stonoverfarm.com

Connecticut's Litchfield Hills

I f ever a small town could be said to have an outstanding antiquing provenance, that town would be Woodbury, Connecticut, located in the Litchfield Hills in the northwestern corner of the state. Some 40-odd years ago, antiques dealers from New York City, Pennsylvania, the Midwest, and the South began moving to Woodbury, attracted by its historic New England ambiance, lovely landscape, and sophisticated local clientele. In a place more noted for reserve than hyperbole, Woodbury has earned the title "antiques capital of Connecticut." The town is home to more than 40 independent dealers offering high-quality antique furniture and decorative arts. Many shops are situated along a six-mile stretch of Route 6, and on Routes 132 and 47, less than two miles from the historic village, and many are housed in buildings dating from the 18th and early 19th centuries. In addition, 30 or more quality antiques stores are located in other towns, notably in Bantam on Route 202. With that tradition, it's no accident that one of the nation's most respected publications in the field, *Antiques and the Arts Weekly* (issued by The Bee publishing company in Newtown, and therefore often called "The Newtown Bee") is located in Litchfield County.

In keeping with the area's legacy, many dealers here specialize in fine American furniture and decorative and folk art of the 18th and 19th centuries. Europe (particularly England and France), Canada, and the Middle and Far East are also represented. Local galleries show contemporary work of artists and artisans. The emphasis here is on quality, often carrying a price tag to match. Antiques malls filled with collectibles are scarce.

The area has several small antiques shows. In Newtown, the Sunday Historical Society show is held the first weekend in April. In mid-August, the Keeler Tavern Museum in Ridgefield sponsors its annual Antiques and Treasures Sale, featuring antique furniture, decorative accessories, textiles, china, and silver. The Glebe House Museum in Woodbury also holds a summer show. Within about an hour's drive are several other important shows. In Wilton, a Saturday/Sunday antiques marketplace held in late June draws 160 exhibitors to "the meadows" north of Wilton High School; in mid-September, the DAR's Sunday show in the high school field house attracts 100 dealers. The Farmington Antiques Weekend, at the town's

Polo Grounds, is a Saturday/Sunday event held in mid-June (and usually also the first weekend in September); it draws about 600 dealers. Hartford hosts a pair of very high-quality Saturday/Sunday shows at the Connecticut Expo Center: the Hartford Antiques Show, with 60 dealers, on the third weekend of October, and the Connecticut Spring Antiques Show, with 70 dealers, in mid-March.

Another local venue worth checking is Litchfield Country Auctions' fine art and antiques auctions. And on Route 7 in New Milford, one of New England's largest outdoor flea markets is held every Sunday from early April through early December, when more than 300 participants sell antiques, "antiques," and a range of other used and new items, starting at 5:45 a.m.

History and nature lovers will find myriad places of interest. Museums in Bristol are devoted to American clocks and watches, carousel animals and art, and firefighting. Antique tools and machinery as well as the work of artist Eric Sloane are displayed in Kent. The birthplace of composer Charles Ives, the father of modern American music, is in Danbury. Museums exhibit antique locks in Terryville, trucks and trucking in Goshen, and ironworking, including cannons, in Lakeville. Washington has a museum of Native American history and culture, and contemporary art is exhibited at the Aldrich Museum in Ridgefield. America's first law school is located in Litchfield. Historic house museums include the 1750 Glebe House Museum in Woodbury, with the only American garden designed by English landscaper Gertrude Jekyll; the Bellamy-Ferriday House & Garden in Bethlehem, a 1754 house cum 20th-century country estate with antique furnishings

AT THE 1789 LONGWOOD COUNTRY INN, IN WOODBURY, PERIOD-STYLE HANGINGS ON A TESTER BED INCORPORATE A FRENCH TOILE, POPULAR IN THE MID-18TH CENTURY. THE GEORGIAN PERIOD IS ALSO RECALLED IN ORIGINAL RAISED FIELD PANELING, AND SHERATON- AND CHIPPENDALE-STYLE FURNISHINGS.

and gardens; General David Humphreys' House in Derby, restored to its mid-18th-century appearance; the Hotchkiss Fyler House Museum, an elegantly furnished Victorian Mansion in Torrington; and Hunt Hill Farm, with ten historic buildings and 84 acres of preserved farmland in New Milford. With rich opportunities for antiquing nearby in the Hudson Valley (New York) and the Berkshires (Massachusetts), collectors will find more than enough to occupy a succession of weekends.

Nature preserves and conservation areas are extensive in this part of Connecticut. They include National Audubon Society holdings in Sharon and in South Britain/Southbury, Nature Conservancy property in New Milford, the Flanders Trust in Woodbury, where seasonal activities include making maple syrup, the Livingston Ripley Waterfowl Sanctuary in Litchfield, and the White Memorial Foundation and Conservation Center; these offer many miles of hiking trails. This is horse country, too, with opportunities to ride and to visit the Second Company Governors' Horse Guard in Newtown, one of the oldest army horse cavalry units in the U.S. You'll also find fine dining, sports activities, car races, cooking classes, and more. An active performing arts calendar includes Armstrong Chamber Concerts in Washington Depot; the annual Music Mountain Summer Festival, the country's oldest summer chamber music festival, in Falls Village; the Summertime Festival of the Arts in Danbury; and the annual Litchfield Jazz Festival in Goshen.

For a place to stay, try the charming Longwood Country Inn, in Woodbury. Built in 1789 and surrounded by rolling fields, this historic inn offers just four guest chambers, some with gas fireplaces and whirlpool tubs, and all with such modern amenities as Internet access and televisions. With its fine restaurant serving American cuisine, and traditional furnishings such as Chippendale-style chairs and tester beds, toile and other reproduction 18th-century fabrics, American Empire bureaus and French brass beds, wing chairs and cherry candlestands, Longwood is a place an antiques aficionado could learn to love.

BEFORE YOU GO, visit
www.litchfieldhills.com

FAVORITE LODGING:
Longwood Country Inn
1204 Main Street South
Woodbury, CT 06798
203-266-0800
www.longwoodcountryinn.com

Cape Cod & Nantucket, Massachusetts

With more than 130 antiques shops that are members of the Cape Cod Antiques Dealers Association (CCADA) and more that aren't, ocean waters warmed by the Gulf Stream, miles of beaches with fine sand and rolling dunes, tidal marshes, beach plums and rugosa roses, quaint cottages clad in weather-grayed shingles, and charming little towns, Cape Cod contains the makings for a perfect antiquing weekend or week. The Cape is a popular summer destination, especially for Boston-area residents—which means traffic, and sometimes a lot of it. On the warm days in early summer and fall, it is quieter, the pace slower. For the crowd-averse, this is the time to come.

Routes 6A and 28, which outline the perimeter of the Cape, are great routes for antiquing. Route 6A, the Olde King's Highway, is the Cape's longest shopping area and one of the nation's longest historic districts; it stretches 39 miles east from Bourne, through Sandwich, Barnstable, Yarmouth, Dennis, Brewster, and Orleans, before continuing up the arm of the Cape to Provincetown. Route 6A is Cape Cod's "antiques

TRADITIONAL ELEGANCE AT THE 1839 CAPTAIN'S HOUSE INN DERIVES FROM WING CHAIRS FRONTING THE HEARTH, A TESTER BED WITH A CROCHETED VALANCE, AND A RED-GREEN COLOR SCHEME, WHICH WAS VERY POPULAR IN INTERIORS OF THIS PERIOD.

row," with some 50 antiques stores inter-spersed with crafts shops (both high-end and less so) and retailers of new Sandwich and Cranberry glass, home decor items, pottery—the list goes on. Route 28, which also boasts a good number of shops, runs along the southern part of the Cape from Bourne through Falmouth, Hyannis, South Yarmouth, Harwich, Dennis, and Chatham, to Orleans. In Barnstable, Dennis, Brewster, Yarmouth, Harwich, and Orleans, antiquers will find eight shops or more, and there are some real finds in Sandwich. Many Cape Cod dealers keep vastly different hours in summer than they do in winter, so do call ahead, especially in the off seasons.

THE WING CHAIR, ONE OF THE 18TH CENTURY'S MOST ENDURING STYLES, WAS ORIGINALLY DESIGNED TO COMFORT THE SICK AND PROTECT FROM DRAFTS. PLACED BY A WARMING FIRE, THIS PAIR AT THE CAPTAIN'S HOUSE INN INVITES RELAXATION OVER A CUP OF TEA.

The CCADA sponsors two annual shows to showcase the wares of member dealers. The first is held the first Saturday in June at Mill Pond Farm in East Sandwich, and the second is held in Orleans during the first full weekend in August. In Wellfleet, from mid-April through the autumn, the flea market on Route 6 takes place on Saturdays, Sundays, and holiday Mondays; during July and August, it is also open on Wednesdays and Thursdays. Cape Cod also has excellent auctions.

Because of its nautical character, the Cape is a good place to look for seascape paintings and maritime antiques, including hand-carved wooden decoys. It's also a place for New England furniture and decorative arts. Early Sandwich glass and Nantucket "lightship" baskets are a specialty here. Among the CCADA dealers, the emphasis is on high-quality decorative arts and fine 18th- and early-19th-century New England furniture, both painted country pieces and higher style woods. Antiquers will also find a range of other items, including jewelry, fine silver, and ceramics from all periods.

A wealth of activities awaits on this sea-conscious peninsula. Museums include Historic New England's antiques-decorated Winslow Crocker house in Yarmouthport and the glass museum in Sandwich. Outdoors, there are whale- and seal-watching cruises, schooner sailing, bicycling, birding and wildlife walks and cruises, canoeing and kayaking, sunbathing and swimming on a number of beaches, Audubon Society tours to Cuttyhunk and the Elisabeth Islands, and marine biological tours that leave from Woods Hole Laboratory. Seasonal activities include house and garden tours, an antique car parade, chowder festivals, county fairs, and road races. Cultural offerings include art galleries as well as theater and symphony performances.

Many delightful bed and breakfasts and small inns are located on Cape Cod. One particularly worth mentioning is the Captain's House Inn in Chatham, an elegant Greek Revival house built in 1839 by a young clipper ship captain for his bride, and now a first-class lodging listed on the National Register of Historic Places. Some rooms in the main building are named after ships, and some are in the historic Captain's Cottage, done in Cape Cod-style with a bow roof, a design that originated here. English gardens with fountains, herb gardens, a heated outdoor pool and a fitness center, traditional furnishings and in-room fireplaces, and an array of creature comforts make the Captain's House an idyllic retreat. After a day of antiquing (or any other day), it's an ideal place to connect with Cape Cod's seafaring past.

Nantucket Island, reachable by plane and by ferry, is also a great place for antiquing. Settled by Quakers and known for its whaling history, Nantucket retains much of its historic character. One of the quaintest places in the U.S., it is home to about 30 antiques dealers, and a listing of shops is available on the island. Museums are devoted to whaling and Nantucket lightship baskets, and a heritage trail leads to one of the oldest African-American church buildings in the nation. Nantucket has many charming bed and breakfasts and small inns, including the wonderful Jared Coffin House. It's wise to reserve space on the ferry in advance, particularly in summer.

One of the current fads is the Nantucket bumper sticker, with a coded reference to the island, which simply reads: ACK. One local wit penned in an initial T and terminal Y. When it comes to antiquing, Nantucket is just the opposite of that.

BEFORE YOU GO, visit
www.massvacation.com
www.capecodtravelguide.com
www.ccada.com
www.nantucketchamber.org
www.mvy.com

FAVORITE LODGINGS:

Jared Coffin House	**The Captain's House Inn**
29 Broad Street	369-377 Old Harbor Road
Nantucket, MA 02554	Chatham, MA 02633
508-228-2400; 800-248-2405	508-945-0127; 800-315-0728
www.jaredcoffinhouse.com	www.captainshouseinn.com

The Connecticut Coast

H ead north along the Connecticut coast from New York, or south from Rhode Island, and before long you arrive in a great antiquing town. One of the joys of this area is that you're never far from the water. This feeling is enhanced in the charming towns where the Connecticut River extends up from Long Island Sound, and in Stonington, the only town on the coast with an active fishing fleet. These seaside towns retain their 18th- and early-19th-century ambiance, with a wealth of authentic Colonial, Federal, and Greek Revival buildings set on tree-shaded streets.

Along the state's lower coast, top-quality dealers are located in New Canaan, Darien, Ridgefield, Westport, and Greenwich. Darien and Greenwich have upscale consignment shops on their Main Streets, excellent sources of stylish vintage furniture and decorative accessories. New Haven has about 30 shops, as well as fine museums. East of New Haven, Westbrook, Old Saybrook, Old Lyme, Essex, East Haddam, Deep

WHO SAYS A TRADITIONAL CHAIR HAS TO BE TREATED IN A TRADITIONAL WAY? AT THE HOMESTEAD INN, A PAIR OF WING CHAIRS, ECHOING THE SYMMETRY OF ARCHITECTURAL COLUMNS, GET THEIR ZIP FROM ZEBRA-PRINT FABRIC.

River, and Stonington are prime antiquing towns, with Old Saybrook and Stonington having the largest concentration of shops. Though there are large antiques malls in New Haven and New London, and some in smaller towns like Old Saybrook, many shops in this area tend to be mid-sized multi-dealer ventures or individual dealers. This area has long been known for Americana, fine formal, high country, primitives, and marine art.

Connecticut has a very full antiques show schedule. Along the coast, some towns have several shows each year, and even the smaller ones can draw 60 dealers or more. Old Greenwich's antiques events include a Sunday show with 60 dealers in early February, a Saturday/Sunday show with 50 dealers in early March, a large ephemera show in late March, a Saturday/Sunday glassware show with 60 dealers in mid-April, and a Saturday/Sunday show with 50 dealers in mid-October. Darien has a Saturday/Sunday show with 30 dealers in late February and a Sunday outdoor show in mid-September. Westport has a Saturday/Sunday show with 53 dealers in mid-April. Madison and Guilford are among the other towns holding seasonal shows.

Three prominent Saturday/Sunday shows are held in Wilton, Farmington, and Hartford, an easy drive inland from the coast. Hartford holds two shows of period American furniture at its Expo Center, one in mid-March and the other in late October. Farmington welcomes 600 dealers for its Antiques Weekend at the Polo Grounds in mid-June and also usually during Labor Day weekend. Wilton has two Saturday/Sunday shows: the Outdoor Antiques Marketplace in late June and the DAR Antiques Marketplace in late September.

Many historic sites and house museums are located in this history-rich corridor, notably in Clinton, Chester, Cromwell, Essex, Guilford, Haddam, Madison, New London, and Old Saybrook; in Hadlyme is the massive Gillette's Castle State Museum. There's also the Connecticut River Museum in Essex and the Florence Griswold Museum in Old Lyme. Dudley Farm, Hyland House, and the Whitfield State Historical Museum are in Guilford. A bit north, off the coast in Mashantucket, the Pequot Museum provides a comprehensive look at Native American culture and history. In Mystic, the Mystic River Seaport, with restored 18th-century houses and a sailing vessel, offers a delightful glimpse into maritime history. The New Britain Museum of Art features the work of American artists, including Benton, Cassatt, Church, Cole, Sargent, Stuart, Whistler, and Wyeth.

New Haven museums include the Yale Center for British Art, with works by Hogarth, Turner, and Gainsborough; the Yale University Art Gallery with Etruscan, Egyptian, and ancient Greek pieces, and masterpieces by Van Gogh, Monet, and Picasso; and the Yale Collection of musical instruments. There's an Ethnic Heritage Center at Southern Connecticut State University, and the New Haven Colony Historical Society Museum traces the state's history back to the 1630s.

AT THE HOMESTEAD INN, VIVID CHARTREUSE IS THE BACKDROP AND DARK WOODWORK THE FRAME FOR A FRENCH SLEIGH BED, A CHINESE RED LACQUER TABLE, AND OTHER INTERNATIONAL FURNISHINGS. AMONG THE OTHER DELIGHTS AT THIS ITALIANATE MANSION IS A SOPHISTICATED GOURMET RESTAURANT.

Other diversions include outdoor activities, performing arts, and festivals. The Victorian-era Goodspeed Opera House, in East Haddam, and the Shubert Performing Arts Center, in New Haven, are favorite performing arts venues. There's golf, horse-back riding, and kayaking tours of the Mystic River. You can swim at Hammonasset Beach State Park in Madison and Harkness Memorial State Park in Waterford. In Essex, you can opt for a steam train or riverboat ride, or a cruise on Long Island Sound.

For accommodations on the lower Connecticut coast, antiquers who like to end the day with a superlative meal won't be disappointed at the Homestead Inn in Greenwich. An Italianate villa, the inn is run by a European-trained chef and his wife, who created a decor as colorful as a candy box filled with marzipan. Each of the inn's seven suites and eleven deluxe chambers has a strong individual personality, with a sophisticated mix of antiques, artifacts, and art culled from China, Indonesia, India, and Morocco. Guest rooms are equipped with cable TV and Internet service. The hand-hewn beams of the inn's earliest section can be seen in the gourmet dining room.

Equally wonderful, mid-coast, is Federal-period Griswold Inn in Essex. Its 30 individually appointed guest rooms and suites meld antiques and complementary furnishings. Rich accents—seascapes in gilt frames, tribal carpets, fireplaces, and period portraits—create a fresh, eye-pleasing decor quintessentially New England in character. The Griswold's gracious style is also evident in its modern amenities. It

THE GRISWOLD INN, IN HISTORIC ESSEX, IS ONE OF THE NATION'S OLDEST CONTINUOUSLY OPERATING INNS. A SHIP CAPTAIN'S PORTRAIT IN A GUEST ROOM AND THE MARINE ART COLLECTION IN ITS DINING ROOMS AND WINE BAR ARE REMINDERS THAT IT HAS SERVED SEAFARERS AND YACHTSMEN SINCE IT OPENED IN 1776.

boasts a new wine bar, a tap room that has been called one of the handsomest in the East, and dining rooms decorated with marine art and serving fine American cuisine.

If time allows, continue up the coast and into Rhode Island, where there's antiquing in West Warwick, Warwick, Barrington, Providence, and Newport. Though known for its grand cottages, Newport is also the site of the Francis Malbone House, designed in the mid-18th-century by America's first architect, now an inn with period furnishings. On this coast, you're never far from the sea, the past, or a fine antique.

BEFORE YOU GO, visit
www.tourism.state.ct.us
www.connecticutcoast.worldweb.com
www.newhavencvb.com

FAVORITE LODGINGS:

Homestead Inn
420 Field Point Road
Greenwich, CT 06830
203-869-7500
www.homesteadinn.com

The Griswold Inn
36 Main Street
Essex, CT 06426
860-767-1776
www.griswoldinn.com

Mid-Atlantic

New York's Hudson Valley

enry Hudson, an Englishman who sailed for the Dutch East India Company, crossed the Atlantic in an 85-foot craft with a crew of 20, explored the Eastern seaboard, and, in 1609, sailed from New York Harbor up the river that now bears his name, seeking the northwest passage to China. He reached the site of Albany, where, in 1614, the Dutch established a trading settlement—six years before the Pilgrims landed at Plymouth Rock. Hudson, New York, located 130 miles upriver from New York City, was founded during the American Revolution by Nantucket families seeking safety for their whaling ships, and it quickly became a bustling port. Shipbuilders devised the Hudson River sloop (from the Dutch term *sloëp*), a single-masted vessel with a mainsail, jib, and usually a topsail. One of these, the *Experiment*, was the first American craft to sail directly from the U.S. to China, setting out in 1785 and returning in 1787, its holds laden with tea, silk, taffeta and satin textiles, and the exquisite porcelains that came to be called, simply, "china."

With over 60 shops, the streets of Hudson recall this early international commerce. Historic shopfronts are filled with formal and country American pieces, English and European furniture, Asian pieces, fine art, ceramics, and decorative objects dating from the 16th through the 20th centuries. The range is vast, from highly decorated Italian chests to Chinese porcelain and Delft, African artifacts, Shaker chairs, and Art Deco dressing tables. A number of shops specialize in or include mid-20th century Moderne furniture and lighting by leading designers, which adds to the fun. Antiques stores line both sides of Warren Street, and many more dealers are located in the Armory at the corner of 5th and State streets. Several do a thriving decorator and interior design trade. While some are high-end, others are more moderately priced, and bargains await shoppers inclined to explore. Along Warren Street are a few restaurants and cafés, and at its foot is a park on the river. Hudson possesses several charming 19th-century brick firehouses and the Museum of Firefighting.

The Hudson River Valley, which inspired early-19th-century landscape painters who collectively became known as the Hudson River School, has been called "the landscape that defined America." Settled by the Dutch, French Huguenots, and the English, and a popular escape for wealthy families in the 19th century, its estates include some of the country's grandest residential buildings. With beautiful scenery, fine estates and house museums with period furnishings, museums, farm stands, towns such as Hyde Park, Kingston, Saugerties, Beacon, Poughkeepsie, Red Hook, and Chatham, each with several antiques stores, it's a fine area to wander. Local auctions worth noting are the Copake Auction in Copake and Meissner's Auction in New Lebanon; check local newspaper listings. Moreover, the antiques-rich Berkshires region of Massachusetts and Connecticut's Litchfield Hills are not far away.

The Hudson Valley's largest antiques shows take place in Rhinebeck, New York, 25 miles south of Hudson. These include a Saturday/Sunday show on Memorial Day weekend, a one-day show called Summer Magic held on a Saturday in late July, and a Saturday/Sunday show on Columbus Day weekend in mid-October. These three shows, all indoors at the Dutchess County Fairgrounds on Route 9, present about 200 diverse dealers from New York, Pennsylvania, New England, the Midwest, the South, Canada, and Europe. The quality is usually excellent, and bargains can be found. There's formal and country French, English, and American furniture, hooked rugs, folk art, paintings, prints, textiles, garden items, period iron, estate jewelry, and, as the saying goes, "much, much more."

CONVENIENT TO HUDSON VALLEY AND BERKSHIRES ANTIQUING, A GUEST ROOM AT THE INN AT GREEN RIVER DISPLAYS LOCALLY SOURCED ANTIQUES AND AN UNFINISHED HOOKED RUG DESIGNED BY PEARL MCGOWN.

FURNISHINGS ARRAYED FOR PREVIEW AT THE COPAKE AUCTION IN COPAKE, NEW YORK, EVIDENCE THE RANGE OF TERRIFIC THINGS YOU CAN FIND AT THIS AND OTHER SMALL, LOCAL AUCTIONS.

Hudson Valley attractions include the Hudson River Maritime Museum and the Stockade Historic District, an area of early Dutch houses, in Kingston; Franklin Delano Roosevelt's home, the Vanderbilt Mansion, and the Culinary Institute of America's restaurant in Hyde Park; Wilderstein Preservation, a Queen Anne Mansion filled with original family furnishings, in Rhinebeck; Boscobel, the stunning Federal mansion, in Garrison; Philipsburg Manor, a late-17th- to early-18th-century complex, and Kykuit, the Rockefeller estate, in Sleepy Hollow; Lyndhurst, the 1840 Gothic Revival castle designed by Alexander Jackson Davis, and Washington Irving's 1835 Sunnyside Cottage in Tarrytown; Montgomery Place, also designed by Davis, in Annandale-on-Hudson; Van Cortlandt Manor, a living-history museum, in Croton-on-Hudson; the Bronck Museum, a Dutch house, in Coxsachie; and the Van Wyck Homestead Museum in Fishkill.

For glimpses into the lives and art of Hudson River School painters, Frederick Church's Moorish-style Olana, designed by Calvert Vaux, is in Hudson, and Thomas Cole's Cedar Grove is in Catskill. In Albany, the New York State Museum's collections include American furniture and decorative arts from 1700 to 1900, women's tools and products, Shaker objects, and artifacts. Several museums, including the Maritime and Boscobel, close in October, so check hours before you go. Old Chatham has a fine Shaker Museum and Library; New Lebanon's Shaker Museum is where the sect, known for its furniture, had its headquarters in the 19th century.

Outdoor activities include occasional hikes on the Hudson River School Art Trail, run by the Thomas Cole National Historic Site (www.thomascole.org/follow_hikes.htm) and the Hudson Valley Ramble (www.hudsonvalleyramble), held two weekends in mid- and late-September in the National Park Service's Hudson River Valley National Heritage area (www.hudsonvalleyheritagearea.com). Seasonal activities also include a Waterfront Festival during the third week of August at the Hudson River Maritime Museum in Kingston.

Hudson River Valley inns range from high style to intimate. Among them are Troutbeck in Amenia, La Chambourd in Hopewell Junction, Bullis Hall in Bangall, and Aubergine, with its fine restaurant, in Hillsdale. Favorite inns with stylish period flair and modern amenities include the Beekman Arms and Delamater Inn in Rhinebeck. Both owned and operated by the same innkeeper, the Beekman Arms was built as an inn in 1766 and has 73 rooms, while Delamater Inn, a rare 1850s Carpenter Gothic designed by Alexander Jackson Davis, has 50 rooms surrounding a courtyard and a fine restaurant. Another favorite, with a rural ambiance, is the Inn at Green River, an 1830 Federal farmhouse in Hillsdale, offering elegance and comfort with romantic period-appropriate furnishings and antiques, guest room fireplaces, and Jacuzzis. A hammock slung between the trees is the ideal vantage point for admiring the landscape and planning the next day's antiquing explorations.

BEFORE YOU GO, visit
www.travelhudsonvalley.org
www.hvnet.com
www.hudsonvalley.org
www.hudsonvalleyheritagearea.com
www.hudsonrivervalley.com
www.hudsonantiques.net
www.rhinebeckantiquesfair.com

FAVORITE LODGINGS:

The Beekman Arms and Delamater Inn
Route 9
Rhinebeck, NY 12572
845-876-7077
www.beekmandelamaterinn.com

The Inn at Green River
9 Nobletown Road
Hillsdale, NY 12529
518-325-7248
www.innatgreenriver.com

Central New York: Bouckville & Madison

I n central New York state on Route 20, west of Albany and about a four-hour drive northwest of Manhattan, the towns of Madison and Bouckville are havens for antiquers. Madison County, with its green farm-dotted landscape, is home to some 50 antiques shops. These range from upscale establishments to barns with items in "as found" condition, all easily reachable by car. It's a great area for farmhouse finds, including painted country furniture, Depression and cut glass, textiles, iron, crockery, linens, and architectural salvage.

The area gets even better during the third weekend in August, when over 1,000 dealers from across the U.S. and Canada come rain or shine to display their wares in tents spread over 90 acres of dairy fields. This is the blockbuster Saturday/Sunday Madison–Bouckville show, New York state's largest outdoor antiques fair.

THE TINY POOLVILLE COUNTRY STORE IN MADISON COUNTY FEATURES COMFORTABLE COUNTRY STYLING, ANTIQUES FOUND LOCALLY, GOURMET FARE, AND EASY ACCESS TO ROUTE 20 AND NEW YORK STATE'S LARGEST OUTDOOR ANTIQUES FAIR.

THE POOLVILLE COUNTRY STORE, BUILT IN 1835, PLAYED A SIGNIFICANT ROLE IN THIS SMALL COMMUNITY. OFFERING MERCHANDISE FROM CUT NAILS TO CALICO, IT WAS ALSO WHERE RURAL PEOPLE GOT THEIR NEWS OF WORLD EVENTS.

The early-bird buying session opens on Friday morning. Early admission, which includes a weekend pass to the show, is $40 compared to $7 for the standard two-day pass—but you may save that much by getting in before merchandise begins changing hands among dealers. With more than 30,000 antiquers shopping at this show, there is some competition for prized items. Other shows tailgate on this one, opening on the Tuesday preceding it, and dealers also set up along Route 20.

On the Friday/Saturday/Sunday of the first weekend of June, there are shows at Bono's Antique Show Field with 90 dealers, and at the East Expo Hayfield, with about 35 dealers. During the June shows, other dealers also set up along Route 20.

Canals played an important part in local history. In Bouckville, you can walk on the original towpath of the historic 168-year-old Chenango Canal and visit the Canal Cottage Museum. In Chittenango, the Erie Canal Landing and Boat Museum is an interpretative archeological site. Another aspect of area history is on view at Munnsville's organic Foothill Hops Farm. Madison County's other rural pleasures include farms where you can pick your own berries, pumpkins, and apples in season; Juravich Farm museum in Oneida; Maple Bush Farm in Eaton, whose maple syrups regularly take prizes at the New York State Fair; and Jewett's Cheese Farm in Earlville. There's horseback riding in Morrisville and Cazenovia. Arts venues include a gallery and summer performances at the Earlville Opera House. In Cooperstown, some 40 minutes away, are the Farmer's Museum, Fenimore Art Museum, and Glimmerglass Opera. Native American culture is the focus at the Shakowi Cultural Center in Oneida, and in Peterboro, the Gerrit Smith Estate and Area Museum present local history related to the Civil War and the Underground Railroad.

With the influx of dealers and shoppers during the Madison–Bouckville show, lodging becomes scarce. If you subscribe to the idea that a day's antiquing is best topped off with a great meal, you won't be disappointed at the Poolville Country Store. Perfectly situated for an exploration of area shops or visiting the show,

it is a tiny place with three guest rooms, and a gourmet restaurant with a national reputation. Freshly styled with finds from local antiques stores, the inn retains its original beams and massive wooden overhead pulley, once used for hauling merchandise to its second-floor loft. Other lodging options include stylish Weathervane Farm, a restored Greek Revival farmhouse in Hamilton; Mansion House, a National Historic Landmark at the utopian Oneida Community; and Bouckville's c.1850 Ye Olde Landmark Tavern, an octagon-shaped cobblestone hotel. A quirky example of this wonderful, if brief, building craze, it was built with sides of unequal length to fit its building lot. It's perhaps the largest antique in New York to have started out as a "make-do."

BEFORE YOU GO, visit
www.iloveny.state.ny.us
www.nyshta.org
www.madisontourism.com
www.bouckvilleantiqueshows.com/html/main.html

FAVORITE LODGING:
Poolville Country Store
1245 Earlville Road
Poolville, NY 13332
315-691-2677
www.poolvillecountrystore.com

New York City & Antiques Week

I f antiques tempt you, take a bite out of the Big Apple. Some of the finest objects in the world are to be found in New York City, along with some of the rarest, some of the most expensive, and many that are great bargains. Christie's and Sotheby's auctions regularly ring up record prices; an 18th-century Newport tea table, for instance, recently went for $8.5 million. At the other end of the spectrum are consignment shops, Sunday-morning flea markets, and sales in parking garages. The number of antiques stores in Manhattan and Brooklyn, the city's two great antiquing boroughs, number in the thousands, but are uncountable, because this huge, energetic, and hardworking city is always changing. Case in point: The Chelsea outdoor flea market recently moved because the parking lot in which it was held became a building site; it's now at 39th Street and Ninth Avenue, but no one knows how long that will last.

Another thing you can depend on in New York City is diversity, and that is as true of its antiques as it is of its people. The range of merchandise here is enormous, representing virtually every place on the globe, and every period and culture. Whether you're in the market for an Amish quilt, West Indies bed, Burmese Buddha, ancient Roman artifact, Japanese tansu, Mexican santo, Navajo rug, Persian carpet, Spanish refractory table, African tribal mask, Middle Eastern inlaid chair, Chinese jade, medieval tapestry, Art Deco lamp, French chaise, or English oak bookcase, you will find it here.

The nation's antiquing calendar begins in this city, in January, with New York Antiques Week, now a jam-packed two-week schedule with shows serving every price range and auctions by major houses. Most of the shows begin with a preview party or gala held the night preceding the show. Some feature "Young Collectors" parties, and a

AT NEW YORK'S WINTER ANTIQUES SHOW, LEIGH KENO ANTIQUES DISPLAYS A FINE FEDERAL CANDLE STAND, A QUEEN ANNE SETTEE, AND A PAIR OF GIRANDOLE MIRRORS.

WEST INDIES FURNISHINGS AT MICHAEL CONNORS ANTIQUES
IN SOHO EVOKE THE TROPICAL ELEGANCE OF THE
CARIBBEAN.

few offer excellent lecture series and special tours. Free shuttle buses provide transportation between several of the shows.

The prestigious New York Winter Antiques Show, at the Seventh Regiment Armory at Park Avenue and 67th Street, begins on the third Thursday of January with an opening night party, opens to the public on Friday, and runs for ten days thereafter. Drawing about 75 leading dealers from the U.S., Europe, and Canada with objects of exquisite quality, this show presents a diverse range of items. Ancient artifacts, fine and religious art, China trade paintings, formal Continental furniture, and Americana are all represented, and prices reflect the quality and rarity of the objects shown.

The focal point for Americana during Antiques Week is the American Antiques Show, sponsored by the American Folk Art Museum and held at the Time Warner Center at Columbus Circle. This outstanding Thursday-through-Sunday show launches with a preview gala on Wednesday night. It brings together some 45 of the nation's finest dealers, exhibiting American furniture (most of it in original condition), folk art, textiles, Native American art and artifacts, early photography, and other pieces.

Collectors of ceramics make it a point to attend the New York Ceramics Fair, a weeklong event beginning on the third Tuesday in January and held at the National Academy Museum at 1083 Fifth Avenue. More than 50 dealers from the U.S., England, and Europe display a range of fine ceramics, from American redware and salt-glaze to Chinese export, Japanese Imari, Majolica, English transferware, mochaware, and Wedgwood, to complementary items such as Baccarat glass.

Other shows during this week include Antiques at the Armory, at the 69th Regiment Armory, located on Lexington Avenue at 26th Street, with 100 dealers presenting a range of objects from early American to Victorian and modern, and Antiques at the Piers at the Passenger Ship Terminal Piers, Twelfth Avenue at 55th Street, a Saturday/Sunday show held during the first weekend of Antiques Week, with about 400 dealers. On the last weekend of January, there's also the Outsider Art Fair and Books at the 25th Street Armory on Lexington Avenue.

New York auction houses, such as Christie's, Sotheby's, and Doyle's, hold major sales during Antiques Week. These are fun events, and auction items can be previewed beforehand. Check the houses' websites for information.

Other New York antiques shows include high-quality Friday-through-Wednesday international shows. Two focusing on Asian and Pacific antiques take place at the end of April. The International Fine Art and Antiques Dealers Show is held in late October. In late May, focus is on the Tribal and Textile Arts Show of antique fine arts and ancient artifacts, a Friday/Saturday/Sunday show presenting 75 international dealers at the Seventh Regiment Armory. Antiques at the Piers presents wares from some 600 dealers in late March and on two weekends in early and mid-November.

New York is a city of neighborhoods, each with a distinct personality. You'll find the largest concentrations of antiques shops among the towering office buildings of Midtown Manhattan, on the well-heeled Upper East Side, in the intimate streets of Greenwich Village, and on Atlantic Avenue in Brooklyn. Though fewer in number, there are also shops in SoHo, Tribeca, Chelsea, and on the Upper West Side. A good city-specific guide is John and Barbara Michel's *Antiquing New York*. For navigation, one good aid is *Flashmaps New York*.

Consignment shops include those run by Housing Works, in several locations around the city. Manhattan's flea markets include Greenflea at 77th Street and

AN EMPIRE SOFA AND OTHER PERIOD FURNISHINGS CREATE AN INTIMATE SPOT AT NEW YORK CITY'S INN AT IRVING PLACE, A SMALL HOTEL IN A 19TH-CENTURY TOWNHOUSE THAT WAS ONCE A PRIVATE HOME.

Columbus Avenue on the Upper West Side (Sunday); the Garage at 112 West 25th Street between Sixth and Seventh avenues (Saturday/Sunday); the Annex on Sixth Avenue from 24th to 27th Streets (Saturday/Sunday); SoHo Antiques Fair at Grand Street and Broadway (Saturday/Sunday); and the aforementioned Hell's Kitchen Flea Market (formerly in Chelsea) at 39th Street and Ninth Avenue (Sunday).

The city is an enormous cultural treasure with a full roster of performing arts and other activities year round, and superlative museums. Of special interest to antiquers is the Metropolitan Museum of Art, with its extensive collections of fine and decorative arts, including furnishings in period rooms, from all periods and every corner of the globe. To name but a few others: New-York Historical Society, Cooper-Hewitt National Design Museum, the Frick Collection, Asia Society, the Museum of Modern Art, and its next-door neighbor, American Folk Art Museum. Local media, such as *New York Magazine*, *The New Yorker*, and the *New York Times* list exhibits at smaller museums and galleries.

Historic hotels are not hard to find here: many of the city's best have long histories or are in refurbished buildings. Two less well-known accommodations are the Inn at Irving Place and Abingdon Guest House. In these small inns, furnished with antiques and located in 19th-century townhouses that were once private residences, you can approximate the experience of living in New York, if only long enough to go antiquing.

BEFORE YOU GO, visit
www.iloveny.com
www.winterantiquesshow.com
www.stellashows.com
www.folkartmuseum.org
www.antiques2.iantiquesguide.com

FAVORITE LODGINGS:

Abingdon Guest House
21 Eighth Avenue
New York, NY 10014
212-243-5384
www.abingdonguesthouse.com

The Inn at Irving Place
56 Irving Place
New York, NY 10003
212-533-4600; 800-685-1447
www.innatirving.com

The Hamptons

F or New Yorkers, Long Island's East End, extending like a fishtail into the Atlantic, has long been the place to be, and be seen, in the summer. The South Fork, as it's known, extends to Montauk Point, through the towns collectively known as the Hamptons—East Hampton, Southampton, Bridgehampton, Hampton Bays, and Westhampton. Beautiful beaches, charming villages, grand Shingle-style summer "cottages" tucked behind privet hedges, freshwater ponds, woods limned with nature trails, vineyards, restaurants serving fresh-caught fish, and family farm stands selling just-picked produce are only some of the area's pleasures. With dozens of antiques stores and a schedule of several shows from spring through fall, this is an ideal place to spend a weekend antiquing.

More than 65 antiques stores are located on the South Fork, in 15 villages along the 48-mile stretch of Route 27 (the Montauk Highway), from East Moriches to Montauk. They offer a wide variety of merchandise from the fine to fun, priced at every point of the spectrum. The best resource for information is Joan Tyor Carlson's "Tour of Antique Shops and Sources of the Hamptons," which is available locally and at www.znap.to/antiques.

Several annual antiques shows take place in this area. In Easthampton, Mulford Farm is the site of Saturday shows held on the last weekend in June, the first weekend in August, and in mid-September. In Bridgehampton, on the first weekend in June is the Garden Antiques Show and Sale; on the last weekend of June and July, the Friday/Saturday Antiques & Design in the Hamptons show; Friday/Saturday/Sunday shows are held in mid-July and late August; and a three-day show in early July is devoted to Modernism and art.

LONG ISLAND'S HERITAGE IS RECALLED IN THE ROOFLINE OF THE MILL HOUSE INN IN EAST HAMPTON. DORMERS PUNCTUATE ITS GAMBREL ROOF, AND FRENCH DOORS OPEN TO ADMIT SEA BREEZES.

IN THE GATHERING ROOM AT MILL HOUSE INN, THE LINES OF ARTS & CRAFTS MISSION-STYLE FURNISHINGS ECHO
THE STRONG LINES OF EXPOSED CEILING JOISTS. BLACK-AND-WHITE PHOTOGRAPHS AND VINTAGE ACCESSORIES ADD
VISUAL APPEAL.

In Amagansett, the Rotary Club holds antiques sales at Miss Amelia's Cottage Museum on Memorial Day and Labor Day weekends. Weekend flea markets are at Elk's Field in Southampton, St. Michael's Church in Amagansett, the East Hampton Middle School, and the Great Lawn on Main Street in Westhampton Beach.

First settled in 1648, the Hamptons retain much of their historic character. Mulford Farmstead, virtually unchanged since 1750, is among the area's historic landmark museums. Montauk, located at the South Fork's eastern tip and renowned for sports fishing, is home to Long Island's oldest lighthouse, and the view from its tower is terrific. Fishing and oystering, whaling, yachting, and shipbuilding have a long tradition here, a history explored at the Long Island Maritime Museum in West Sayville. In Sag Harbor there is a c.1790 Customs House and the Whaling Museum, where visitors enter through the jawbones of a whale.

Among the most glorious in the country, the beaches in this area offer miles of white sand and Gulf Stream—warmed waters; some are very social, some very private. You can enjoy water activities, play golf or tennis, pick your own fruit at local farms, ice skate in winter, go on nature hikes, take cruises for deep sea sport fishing or whale- and seal-watching, and horseback ride at Deep Hollow Ranch, a working cattle ranch on land used for that purpose since 1660. Annual events include Bridgehampton's Hampton Classic Horse Show on the last week of August, East

Hampton's Artists and Writers softball game in mid-August, the Hamptons Film Festival in mid-October, and, on Labor Day weekend, the annual pow-wow on the Shinnecock Reservation in Southampton.

The North Fork is quieter and more rural than the South and has a number of antiques shops. Most of Long Island's two dozen wineries, which cultivate nearly 3,000 acres and produce award-winning wines, are on the North Fork; from East Hampton, take Route 114 North to 25 West, which meanders through wine country. You'll find antiques stores starting in Jamesport and extending east to Greenport.

Antiques-minded lodgings include Maidstone Arms, where antique furnishings are for sale. For comfort and style, none surpasses the c.1790 Mill House Inn, located in East Hampton's historic district. It stands opposite Hook Mill, built in 1806 by noted furniture and clock maker Nathanial Dominy V (whose family's furniture is on view at Amagansett's c.1725 Miss Amelia Cottage Museum). The Mill House Inn's cozy, well-appointed rooms, feather beds, down quilts, gas fireplaces, whirlpool baths, and delicious breakfasts—coupled with the innkeepers' knowledge about local antiquing destinations—make a winning combination. Nearby is the salt-box style home of John Howard Payne, who, in 1823, wrote the popular song, "Home Sweet Home." You might not purchase any Dominy furniture, but your antiquing finds in the Hamptons may make your own home that much sweeter.

BEFORE YOU GO, visit
www.hamptonsantiques.com
www.znap.to/antiques
www.stellashows.com
www.flamingoshows.com
www.northforkantiques.com

FAVORITE LODGING:
The Mill House Inn
31 North Main Street
East Hampton, NY 11937
631-324-9766
www.millhouseinn.com

Lambertville & Hunterdon County, New Jersey; New Hope & Bucks County, Pennsylvania

T he Delaware River cuts a sparkling swath between Bucks County, Pennsylvania, and Hunterdon County, New Jersey, creating a lush landscape. On its opposite banks, two towns have been known as antiquing destinations for decades: New Hope, Pennsylvania, and Lambertville, New Jersey. The first to establish its reputation was New Hope, thanks to its high-quality dealers in American, English, and European furniture and folk art. Lambertville, nicknamed "the antiques capital of New Jersey," is its complement, and the two antiquing districts are connected by a short bridge. There's also good antiquing elsewhere in Bucks County, Pennsylvania, and Hunterdon county, New Jersey.

William Penn, who founded the Pennsylvania Colony, began building his Bucks County home in 1683, the year he established Philadelphia's First Quaker Meeting House. Lambertville was settled in 1705. The river, and later the Delaware and Raritan Canal, provided water power and transportation for early industries, and the Delaware River Valley's fertile soil attracted farmers. Since then, the area has drawn settlers and visitors: historically, the well-to-do lived in New Hope and the working class in Lambertville.

AN 18TH-CENTURY SLANT-TOP DESK
WITH GILT "JAPANNED" DECORATION.

ACCOMMODATIONS AT THE CHIMNEY HILL ESTATE ARE IN A FIELDSTONE HOUSE BUILT IN 1820, SET ON EIGHT ACRES, AND LOCATED A HALF-MILE FROM ANTIQUES SHOPS IN LAMBERTVILLE AND NEW HOPE.

Each town has about 40 shops (not all downtown). Filled with shops and restaurants, 18th- and 19th-century buildings create intimate streetscapes. In New Hope, antiques stores cluster on Bridge, Ferry, and Main streets; in Lambertville, they are on Union Street and the streets around it. In New Hope, there's a flea sale on Tuesday at Rice's Market, and Lambertville's Wednesday/Saturday/Sunday Golden Nugget market is excellent. Elsewhere in both counties are many more individual dealer shops, antiques malls, and multi-dealer facilities. Frenchtown, 16 miles north of Lambertville, has about five quality shops, offering a range of formal American and European furniture, Victorian and 20th-century garden and architectural items, and collectibles. Lists of antiques shops are available locally.

This area has a full calendar of small, quality shows. On the first Saturday in February, the Heart of Bucks Winter Antique Show, in Newtown, Pennsylvania, draws 45 exhibitors. In late February, the Saturday/Sunday Heritage Conservancy Annual Antiques Show, usually held in Jamison, Pennsylvania, features 50 dealers specializing in Americana. The first Sunday in June, the Tinicum (Pennsylvania) County Outdoor Antiques Show draws 100 dealers. Also in June on Father's Day Weekend, and again in mid-October, the Saturday/Sunday Prallsville Mills Antiques Show in Stockton, New Jersey, presents 35 dealers. On the fourth weekend of November, the Saturday/Sunday Bucks County Antiques Dealers Show in Doylestown, Pennsylvania, features about 40 dealers. And on the first weekend of December in Oldwick, New Jersey, the Saturday/Sunday Christmas Antiques Show presents 55 dealers.

CHIMNEY HILL'S FRONT HALL EXHIBITS A GRACEFUL STAIRCASE, A SHELF WITH A CHIPPENDALE-STYLE BROKEN PEDIMENT, AND A BABY GRAND PIANO. BEYOND, A FIELDSTONE FIREPLACE AND WALL STRIKE A CASUAL NOTE.

One Bucks County site history-lovers won't want to miss is the Mercer Museum, Henry Mercer's massive 1916 castle, built to house his collection of implements, folk art, and furnishings of early America. A National Historic Landmark, its vast interiors feature dramatic displays, which include a whaling boat, a Conestoga wagon, and 40,000 tools representing more than 60 trades. Fonthill, Mercer's home, a 44-room concrete castle with 18 fireplaces, showcases handcrafted Arts & Crafts tiles his company made.

Pennsbury Manor, an impeccable replica of William Penn's home based upon extensive archeological study, features period 17th-century interiors; its mid-September festival showcases 12 cultures, and embodies Penn's ideas of ethnic and religious harmony. Other house museums include the 1834 Marshall House and the Holcombe-Jimison Farmstead, in Lambertville; the 1722 stone Keith House, with mid-18th-century period interiors, at the Graeme Park Historic Site in Horsham; and the 1784 stone Parry Mansion, where furnishings reflect 125 years of family life, in New Hope. You can explore historic 18th-century gristmills, take in dinner and a show at the c.1894 Victorian Sellersville Theater, or stop at the Lumberville Store, a Delaware River landmark, to rent a bike and get sandwiches for a picnic. Bucks County has several sites related to African American history, the Quakers, and their Abolitionist efforts, and holds an annual African American Heritage Festival in August. The Churchville Nature Center has a living-history Lenape Indian Village and offers Saturday-morning bird walks.

Other diversions include theater, symphony, ballet, festivals, the Michener Art Museum, farmers markets, wineries, and a micro-brewery. Several miles south of New Hope is Washington Crossing Historic Park, where in 1777 George Washington crossed the Delaware to storm the Trenton outpost held by Hessian mercenaries fighting for the British, a pivotal moment in the American Revolution. The Delaware River now invites tubing, canoeing, and kayaking, and there are numerous other recreational activities. Stone farmhouses and covered bridges are focal points for photographers.

If you dream of staying in one of those classic stone farmhouses, consider Chimney Hill, a fieldstone gem built in 1820, now a luxury bed and breakfast set on eight acres of landscaped grounds and fields. Each of its 12 guest rooms is elegantly decorated with period furnishings and has a private bath; many have canopied beds, fireplaces, and Jacuzzis. Delicious breakfasts are served by candlelight in the 1820 dining room. It's enough to put one in the mood to shop for early American antiques, and to make one understand William Penn's choice of place for his country home.

BEFORE YOU GO, visit
www.bccvb.org
www.visitbucks.com
www.buckscounty.org
www.frenchtowner.com
www.lambertville.org
www.pa-antiques.org

FAVORITE LODGING:
Chimney Hill Estate & The Ol' Barn Inn
207 Goat Hill Road
Lambertville, NJ 08530
609-397-1516; 800-211-4667
www.chimneyhillinn.com

Philadelphia, Pennsylvania

P hiladelphia, established in 1682 by Quaker William Penn, who called it "The City of Brotherly Love," is where America's founding fathers drafted the Declaration of Independence and the U.S. Constitution. It was the first capital of the U.S., and, until 1800, the largest city in the country. In 1805, not far from the spot where the first U.S. Congress met, Tristram Freeman established the first auction house in America: Freeman's 200 is now in its seventh generation of family management. As an antiquing city, Philadelphia has an impeccable provenance. It is home to an estimated 100 antiques shops and some of the country's foremost dealers. The annual Philadelphia Antiques Show, a weeklong event founded in 1962, has been called the country's premier antiques and decorative arts event.

Held in the first part of April in the historic 33rd Street Armory, the Philadelphia Antiques Show features 60 exhibitors, draws serious collectors from around the world, and is the centerpiece of what has become known as Americana Week. On display are formal European and American furniture; folk art; fine early American and country furniture; Arts & Crafts furniture and textiles; quilts, samplers, and needlework; silver, porcelains, and ceramics; Native American arts; Asian art and antiquities; fine art; Oriental rugs; and garden antiques. Prices are generally high, reflecting quality, and this show is an ideal place to study the best of the best. Its sell-out preview gala is one of the city's leading social events, and programs include lectures on antiques, art, decoration, and history.

This show serves as the centerpiece for three others. The first is Antiques at Philadelphia's Navy Pier, offering 70 dealers with American and English formal and country furniture, folk art, architectural and garden items, art, ceramics, jewelry, Native Indian antiques, textiles, rugs, and other decorative items. The second is the Original 23rd Street Armory Antiques Show at the armory between Market and Chestnut streets, with 40 exhibitors showing formal and rural furniture, folk art, textiles and carpets, garden items, fine art, porcelain, jewelry, and accessories. The third is Antiques at the Highlands, started in 2005 at the Highlands Mansion in Fort Washington; held the last weekend in April, it comprises 25 dealers.

Philadelphia antiques shops include high-end enterprises, owned by dealers who exhibit at the Philadelphia Antiques Show, and multi-dealer venues with a range of merchandise. The city's Antiques Row, with many prestigious shops, is on Pine Street between Ninth and Broad, also known as the Avenue of the Arts, a few blocks from

Independence Hall. You'll also find shops on Third, Walnut, and Chestnut streets and on Germantown Avenue, where merchandise is varied and prices are moderate. Flea markets include the Big T at 2600 East Tioga Street, the Capitolo Playground at Ninth and Federal streets, and Quaker City Flea Market at State Road and Comly Street near Tacony.

Philadelphia's landmarks of American democracy include Independence Hall and the Liberty Bell. But, more evocative of 18th-century urban life is the Old City, between Second and Sixth streets south of Walnut, where Washington, Madison, and other founding fathers lived. At Christ Church on Second Street are the pew Washington used and the gravesite of Benjamin Franklin. The latter is remembered in many exhibits and statues, such as those at the National Constitution Center and the Franklin Institute Science Museum. Other sites of interest include Elfreth's Alley containing c.1702 artisans' homes, the Betsy Ross House, the American Indian Cultural Center, the African-American Museum, the National Museum of American Jewish History, the Chinese Cultural Center, the Polish American Cultural Center Museum, and a Japanese house and garden. The Free Quaker Meeting House (a museum), the 1804 Arch Street Meeting House (still in use), and the Congregation Mikvah Israel, one of the nation's first synagogues, recall Penn's idea that Philadelphia was a "holy experiment" in coexistence.

Noteworthy museums include the Pennsylvania Academy of the Fine Arts, with its collection of early American paintings. The Philadelphia Art Museum's holdings include American art, European decorative arts, prints and drawings, and Asian art, as well as seven 18th- and early-19th-century historic houses, all important restorations

NEAR ONE OF PHILADELPHIA'S CHARMING PARKS, RITTENHOUSE SQUARE BED AND BREAKFAST DISPLAYS ANTIQUES, SUCH AS THE PIER TABLE UNDER A PAINTING AT THE LEFT SIDE OF THE PARLOR.

with period interiors and antique furnishings. Also of note are the gardens of John Bartram, America's first botanist, and two exquisite mid-18th-century Georgian mansions: the National Trust's Cliveden (aka Chew House) in Germantown, and the Art Museum's Mount Pleasant in Fairmount Park. Philadelphia boasts excellent theaters, and symphony and ballet companies.

For antiquing side trips, the Brandywine Valley and Mullica Hill, New Jersey, a historic village with a number of shops and multi-dealer malls, are about 30 miles away; Bucks County is about 40 miles away; and Lancaster County and Berks County are about 70 miles distant.

A favorite Philadelphia hostelry among antiquers is the posh Rittenhouse Square Bed and Breakfast, built by well-known architect Walter Cope in 1911 and within walking distance of Antiques Row, restaurants, cafés, museums, historical attractions, and Rittenhouse Square. This is one of five public squares laid out by William Penn, with acres of trees, fountains, and English perennial gardens. The inn's 24-hour concierge service provides access to restaurant and event reservations, and advises on shopping and cultural options. Each of its eight rooms and two suites has a private marble bath, four with Jacuzzis. Sumptuous breakfasts await in the morning, and several gourmet restaurants will deliver meals upon request. The luxe atmosphere includes Louis XVI-inspired chairs, Chippendale-influenced tables, taffeta valences, vintage mirrors, Italian ceramics, and Neoclassical rugs. As you slide into a bed triple-sheeted with Frette linens, thinking of the wonderful antiques you've seen, you may feel a twinge of pity for those who'd rather be in Philadelphia, but aren't.

BEFORE YOU GO, visit
www.gophila.com
www.antique-row.org
www.pa-antiques.org
www.philaantiques.com
www.barnstar.com/pnp.htm
www.b4rtime.com

FAVORITE LODGING:
Rittenhouse Square Bed and Breakfast
1715 Rittenhouse Square
Philadelphia, PA 19103
215-546-6500; 877-791-6500
www.rittenhousebb.com

Adamstown & Lancaster County, Pennsylvania

Lancaster County, the heart of Pennsylvania "Dutch" Country, regularly shows up on lists of the best places in the U.S. to go antiquing. Thanks to the prosperous farms, German (not Dutch) heritage, and tradition of craftsmanship, the objects that turn up in Lancaster County are many and wonderful. Within 25 miles of the town of Lancaster are more than 150 antiques dealers along country roads (especially Route 272) and in several towns, including Adamstown (nicknamed "antiques capital USA") and Lancaster. Ephrata, Strasburg, Lititz, and Columbia have many antiques shops along their Main Streets. The antiquing landscape includes large antiques malls, multi-dealer ventures, individual dealer shops, antiques shows, flea markets, and farm auctions.

Though this area has its share of early-20th-century furnishings, it's better known as a source for 19th-century farmhouse and country finds, including high country and rustic pieces. One thing to look for is folk art. Amish women transformed the quilt into high art with their fine needlework and preference for strong graphic designs and deep coloration; antique and vintage quilts and quilt tops can be found at antiques stores and country auctions. Many a museum treasures its Pennsylvania German painted furniture and *fraktur*, decorated records of births and marriages.

On weekends, Lancaster County is an antiquing hot spot. The two largest weekend antiques and flea markets are run by Renningers. In Kutztown, the regular Saturday antiques market features 250 dealers and a

THE NEOCLASSICAL BRICK SHEPPARD MANSION BED AND BREAKFAST, IN HANOVER, PENNSYLVANIA, IS A BEAUTIFUL EXAMPLE OF HIGH STYLE COLONIAL REVIVAL ARCHITECTURE.

wide variety of country furnishings; on the last full weekends of April, June, and September, over 1,200 dealers from 42 states converge there for Thursday/Friday/Saturday "Extravaganzas." In Adamstown, the Sunday Antiques and Collectibles Market presents more than 375 dealers indoors; in the spring, summer, and fall, more than 400 dealers also set up outdoors. Five "special" Sunday markets are held on Memorial Day and Labor Day weekends, the first weekend of May, the last weekend of June, and the last weekend of September. These markets open at 7:30 a.m., and early shoppers are often armed with flashlights, as items are bought and sold as dealers set up.

Another favorite is the Saturday/Sunday Shupp's Grove Antique Market, held every weekend from late April through the end of October. Each weekend it features a different specialty, whether it's vintage kitchenware, art glass and pottery, folk art and primitives, textiles and linens, glassware and silver, lighting and timepieces, desktop and writing accoutrements, or something else. Also look for Saturday-morning auctions. Horst Auctions in Ephrata is one good bet, but it's best to check a local newspaper. A typical auction might include farm items, high country furniture, quilts, kitchenware, fine china, and glassware, and you might be bidding against Amish and Mennonite farmers and their wives.

This area is also known for its antiques shows. On the last weekend in February, Renningers holds its Saturday/Sunday Mid-Winter Classic, featuring over 500 dealers, at the Valley Forge Convention Center in King of Prussia; early buying is Saturday morning before the show. On the third weekend of March, the Lancaster Heritage Antiques show, a Friday/Saturday/Sunday event held at Franklin and Marshall College's sports center, presents quality Americana.

Other shows are held in York, southwest of Lancaster, and throughout York County. On the first weekend of March is the Friday/Saturday/Sunday Antiques at York show, with over 50 dealers exhibiting quality period and country furnishings and folk art, held at the York Fairgrounds; the same show reprises the third weekend in November. On the first Saturday in May, the York Pickers Market Antiques Show draws more than 100 dealers to the York Expo Center. The big event in York comes on the first weekend in November, when top-quality Friday/Saturday/Sunday shows take place at the York Fairgrounds; in all, they present over 200 dealers with high-quality American country and formal furniture, early folk art, paintings, textiles, and period accessories. In Harrisburg, two events at the Farm Show Complex are worth noting, both in April: The Friday/Saturday Mennonite Relief Sale includes quilts and is held on the first weekend, while the Friday/Saturday/Sunday Eastern National Antique Show takes place on the third weekend.

Lancaster County contains 29 covered bridges and nearly 3,000 acres of nature preserves. Museums in Lancaster include the Americana Museum of Bird-in-Hand;

THE GENTLEMEN'S PARLOR AT SHEPPARD MANSION BED AND BREAKFAST, BUILT IN 1913, DISPLAYS VIRTUOSO INTERIOR DETAILS AND COLONIAL REVIVAL FURNISHINGS DATING FROM THE EARLY 20TH CENTURY. THESE INCLUDE A PALLADIAN WINDOW WITH FLUTED COLUMNS, DENTIL MOLDINGS, AND PERIOD LIGHTING.

Rock Ford Plantation, an 18th-century home with period furnishings; the Lancaster Cultural History Museum; Amish Farm and House; and President James Buchanan's Wheatland, a Federal-style mansion with period furnishings. Other historical museums include the Amish Village in Strasburg, Ephrata Cloister (one of America's earliest communal societies), the Gemberling-Rex House in Schaefferstown, and Cornwall's Iron Furnace, which operated from 1742 to 1883 and made cannons for the American Revolution. The People's Place Quilt Museum in Intercourse exhibits antique Amish and Mennonite quilts and decorative arts. There are buggy and sleigh rides, outdoor activities, performing arts, and festivals, such as Kutztown's weeklong festival at the fairgrounds in early July. The Amish are part of the landscape here, and their horse-drawn buggies are to be seen on many a country road. Though the scenery invites snapshots, Amish people prefer not to be photographed, regarding it as an invasion of privacy. You can take Old Order Amish tours in Ronks or visit a contemporary Amish home at the Amish County Homestead on Route 340 in Bird-in-Hand.

Places to stay with historic ambiance and ample modern amenities include the E. J. Bowman House and Lovelace Manor in Lancaster, and Kimmel House Bed and Breakfast in Ephrata. To experience authentic Colonial Revival interiors firsthand, the place to stay is the 1913 Sheppard Mansion in Hanover. With period architectural details, stunning woodwork, decorative ceilings, and lighting, this upscale inn combines period furnishings original to the house with new accessories and modern conveniences, such as cable TV and data ports. You can watch a classic movie in the den, relax in the ladies' and gentlemen's parlors, or simply enjoy the privacy of one of the inn's nine guest rooms. Its rooms and intimate 17th-century guest cottage are comfortably outfitted with deluxe linens and private baths, and elegant country breakfasts focus on local produce and meats from Lancaster County farms.

BEFORE YOU GO, visit
www.800padutch.com
www.pa-antiques.org
www.antiquescapital.com
www.goodrichpromotions.com/york_antiques/index.html
www.antique-central.com/pennsylvania.html
www.newoxfordantiques.com

FAVORITE LODGING:
The Sheppard Mansion Bed and Breakfast
117 Sheppard Street
Hanover, PA 17331
717-633-8075; 877-762-6746
www.sheppardmansion.com

The Brandywine Valley & Wilmington, Delaware

he Brandywine Valley, extending from Wilmington, Delaware, to the area south of Philadelphia—about 20 miles from those cities and 125 miles from New York City and Washington, D.C.—is beautiful countryside, with fine estates, gardens, museums, historic towns and houses, and quality antiques shops. One reason to visit is the awe-inspiring collection of American period rooms and decorative arts that Henry Francis Dupont assembled and established as a museum in 1951.

Winterthur (pronounced "winter tour") museum could, without much of a stretch, be called "Winter*tour de force*." One of the best places in the nation to see and learn about American antiques of surpassing quality, it possesses approximately 85,000 objects dating from 1640 to 1860. These are displayed in 175 period rooms, and in galleries that focus on furniture and stylistic movements, textiles, metalwork, paintings, ceramics, and glass. A grand mansion set on 1,000 acres of varied landscape, Winterthur is a center for scholarly study and education, including degree programs

A BUCOLIC VIEW AT SWEETWATER FARM BED & BREAKFAST, AN 18TH-CENTURY STONE MANOR HOUSE SET ON 50 ACRES, MIDWAY BETWEEN PHILADELPHIA AND WILMINGTON.

and seminars for collectors and curators. Special tours are geared to particular inter-
ests, but any visit to Winterthur is a crash course in American decorative arts.

The Brandywine Valley in Pennsylvania has more than 60 shops, including
antiques malls and individual dealers of national repute who offer high quality and
good value. You'll find fine formal and informal American and European objects,
and, particularly in area antiques malls, furnishings up through the mid-20th century.
In Delaware, Wilmington has about 15 varied and interesting shops and a charming
Quaker Historic District. Six miles to the south is New Castle, with brick and cobblestone streets, centuries-old Dutch, English, and Federal buildings, and about six
antiques shops. One bonus of shopping in Delaware is that it's tax-free.

Three excellent annual antiques shows are held. On Memorial Day weekend, the
Saturday/Sunday/Monday Brandywine River Museum Antiques Show in Chadds Ford,
Pennsylvania, attracts 32 exhibitors with 17th-, 18th-, and 19th-century English and
American furniture, paintings, Georgian silver, Delft and other ceramics
(including Chinese export wares), pewter, tall clocks, and accessories. In
mid-October, the Saturday/Sunday Historic Yellow Springs Show is held
in Chester Springs, Pennsylvania; it draws 50 dealers from ten states,
exhibiting 18th- and 19th-century American pieces, including country
items and folk art. In mid-November, the annual Delaware Antiques Show,
a Friday/Saturday event in Wilmington, benefits Winterthur, and presents 60
prestigious dealers, who specialize in fine 17th-, 18th- and early-19th-century English
and American furniture, folk art, Native American art, ceramics, needlework, jewelry,
art, and rugs.

The Brandywine's earliest permanent European settlers were Swedes and Finns
who arrived in 1638, introducing the log cabin to America. The Dutch founded New
Castle in 1651; Quaker William Penn arrived in 1682; the English followed.
Wilmington's 1698 Old Swedes Church is still in use for regular worship; its stone 1690
Hendrickson Farmhouse is a museum of 17th-century life. The Conestoga wagon, the
"prairie schooner" that carried so many pioneers west, was developed to haul grain to
the Brandywine River's water-powered mills. Some of the mills supplied the paper on
which the Declaration of Independence and U.S. Constitution were written.

Historic house museums with period furnishings include several in Chadds Ford:
the 1714 Barns-Brinton House and John Chad's 1725 stone house. George
Washington's headquarters at Ring House and General Lafayette's quarters at Gideon
Gilpin's farmhouse are both in Brandywine Battlefield Park. Also of interest are the
1704 Brinton House in Dilworthtown and the 1704 Newlin Grist Mill and Miller's
House in Glen Mills Park. Of note in Delaware are the c.1852 Gothic Revival
Rockwood Mansion in Wilmington; and the 17th-century Dutch House, the 1738
Amstel Mansion, and 1804 George Read II House and Gardens, all in New Castle.

The fortune that underwrote Winterthur originated with a French immigrant who established black powder mills on the Brandywine River in the late 1700s, beginning the Dupont Company. Other museums associated with the Duponts are the Hagley Museum, with historic mills and an 1803 Georgian-style mansion; the Nemours Mansion and Gardens, a 1910 Louis VXI chateau; and Longwood Garden, with over 1,050 landscaped acres, 20 indoor gardens, and an open air theater. The Brandywine River Museum's collections of American art include work by the Wyeths.

USED AS AN INFIRMARY DURING THE CIVIL WAR, SWEETWATER FARM'S MOST MODEST GUEST ROOM IS ALSO ONE OF ITS MOST CHARMING.

In Wilmington, the Delaware Art Museum exhibits English pre-Raphaelite art and 19th- and 20th-century American paintings and illustrations, while, in Dover, the Briggs Museum exhibits fine American antiques.

Seasonal events include Old New Castle Day and Winterthur's steeplechase horse races, both in May. You can also enjoy blues and jazz festivals; a Revolutionary War reenactment at the Battle of Brandywine Park; theater, opera, ballet, musical performances; outdoor activities; and the Brandywine Valley Wine Trail.

There are two favorite lodgings among antiquers, one in Delaware and the other in Pennsylvania. In Brandywine County, Sweetwater Farm Bed and Breakfast is an idyllic 50-acre estate encompassing a 1734 Quaker stone farmhouse with an 1818 wing and several cottages. Its 12 inviting guest rooms feature fresh interior styling and period ambiance, private baths, and high-speed Internet access. Amenities include a billiard room, a swimming pool, and a wicker-filled porch overlooking acres of peaceful, rolling fields, ponds, and woods. In Delaware, the Inn at Montchanin Village, once

BUILT BY THE DUPONT FAMILY, THE INN AT MONTCHANIN VILLAGE, A RESTORED 19TH-CENTURY HAMLET, WAS ONCE PART OF THEIR WINTERTHUR ESTATE. A MEMBER OF HISTORIC HOTELS OF AMERICA, ITS ANTIQUE FURNISHINGS INCLUDE THIS BARONIAL BED.

part of the Winterthur Estate, is listed on the National Register of Historic Places and a member of the National Trust's Historic Hotels of America. This 19th-century hamlet, built to house Dupont mill workers, comprises 11 restored buildings set among gardens and containing 28 guest rooms and a restaurant. Sophisticated appointments include antique and reproduction furnishings, marble baths, high-speed Internet access, cable TV, and a wet bar; many rooms have private courtyards and gas fireplaces. At both of these inns, comfort and historic ambiance will enhance any weekend.

BEFORE YOU GO, visit
www.visitwilmingtonde.com
www.thebrandywine.com/special/index.html
www.pa-antiques.org
www.winterthur.org

FAVORITE LODGINGS:

Sweetwater Farm Bed and Breakfast
50 Sweetwater Road
Glen Mills, PA 19342
610-459-4711; 800-793-3892
www.sweetwaterfarmbb.com

The Inn at Montchanin Village
Route 100 and Kirk Road
Montchanin, DE 19710
302-888-2133; 800-269-2473
www.montchanin.com
www.historichotels.org

Annapolis & Maryland's Eastern Shore

nnapolis, Maryland, became a maritime center shortly after it was founded over 300 years ago and remains so today. Established as a Puritan settlement in 1670 and chartered by Queen Anne in 1708, 18th-century Annapolis was known for its elegant homes and gracious social life. Sailing vessels came here to pick up tobacco, bringing furnishings and decorative arts from other American cities and from abroad. The city's antique character is preserved in a National Historic District that retains its unique early-18th-century street plan and encompasses three

centuries of buildings, many now containing shops and restaurants. With the presence of the U.S. Naval Academy and an active yachting community, sailing and maritime traditions remain an important part of Annapolis life. Antiques stores tucked into historic brick shopfronts are perfectly in keeping with the city's historic ambiance.

Some of Annapolis' upscale antiques shops include stores oriented to decorators. Across the Eastport Bridge, on the opposite side of Chesapeake Bay, the Eastern Shore has more multi-dealer shops and malls. In this area, you can find fine formal and high country Federal period furniture and a variety of other items up through the Colonial Revival period. In mid-January, the Historic Annapolis Foundation holds its annual antiques show. This Friday/ Saturday/Sunday event at the National Guard Armory showcases dealers from around the country, who display fine American, English, and Continental period furniture and decorative accessories.

IN THE STATELY PARLOR OF THE GEORGIAN C.1770
ANNAPOLIS INN, PERIOD DÉCOR HARMONIZES WITH
NEOCLASSICAL ARCHITECTURAL DETAILS, WHICH INCLUDE
A MARBLE MANTEL AND GILDED ROSETTE MOLDINGS.

Named Maryland's state capital in 1694, Annapolis was home to every Maryland signer of the Declaration of Independence, and in 1783–84 served as the nation's capital. In its State House, the Continental Congress ratified the Treaty of Paris, ending the Revolutionary War, and accepted George Washington's resignation as the Army's commander in chief. The 1786 Annapolis Convention led to Philadelphia's Constitutional Convention the following year.

Historic house museums include several impressive mid-18th-century Georgian buildings: the William Paca House and Gardens; the Charles Carroll House; the Chase-Lloyd House; and the Hammond-Hardwood House, which exhibits Charles Wilson Peale paintings and John Shaw furniture. In Edgewater, the William Brown House is at London Town & Gardens, an important archeological site. Maritime history is the focus of the Annapolis Maritime Museum, the Naval Academy Museum, and the Captain Salem Avery House and Museum. African American history is recalled in the city's historic tours and at the Banneker-Douglass Museum.

IN A GUEST SUITE AT THE ANNAPOLIS INN, ETCHED GLASS DOORS OPEN TO AN OPULENT SITTING ROOM, WHERE ANTIQUE FURNISHINGS INCLUDE A PERIOD SETTEE AND A GILDED FRENCH SECRETAIRE.

Maryland's Eastern Shore is more rural and quieter than Annapolis, but equally historic and tied to the sea. Just over the bridge, in Stevensville, is a charming Carpenter Gothic church, built in 1880. The distance from Annapolis to Cambridge, on the Eastern Shore, is a mere 60 miles along the "fast" road; take a slow meander through Easton, St. Michael's, and Oxford, and you'll find antiquing stops along the way. Thirty miles beyond Cambridge is Salisbury, which has about eight shops. From Salisbury, it's another 30 miles to Ocean City, the gateway to the Assateague Island National Seashore, one of the most beautiful on the Eastern seaboard. Along this route, St. Michaels, established in the mid-1800s, is a favorite place for antiquing. This tiny waterside town saved itself during the

War of 1812, when residents hoisted lanterns to the masts of ships and tops of trees, foiling the aim of British cannons: Only one house was struck. St. Michaels has two museums: the historical museum on the town's 1778 St. Mary's Square and the Chesapeake Bay Maritime Museum. Also on the Eastern Shore, west of Chestertown, Mount Harmon Plantation offers tours of its Georgian mansion.

This area offers fine dining, opera, symphony, jazz and other types of music, theater, dance, and many festivals, including an oyster festival in October. Activities on and about the water include boat tours, fishing charters, sailing instruction, and cruises. The Eastern Neck Wildlife Refuge, a beautiful marsh, field, and woodland area, has miles of hiking trails.

A charming lodging on the Eastern Shore is the Cherry Street Inn, with porches overlooking a quaint street, guest rooms with private baths, and period-appropriate furnishings such as sleigh beds and French toiles. In Annapolis, the choice for its period elegance is the Annapolis Inn, a beautiful c.1770 Georgian townhouse located in the Historic District. Featuring original rosette moldings, marble fireplaces, Greek Revival interior windows with rolled glass, French and English antiques, and European paintings, and offering amenities such as afternoon tea, an enclosed garden with a koi pond, concierge service, claw-foot whirlpool tubs, and modem access, the inn pampers the antiquer both physically and visually.

BEFORE YOU GO, visit
www.maryland.com
www.visit-annapolis.org
www.antiquesinmd.com

FAVORITE LODGING:
The Annapolis Inn
144 Prince George Street
Annapolis, MD 21401
410-295-5200
www.annapolisinn.com

Washington, D.C.; Kensington, Maryland; & Alexandria, Virginia

J ust as there are three branches of government, there are three outstanding antiquing destinations in and around the U.S. capital: Alexandria, Virginia, Kensington, Maryland, and Washington, D.C. itself.

Alexandria was part of the District of Columbia until 1847, when its residents voted to become part of Virginia. In 1946, Alexandria became the country's third historic district, and it still retains its 18th-century character. The city contains about 20 antiques shops, including several of national prominence. Alexandria is also home to two high-quality antiques shows, presenting outstanding American, English, Continental, and Asian furniture and decorative arts of the 17th through 19th centuries. The Antiques in Alexandria Antiques Show, with 60 dealers, takes place in early March; the Historic Alexandria Antiques Show, with about 45 dealers, is held the third weekend in November. On the third weekends of February and August, the Lee District Antiques Shows bring together 80 dealers, with American, European, and Asian 19th- and 20th-century furniture, decorative arts, fine art, and jewelry.

Kensington's Antique Row, which claims to have been the first antiquing district in the metropolitan area, contains an estimated 80 shops on Howard Avenue East and adjacent streets. These offer a range of merchandise from 18th- through 20th-century American and Continental furnishings to vintage fountain pens, political memorabilia, and rare books.

In Washington, D.C., concentrations of antiques shops are in Dupont Circle, Georgetown, and Adams Morgan, and shops reflect the city's international character. The Washington Antiques Show, held in early January, attracts 45 top dealers with a range of high-quality furnishings and decorative arts. The Historic Indian and World Tribal Arts Show, held in mid-October, brings together 45 dealers with ethnographic antiques and art of the Americas, Africa, Asia, and Oceania, and Western, Spanish Colonial, and Pre-Columbian art. In early December and March, the D.C. Armory on East Capitol Street is the site of a show featuring some 150 dealers. Other area shows include the District's Stephens-St. Agnes Antiques Show, held in early January, and the Chevy Chase Women's Club Antiques Show in early September. The Northern

Virginia Antiques Show, held in mid-June in Arlington, presents some 160 dealers; a mid-November show in McLean, Virginia, draws 60 dealers. Flea markets include the year-round Sunday Georgetown Flea Market on Wisconsin Avenue north of S Street, and the Saturday/Sunday Big Flea Market, with over 1,100 booths, held in mid-July and mid-September at the Dulles Exposition and Convention Center in Chantilly, Virginia.

The Smithsonian Institution, in Washington, D.C., is the largest museum complex in the world, and its artistic and historic treasures are legion. Antiquarians take note of the National Gallery of Art, Corcoran Gallery of Art, Smithsonian's American Art Museum, the Textile Museum, the Octagon House (the nation's oldest museum dedicated to architecture and design), National Museum of American History, National Museum of the American Indian, Freer Gallery of Art and The Arthur M. Sackler Gallery (Asian art), Phillips Collection (museum of 20th-century art, especially Modernism), Dumbarton Oaks (Byzantine and pre-Columbian collections and gardens by Beatrix Ferrand), the Library of Congress, and the National Archives. Historic homes with period furnishings include the White House, the c.1795 Old Stone House (furnished with c.1765–1810 antiques), and the Federal-period Decatur House. The homes of Frederick Douglass and Clara Barton are both National

A TABLE SET FOR BREAKFAST AT THE SWANN HOUSE INN IN WASHINGTON, D.C., AFFORDS A VIEW OF ITS MAGNIFICENT C.1883 ROMANESQUE REVIVAL EXTERIOR.

Historic Sites. Recreation in Washington's Rock Creek Park includes horseback riding, bicycling, jogging, and tennis. If you're visiting in July, the Smithsonian's Festival of American Folklife is a must.

In Alexandria, period restorations in Old Town, founded by Scottish merchants in 1749, include the 1752 Georgian Palladian Carlyle Manor House; the c.1785 Gadsby's Tavern, frequented by the founding fathers; and the Lee-Fendall House, with furnishings dating to 1850–70. Also of interest are two museums of African American history, an apothecary museum, and an archeology museum. Nearby are Mount Vernon, Washington's home, and the c.1805 Woodlawn Plantation, which encompasses the house Washington built for his nephew, as well as Frank Lloyd Wright's Pope-Leighey House. Gunston Hall, the home of George Mason, father of the Bill of Rights, is in the town of Mount Vernon.

Among the District's historic hostelries are the Willard Hotel, the Taft Bridge Inn, the Morrison-Clark Inn, and Swann House, a magnificent Romanesque Revival mansion. With crystal chandeliers, ornate woodwork, carved marble fireplaces, and molded plasterwork, its c.1883 interiors recall the Gilded Age. Period ambiance and sensitive styling combine with personal comforts and conveniences (a swimming pool, French doors opening to private decks, featherbeds, Internet access, and baths with whirlpools and claw-foot tubs) to make an antiquer feel as pampered as a visiting head of state—and probably much more relaxed.

BEFORE YOU GO, visit
www.masondixonantiquetrail.com
www.antiquescouncil.org
www.virginiastatewebsite.com
www.ci.alexandria.va.us
www.kensingtonantiquerow.com
www.antiquesinmd.com
www.washingtonantiques.org
www.georgetownfleamarket.com
www.ArmacostAntiquesShows.com
www.pappabello.com
www.damorepromotions.com

FAVORITE LODGING:
Swann House Historic Dupont Circle Inn
1808 New Hampshire Avenue, NW
Washington, D.C. 20009
202-265-4414
www.swannhouse.com

South

Loudoun County, Northern Virginia's Hunt Country

orthern Virginia's Loudoun County is known as Hunt Country. First settled in the early 18th century, western Loudoun County is a place of rolling hills and stone houses. Chestnut and bay thoroughbreds, some of them Olympic competitors, graze in its emerald pastures edged by tall trees and fences. Horseback riding is a high art, and fox hunts, introduced from England in 1748, are still held. Located in the foothills of the Blue Ridge Mountains, Loudoun County is flanked by Washington, D.C., to the east, and by the Shenandoah Valley on the west. Part of the John Mosby National Heritage Area, it is a beautiful place to visit, with many historic attractions and good antiquing. The heart of Hunt Country is Middleburg, so named because it is midway between Winchester and Alexandria on the Ash Gap Road, now Route 50, once a Native American trail.

Loudoun County has about 24 antiques stores, with the largest concentrations of shops in Leesburg, Middleburg, Hamilton, Purcellville (on 21st Street), and Lovettsville. There are multi-dealer and individual antiques shops here, and antiques

NEAR THE BLUE RIDGE AND BULL RUN MOUNTAINS, THE RED FOX INN IN MIDDLEBURG, VIRGINIA, WAS ESTABLISHED 1728. ITS PERIOD-STYLE GUESTROOMS, FINE RESTAURANT, AND ART GALLERY, SPECIALIZING IN 19TH-CENTURY AMERICAN PAINTINGS, MAKE IT A FAVORITE.

malls with up to 45 dealers. Quality is generally quite good. This area favors "shiny brown" furniture, and a couple of stores focus on shabby chic style. Nearby, but outside Loudoun County, two shops carry period country furnishings and folk art, a relative rarity in these parts. During Leesburg's First Friday Gallery Walk, held every month except January, many shops extend their hours.

Several notable antiques shows take place in Loudoun County. In January, a Saturday/Sunday show with about 35 dealers is held at the Leesburg Armory. The Morven Park Equestrian Center in Leesburg is the setting for two Saturday/Sunday shows, which attract about 150 dealers; these take place on the third weekend in April and the second weekend in October. The following weekend, the same venue is the site of a Saturday/Sunday rummage sale, recommended for antiques and home furnishings—it's wise to arrive early. In Purcellville, a Friday/Saturday/Sunday show with 35 dealers is held the first weekend in November at the skating rink. There's a weekend flea market in Aldie, and a summer Saturday flea market in Sterling.

Virginia's "antiques capital," Strasburg, with about 20 malls and shops, is 45 miles west of Middleburg. En route, Front Royal has about ten shops. Just over the border in West Virginia is Harper's Ferry, with its National Historic Park and village containing some antiques stores.

One reason this area is fun to explore is the varied character of its small towns. Leesburg, the county seat, just 35 miles from Washington, D.C., is a busy town with a charming historic district and a mix of 18th- and 19th-century buildings. Shop signs, with names like Cuppa Giddyup (a coffee shop), on Middleburg's chic main street emphasize equine associations. Lincoln, Purcellville, and Waterford (a National Landmark Village) were settled in the 1700s by Quakers and have historic Friends Meeting Houses. Lovettsville retains many of its early German buildings, while Hamilton boasts fine Victorians. Aldie and Bluemont are quiet rural towns, and Round Hill, the gateway to the Blue Ridge Mountains and the Appalachian Trail, is known for its spectacular scenery and active arts scene. Historic gristmills and sites commemorating the American Revolution and Civil War are among other attractions. Historic homes with period furnishings include the 22-room 1804 antebellum Oatlands Plantation, a 330-acre National Trust property; the grand early-20th-century Neoclassical mansion at Morven Park, which also has a Museum of Hounds and Hunting and a carriage museum; and Dodona, the former home of George Marshall, who authored the post-WWII Marshall Plan.

This countryside is ideal for cycling and, with the Appalachian Trail close at hand, there's plenty of hiking. Other outdoor activities include golf, skating, river trips and whitewater rafting, nature and bird walks at the Audubon Society's Rust Sanctuary and elsewhere, and horseback riding at Georges Mill Farm. As you'd expect in Hunt

Country, horse shows and equestrian sporting events are numerous, and include polo matches and steeplechase races in the spring and fall. The Middleburg Hunt Country Stable Tour takes place during Memorial Day weekend.

You can also tour area wineries, enjoy an organic al fresco dinner in the garden at Patowmack Farm, stop for lunch at Planet Wayside, a funky old diner in Hamilton, visit some of the area's old-fashioned general stores, ride on an early railroad, or poke around in one of Virginia's oldest hardware stores. In mid-September, rural Bluemont holds its Country Fair, and, in mid-October, the 200-year-old village of Aldie hosts its Saturday harvest festival. The arts scene includes local theater, symphony, ballet, chorale concerts, and jazz.

Loudoun County's oldest accommodation is Middleburg's Red Fox Inn, established in the early 1700s. This romantic country inn, with 23 tasteful, traditionally appointed rooms, an excellent restaurant, and a fine arts gallery, is much loved by local residents and visitors. The area's historic bed and breakfasts include Creek Crossing Farm in Lincoln, Little River Inn in Aldie, Georges Mill Farm in Lovettsville, and the Longbarn in Middleburg, an authentic period barn restored as an inn. At each of these places, you'll find comfortable rooms with antique or country furnishings, good breakfasts, and peaceful vantage points from which to enjoy spectacular scenery. For antiquers, the nickname Hunt Country might take on a whole new meaning.

BEFORE YOU GO, visit
www.visitloudoun.org
www.leesburgantiques.com

FAVORITE LODGING:
Red Fox Inn
2 East Washington Street
Middleburg, VA 20118
540-687-6301
www.redfox.com

Asheville, North Carolina

T his thriving resort town in the Blue Ridge Mountains has been a tourist destination since the late 19th century, when George Vanderbilt established his magnificent Biltmore estate. Its 255-room French Renaissance chateau, designed by Richard Morris Hunt, was the largest private residence in the U.S. at the time. The spectacular scenery and cool, healthful climate of the "land of the sky" made Asheville a popular getaway for millionaires. Add to its natural attractions the town's 30 antiques stores, and you have the makings of a perfect antiquing weekend. Asheville antiques dealers, whether in multi-dealer malls or high-end shops, offer a range from fine European and American pieces to art pottery and Appalachian folk art. Brunk Auctions, with eight to ten sales a year, attracts buyers nationally and internationally.

For aficionados of early-20th-century architecture and arts, downtown Asheville is second to only one other southeastern town, Miami Beach, in its abundance of Art Deco buildings, and the Grove Park Inn's annual symposium on the Arts & Crafts movement is excellent.

First settled in 1784, Asheville was a Confederate center during the Civil War. It boasts numerous restaurants, a vibrant nightlife, and over 150 boutiques, shops, and galleries. The stunning Biltmore estate is now a museum; it offers tours of its

JUST MINUTES FROM ASHEVILLE, THE RICHMOND HILL INN IS A BEAUTIFULLY RESTORED C.1889 COUNTRY ESTATE, WHERE PLEASURES INCLUDE VIEWS OF THE BLUE RIDGE MOUNTAINS, OPULENT INTERIOR DETAILING, AND FINE DINING.

antiques-filled interiors, as well as biking, horseback riding, and rafting on its 8,000 acres, which include landscapes designed by Frederick Law Olmstead.

Other places to visit are a contemporary art museum, a botanical garden, the North Carolina Arboretum, and the house, now a museum, that Thomas Wolfe, an Asheville native, immortalized in *Look Homeward Angel*, incurring local ire. The Blue Ridge Mountains are one of the most visited sites in the National Park system. Outdoor activities include golf, hiking at Chimney Rock Park (known for its 400-foot waterfall), and winter skiing at Wolf Laurel. Other diversions include the National Park Service's Folk Art Center, which sponsors craft sales, exhibits, and demonstrations, and the WNC Farmers Market with its mountain crafts, jams, garden supplies, and plants.

Other antiquing destinations in North Carolina include Charlotte (which hosts an Antiques & Collectibles show on the first weekend of each month), Wilmington, Raleigh, Greensboro, Durham, Blowing Rock, and Winston-Salem, where the Museum of Early Southern Decorative Arts is a fine place to learn about antique furniture of the South.

Asheville's historic lodgings include the c.1913 Grove Park Inn resort, where guest rooms showcase decorative styles of various periods, the lovely Colonial Revival Chestnut Street Inn, the Victorian Cedar Crest Inn, and the Queen Anne-style Richmond Hill Inn. Built in 1889 for congressman and diplomat Richard Pearson, Richmond Hill was rescued in 1984 by Asheville's Preservation Society and treated to an extensive restoration, which included reinstalling original Belcher stained-glass windows above its grand staircase and creating an octagonal ballroom. A short drive from downtown Asheville, the Richmond Hill Inn retains the character of a country estate, with a gourmet restaurant, 36 antiques-decorated guest rooms, a formal parlor and library, six acres of English cottage-style gardens, a parterre garden, a nine-foot waterfall, and 40 acres of woodland. Enjoying the view from one of the rocking chairs on its wide porch, you'll experience the same scenery enjoyed by Asheville's Gilded Age millionaires, even if you can't afford to shop like them.

BEFORE YOU GO, visit
www.exploreasheville.com
www.cr.nps.gov/nr/travel/asheville
www.southfest.com

FAVORITE LODGING:
Richmond Hill Inn
87 Richmond Hill Drive
Asheville, NC 28806
888-742-4536; 828-252-7313
www.richmondhillinn.com

Charleston, South Carolina

A local joke goes like this: How many Charleston women does it take to screw in a light bulb? Three—one to replace the bulb, one to mix the cocktails, and the third to talk about how much better the old light bulb was than the new one. Charleston, founded in 1670, loves its history and its antiques. It was the first city in the U.S. to establish a museum (1773) and the first to zone a historic district (1931).

One of 18th-century America's busiest ports, Charleston quickly became a cosmopolitan city with a taste for fine things. Englishmen came from Barbados, introducing the plantation system, and French Huguenots planted rice as an experiment, originating Carolina rice. With wealthy planters and merchants whose homes displayed their status, and access to prized West Indian *Swietenia mahogani*, Charleston was soon employing hundreds of cabinetmakers and craftsmen. One was silversmith Solomon Le Gare, whose name writer Harriet Beecher Stowe appropriated for Simon Legree, the famous villain of *Uncle Tom's Cabin*. (A Le Gare descendent in New England possesses her letter of apology.)

The work of these craftsmen can still be seen in some of the city's finer antiques stores. More than 40, many of surpassing quality, are located in Charleston's historic lower peninsula, along lower King Street and intersecting streets, and on Church and Broad streets. You'll find excellent 18th- and early-19th-century American, English, and Continental pieces, along with decorative arts, silver, and porcelain. Paintings and prints by naturalists Mark Catesby and John James Audubon are a specialty. Greater Charleston has over 150 dealers, accommodating virtually every taste and purse; the city's Antiques Dealers Association publishes a directory, available at shops and the visitor center. Mount

IN HISTORIC CHARLESTON, AN ELEGANT PIANO AWAITS ITS OPPORTUNITY TO ENTERTAIN AT THE GOVERNOR'S HOUSE INN, A GEORGIAN MANSION BUILT IN 1760 FOR EDWARD RUTLEDGE, THE YOUNGEST SIGNER OF THE DECLARATION OF INDEPENDENCE.

Pleasant and Summerville have numerous antiques malls, and many shops dot Savannah Highway.

March is prime time for antiquing here. Mid-month, the College of Charleston holds its five-day antiques symposium. This kicks off the Historic Charleston Foundation's Annual Antiques Show, which attracts 30 American and European dealers exhibiting European, American, and Asian antiques.

Superb house museums with period furnishings include the 1772 Heyward-Washington House, which contains the Holmes Bookcase, one of the finest pieces ever

made in America; the 1803 Joseph Manigault House; and the Aiken-Rhett House, with crystal chandeliers and classical sculpture. Outside the city are Middleton, with furnishings from the 1740s–1880s, and Drayton Hall, an unfurnished National Trust Historic Site, one of the nation's finest examples of Georgian-Palladian architecture. The Gibbes Museum of Art displays colonial and antebellum pieces. The National Monument at Fort Sumter is where Confederate soldiers fired the first shots of the Civil War.

The internationally acclaimed Spoleto Festival and its offshoot, Piccolo Spoleto, run from Memorial Day weekend through mid-June. An active musical calendar runs all year. Gourmet restaurants and food festivals abound. Quaint Daniel Island and Folly Beach offer recreational activities.

CHINESE BLUE-AND-WHITE EXPORT PORCELAIN AND A CHIPPENDALE-STYLE SECRETARY ARE AMONG THE PERIOD-APPROPRIATE FURNISHINGS AT THE GOVERNOR'S HOUSE INN. A NATIONAL HISTORIC LANDMARK, IT IS JUST A SHORT WALK FROM FINE ANTIQUES SHOPS.

One of the best forms of recreation is simply exploring Charleston's seven historic districts, which occupy 1,000 acres and contain as many pre-Civil War buildings, many with Caribbean and French architectural influences, and all, including the Old Market, still in use. The Huguenot Church and the Kahal Kadosh Beth Elohim (the oldest surviving Reform synagogue in the world) are the oldest of their kinds in the U.S. still in continuous use; Charleston's Coming Street Jewish cemetery dates to 1762. Historic African American churches include the Old Bethel United Methodist

Church, founded by whites and blacks, and the A.M.E. Church, founded by free blacks and slaves. Charleston's First Baptist Church was also the South's first Baptist church.

Among lodgings, a jewel in Charleston's crown is the Governor's House Inn, a National Historic Landmark and a short walk from King Street's shops, the Old Market, and Spoleto performance venues. The Inn's split front staircase was borrowed from Caribbean architecture, and its double verandas are a feature seen on grand and humble homes throughout the city. This Georgian mansion, built in 1760 for Edward Rutledge, the youngest signer of the Declaration of Independence and husband of Henrietta Middleton (whose family owned Middleton Plantation) is a magnificent place. Twelve-foot ceilings, a crescent staircase, nine fireplaces, crystal chandeliers, marble baths and period-appropriate furnishings create an elegant setting for low country treats at afternoon tea, sherry in the parlor, and a luxurious night's sleep. Southern hospitality at its most gracious is what you'd expect in Charleston, and it's what you'll find.

BEFORE YOU GO, visit
www.celebratecharleston.com
www.discovercharleston.com
www.historiccharleston.org
www.cofc.edu/sota/symposium
www.charlestonsfinest.com/sc/antiques.htm

FAVORITE LODGING:
Governor's House Inn
117 Broad Street
Charleston, SC 29401
843-720-2070; 800-720-9812
www.governorshouse.com

Atlanta, Georgia

I
f any city in the U.S. has an appetite for antiques, it's Atlanta. Rebuilt—and refurnished—after the Civil War, Atlanta's enthusiasm for home furnishings seems only to have increased over time. Atlanta has three antiquing neighborhoods and more than enough shops to occupy a weekend. Many of the city's finer shops are located on Bennett Street and on the Miami Circle cul de sac, a decorator destination. The Antiques Row in Chamblee, 15 miles north of Atlanta, has about 15 stores, including malls, multi-dealer enterprises, and consignment shops, many of which carry collectibles. Chamblee holds an Antiques Festival the first Saturday in June.

With its antiquing districts, Atlanta is an antiquing destination at any time. But, on the second weekend of the month, two Friday/Saturday/Sunday antiques shows attract buyers from around the country (make that the world). Held every month of the year, the Lakewood Antiques Market, at the old fairgrounds at Lakewood Park in downtown Atlanta, is an indoor and outdoor show with some 1,500 dealers who set up in seven buildings and five courtyards on 13 acres. Items range from furniture and household objects to architectural antiques and garden accessories.

From August through December, the enormous Scott Show occupies 364,000 square feet of space (a total of 2,400 booths) in two buildings at the Atlanta Expo Center. Incredibly diverse in quality and price, it includes furniture, decorative arts and accents, carpets, lighting, ceramics, jewelry, and art. Check the South building for

THE SHELLMONT INN, A GRACEFUL COLONIAL REVIVAL MANSION BUILT IN 1891 AND LOCATED IN ATLANTA'S CULTURAL DISTRICT, SHOWCASES ORIGINAL DETAILS SUCH AS STAINED- AND LEADED-GLASS WINDOWS AND CARVED WOODWORK. ANTIQUE FURNISHINGS, ORIENTAL CARPETS, AND WICKER-FILLED VERANDAS CREATE PERIOD AMBIANCE.

French, American, and English furniture, including armoires, beds, and chests, and the North building for dealers specializing in silver. Outside, where things are more eclectic and less expensive, are interior and garden furnishings, and architectural salvage. Thursday, when the dealers are setting up, is "dealer day," when Atlanta antiques dealers source pieces that may increase fivefold in price the next time they're sold; the general public can enter the buildings at this time, too.

Atlanta is home to wonderful cultural and performing arts activities. Museums include the (Martin Luther) King Center, the botanical society, and the High Museum of Art, with its significant collection of 19th- and 20th-century American furniture and decorative arts, including late-19th-century masterpieces by the Herter Brothers. The Atlanta History Center exhibits include decorative arts and domestic culture, textiles, and urban history, as well as two historic properties with period furnishings: the 1840s Tullie Smith Living History Farm and the 1928 Swan House, both listed on the National Register of Historic Places. The Margaret Mitchell Home and Museum is a two-block site devoted to *Gone With the Wind*; the museum's Center for Southern Literature presents lectures and literary events.

For lodgings, a top choice among antiquers is the Shellmont Inn, listed on the National Register of Historic Places and a recipient of a city preservation award. Located in the cultural district, this 1891 mansion displays ornate woodwork, beveled- and stained-glass windows, stenciling, period wallpaper, and antique furnishings, some original to the house. You can soak up Southern atmosphere in a music room with a coved ceiling and a 12-foot floor-to-ceiling wooden mantel with carvings of musical instruments, in the "Turkish" library, or on wicker-filled porches overlooking lush gardens. Other historic Atlanta lodgings with antique furnishings include the Ansley Inn, the Beverley Hills Inn, and the Laurel Hill Bed and Breakfast.

BEFORE YOU GO, visit
www.atlanta.net
www.escapetothesoutheast.com
www.scottantiquemarket.com
www.atlantaantiquedealers.com
www.lakewoodantiques.com
www.antiquerow.com

FAVORITE LODGING:
The Shellmont Inn
821 Piedmont Avenue, NE
Atlanta, GA 30308
404-872-9290
www.shellmont.com

Savannah, Georgia

I ronically, most tourists who visited Savannah in the last decade were attracted by a story about an antiques dealer, but didn't come to shop. *Midnight in the Garden of Good and Evil,* John Berendt's 1994 nonfiction bestseller about Jim Williams's murder of his gay lover, has been the magnet. But for antiquers, historic Savannah—languorous, seductive, and hauntingly beautiful—has much more to offer.

This seaport city is salted with small shops, antiques malls, and galleries offering opulent, high-style Continental and Southern furniture, fine Chinese porcelains, estate jewelry, collectibles, and all manner of things in between. Many of its antiques shops are located in the city's National Historic Landmark District. Founded in 1733, Savannah possesses one of the country's largest: over two square miles of 1,500 preserved historic structures now used as residences, businesses, museums, and inns. Among them are a number of 200-year-old Regency buildings, including the 1818 Neoclassical mansion housing the Telfair Museum of Art and its American Impressionist collection.

ELEGANCE AND REFINEMENT ARE THE HALLMARKS OF SAVANNAH'S HISTORIC BALLASTONE INN, WHERE PARLOR FURNISHINGS INCLUDE AN 18TH-CENTURY FRENCH HARP, RECALLING MUSICAL RECITALS POPULAR IN THAT CENTURY.

Savannah's historical attractions include the 1850 Gothic Revival Green-Meldrim House and the 1820 Davenport House. The Owens-Thomas House veranda represents the first architectural use of cast iron in the U.S.; its intact slave quarters are among its outbuildings. The city's ecclesiastical architecture includes the 1788 First African Baptist Church, one of the nation's oldest continuously functioning African American churches; the 1802 Second African Baptist Church where Union General Sherman read the Emancipation Proclamation and Martin Luther King first preached his "I Have a

Dream" sermon; and the 1876 Temple Mickve Israel, the only Gothic Revival-style synagogue in the U.S.

Savannah was laid out on a grid system by its founder, Englishman James Oglethorpe, who wrested this city out of marshland. It is eminently walkable, its geometry softened by wisps of Spanish moss hanging from venerable oaks and by the lush greenery of its 21 squares, which contain azaleas, oleander, and jasmine, fountains, statues, and gazebos. Many diversions await here, too: gourmet restaurants, the City Market's jazz and blues clubs, music festivals, Tybee Island beaches (18 miles away), and islands rich in Gullah African American culture. One of the city's most delightful spots is its historic riverfront district and River Street, where you can relax at a café, watch ships come and go, and enjoy sunsets over the Savannah River.

Savannah's historic inns include the Hamilton-Turner Inn, the Eliza Thompson House, and the Olde Harbour Inn. Romance and refinement are nowhere more evident than at the Ballastone Inn. Named for the ships' ballast stones that form the loading ramps on the Savannah River, this gracious townhouse, now a luxurious bed and breakfast, traces its origins to 1838 and is listed on the National Register of Historic Places. Located on a street laid out by Oglethorpe, its lineage includes ownership by cotton planters and wealthy merchants, and use as a speakeasy and bordello. Beautifully restored interiors feature elegant period-influenced colors and furnishings, as well as modern amenities. In this elegant setting, you'll find that Savannah lives up to its nickname "Hostess City of the South."

BEFORE YOU GO, visit
www.savannahvisit.com
www.savannahchamber.com
www.coastalantiques.com

FAVORITE LODGING:
The Ballastone Inn
14 East Oglethorpe Avenue
Savannah, GA 31401
912-236-1484; 800-822-4553
www.ballastone.com

Northern Florida: The Treasure Coast

F rom an antiquer's point of view, it's easy to understand why Northern Florida has been nicknamed the Treasure Coast. The area, which includes St. Augustine and Jacksonville as well as noncoastal towns such as Orlando and Mount Dora, has well over 100 antiques stores. Florida's largest flea market/antiques fair, Renningers, is located in Mount Dora. Explorer Ponce de Leon was the first European to land on this coast, in 1513. The "antique city" of St. Augustine, founded by the Spanish in 1565, is the oldest continuously occupied city in North America. The nation's first free black community was formed just north of St. Augustine in 1738. Located 40 miles south of Jacksonville and 100 miles northeast of Orlando, St. Augustine is an antiquing destination, as well as an excellent base for antiquing on the Treasure Coast. Most of its 24 antiques shops are located in its Antiques District along San Marco Avenue. Others are also located on Granada and Aviles streets and King Street, where a mall at the Lightner Museum contains some shops. Antiques shows are held the Friday/Saturday/Sunday of the last weekend in December and in mid-March at the National Guard Armory.

In Jacksonville, about 50 antiques stores are spread throughout several older neighborhoods: Avondale, Riverside, and Five Points. The Avondale Mall on Beach Boulevard is worth a look, too. *The Antique Shoppe Newspaper*, distributed in most shops, offers information on local dealers, auctions, and shows. Jacksonville's antiques shows include two Friday/Saturday/Sunday shows; one is held on the third weekend in January at the Prime Osborn Convention Center, the other in mid-July at the Morocco Temple.

In Orlando, you'll also find about 50 antiques shops. Roughly half of these are located along North Orange Avenue in its Antique Row, an eminently strollable neighborhood of shops, boutiques, and restaurants, and a welcome antidote to Disney World, the biggest show in town. Shops are also located on South Orange and throughout town. In Sanford, founded in 1837, 28 miles north of Orlando on Lake Monroe, are a few antiques shops as well as cruises on the St. John's River. In Deland, between St. Augustine and Orlando, an Antiques Market at the Fairgrounds is held Friday/Saturday/Sunday of the last weekends in November, December, and January.

Mount Dora, near Orlando, a lovely historic town on Lake Dora, is another terrific antiquing town. Its attractions include about 24 antiques stores, carriage rides, a boardwalk, and a downtown nature park. The biggest show here is Renningers (the Adamstown, Pennsylvania, company), which holds a year-round Saturday/Sunday indoor flea market with 180 dealers. On the third weekend of the month, Renningers indoor/outdoor fair attracts 400 dealers; in January, February, and November, its "third weekend" fairs swell to 1,400 dealers.

Because Florida has long been a popular choice for second homes and retirement, a wide variety of home furnishings have come here and continue to arrive. It's not uncommon for people moving to Florida to find that the furniture they've brought with them doesn't fit in, in terms of space or style. Moreover, Floridians have always collected antiques. Thus, you can expect the unexpected. You'll see early-20th-century furnishings, decorative items, and collectibles, including Art Deco and Art Nouveau objects, vintage lighting, art pottery, Mission furniture, vintage linens, architectural and garden items, shabby chic furnishings, prim-

WITH ITS ITALIANATE ROOF BRACKETS, DOUBLE PORCHES FEATURING GINGERBREAD TRIM, AND TROPICAL COLOR SCHEME, OUR HOUSE OF ST. AUGUSTINE IS RICH IN CURB APPEAL.

itives, Florida pieces from the 1940s and 1950s, European furnishings, Oriental rugs, and Asian objects. There's a wonderful sense of serendipity about antiquing in Florida.

The most impressive antique in the state may be the city of St. Augustine itself, a prime destination for historic travel. Its museums include Old St. Augustine Village, a collection of nine houses dating from 1790 to 1910; the Oldest House Museum Complex, containing the early-1700s Gonzalez-Alvarez House, a National Historic Landmark; and the Mauncy Museum, covering over 400 years of Florida history. The Lightner Museum has a comprehensive collection of decorative arts from America's Gilded Age, including an escritoire made for Louis Bonaparte; late-19th-century cut glass; Art Nouveau furniture; 19th-century paintings; Victorian art glass; and stained-glass by Louis Comfort Tiffany. Built in 1885 as a hotel in the Spanish Colonial style by Henry Flagler, the fabulously wealthy cofounder of Standard Oil who established St. Augustine as a resort, it is one of the city's defining landmarks.

VICTORIAN AND TURN-OF-THE-CENTURY FURNISHINGS ARE PERFECTLY SUITED TO THE SENSIBILITY OF THE 1880S, WHEN OUR HOUSE OF ST. AUGUSTINE WAS BUILT.

St. Augustine also has live theater, concerts, jazz and swing performances, art shows, historical reenactments, and festivals celebrating Spanish, Minorcan, British, Greek, African American, and other ethnic cultures. Coastal pleasures include water sports, golf, tennis, scenic cruises, and fishing charters. State parks offering recreational activities include Anastasia Park on St. Augustine Beach, Fort Matanzas, and Faver-Dykes Park.

In Jacksonville, Kinsley Plantation museum on Fort George Island may be Florida's oldest plantation. Jacksonville's historic Ritz Theatre presents music, theater, and movies. African American history is remembered at the Bethel Baptist Church, the La Villa Museum, the Clara White Mission, and the Olustee Civil War Battlefield, where Massachusetts' 64th black regiment fought. On the campus of the 1866 Edward Waters College, Florida's first African American college, Centennial Hall houses an African art collection. Several educational institutions in this area played a significant role in African American history and culture.

Orlando's art museum houses American art from the 19th century to the present, African art, and art of the ancient Americas. The 50-acre Harry P. Leu Botanical Garden displays tropical plantings that include the largest camellia collection in North America. Nearby, in Winter Park, the Charles Hosmer Morse Museum of American Art displays late-19th- to early-20th-century American paintings and decorative arts, including American art pottery and works by Louis Comfort Tiffany. Around Orlando, activities include golf, and on the area lakes, water sports and fishing. In

Winter Garden, West Orange Trail is the place for recreation, including bird watching and horseback riding.

Several area bed and breakfasts make antiquers feel right at home. These include the Thurston House in Maitland, 11 miles from Orlando; the c.1883 Lakeside Inn in Mount Dora; and the Kenwood Inn and Saragossa Inn in St. Augustine. One of the loveliest is Our House of St. Augustine, located behind a picket fence in the city's antiquing district. A charming 1880s wood-frame classic, with two-story gingerbread-trimmed porches, Our House of St. Augustine was one of the first houses built when this area was still an orange grove. Its interiors combine vivid color with a well-styled selection of antique furnishings. Amenities include off-street parking, wireless Internet access, private baths, and breakfast served on 19th-century English ironstone plates. Just minutes away are Atlantic Ocean beaches, Cathedral Place, the ancient Castillo de San Marcos, and an array of antiques from St. Augustine's five centuries of history.

BEFORE YOU GO, visit
www.staugustine.com
www.adasta.org
www.aarf.com
www.visitoldcity.com
www.renningers.com

FAVORITE LODGING:
Our House of St. Augustine
7 Cincinnati Street
St. Augustine, FL 32084
904-824-9204
www.ourhousestaugustine.com

ROSES DECORATE A VINTAGE TEAPOT.

West Palm Beach, Florida

(P)alm Beach is the Grace Kelly of American towns—beautiful, moneyed, refined, with a soft-spoken confidence and an old school sort of glamour. Its Worth Avenue is the princess of high-style shopping, and its antiques stores have long enjoyed a blue-chip reputation. West Palm Beach, next door, is more Lana (aka Julia Jean Mildred Francis) Turner, who was born in Idaho and "discovered" at a soda fountain. West Palm Beach is working all the time: With 45 shops, its design-conscious Antique Row on South Dixie Highway (Route 1) is a decorator destination. And it tries even harder in winter, when even those who aren't habitual snowbirds are ready to trade up to a warmer clime.

Several major antiques shows take place in West Palm, beginning the second weekend in January and running through March. First among them is the Palm Beach Winter Antiques Show, a Friday/Saturday/Sunday/Monday event, with a Thursday night preview. Held in early January at the Crowne Plaza Hotel, it attracts some 50 U.S. and international exhibitors who offer top-quality items, ranging in time and place from Ancient Egyptian to English Regency to Federal New England. This show is bracketed by two other four-day shows: the Palm Beach Connoisseur Fair, held at the Kravis Center the previous week, and the Palm Beach International Fine Art Exposition at the Convention Center, held during the third weekend in January.

THE CHESTERFIELD PALM BEACH, JUST STEPS FROM WORTH AVENUE, IS DECORATED WITH TRADITIONAL FURNISHINGS THAT SUGGEST GOOD BREEDING AND AN "OLD MONEY" PEDIGREE.

Smaller shows augment this schedule. Antiques and collectibles shows are held Friday/Saturday/Sunday of the first two weekends of nearly every month at the West Palm Beach fairgrounds. On the fourth weekend of January, an Antique & Collectible show is held at St. Catherine's Greek Orthodox Church. The first weekend in February, the three-day, Friday/Saturday/Sunday West Palm Beach Antique & Collectibles Spectacular is held at the fairgrounds. Starting the first Monday of February is the important ten-day show, America's International Fine Art & Antique Fair, at the Convention Center. Running for five days during the third week of February is an Antique & Jewelry show. And on the first and third weekends of March,

THE MEDITERRANEAN-STYLE CHESTERFIELD PALM BEACH HOTEL WAS ONCE A PRIVATE RESIDENCE. IT IS AN EASY DRIVE FROM WEST PALM BEACH'S ANTIQUES STORES.

January's three-day Antiques and Collectibles Show is reprised at the fairgrounds and St. Catherine's, respectively. Delray Beach also has several shows each year, including one in early February sponsored by its Historical Society. *Antiques & Art Around Florida* (www.aarf) is a great source of information about shops and shows.

West Palm Beach's Antique Row begins at the corner of Southern Boulevard and South Dixie Highway and runs along the highway for about seven blocks. Its 45 shops present a wide range of antique furniture and decorative objects, sourced from the U.S., England, France, Italy and elsewhere in Europe, and from Japan, China, and elsewhere in Asia. On display are furniture, lighting, clocks, ceramics, architectural items, fine art and engravings, glass, jewelry, rugs and carpets, pewter, bronze, pottery, porcelain, textiles, books, and silver, in a variety of styles and range of periods. This

town has a sense of humor, so you're likely to find fun objects that put a creative spin on an interior. Every year, during the first weekend in February, there's an "Evening on Antique Row" street festival.

West Palm is a lively scene, with festivals, jazz and blue-grass, and fun dining spots. Outdoor activities include beaches, swimming, biking, bird watching, tennis, golf, and polo matches. Its historic neighborhoods— Prospect Park, El Cid, and the Mango Promenade—contain lovely Florida bungalows, frame vernacular houses, and Mediterranean-style houses.

Area museums include Palm Beach's Flagler Museum, a 55-room Edwardian mansion built in 1902 by the

THE PALM BEACH WINTER ANTIQUES SHOW PRESENTS OBJECTS LIKE THIS 9-INCH-TALL WEDGWOOD VASE, FROM ELISE ABRAMS ANTIQUES.

cofounder of Standard Oil and featuring a Louis XIV music room and art gallery, a Louis XV ballroom, and 14 bedrooms with their original European antique furnishings. The Norton Museum in West Palm Beach has a distinguished collection of 19th- and 20th-century European and American art, Chinese art, and contemporary art and photography. Thirty miles south is the Boca Raton Museum of Art, where collections include European and American art from the 19th century to the present, photography from 1850–2000, West African and pre-Columbian art, and Peruvian textiles. In Delray Beach, you'll find the Morikami Museum and Japanese Gardens.

Two accommodations in the area seem to suit antiquers very well. One is the Chesterfield Palm Beach, two blocks north of Worth Avenue, a boutique hotel in a historic landmark property that began its life as a private residence. This small, well-appointed luxury hotel has 41 guest rooms and 11 suites, freshly styled, traditional interiors that feel more like a home than a hotel, an attentive staff, and all the creature comforts one could wish for. In West Palm Beach, Hibiscus House Bed and Breakfast is a typical Florida frame house, with double porches and a tiny swimming pool overhung with palms—a charming, well-decorated jewel of a place. Add some freshly squeezed Florida orange juice to the breakfast menu and you'll wish you'd thought of spending the winter antiquing here a whole lot sooner.

BEFORE YOU GO, visit
www.palmbeachfl.com
www.2chambers.com
www.aarf.com
www.westpalmbeachantiques.com

FAVORITE LODGING:
The Chesterfield Palm Beach
363 Coconut Row
Palm Beach, FL 33480
561-659-5800
www.chesterfieldpb.com

New Orleans, Louisiana

ew Orleans has a cachet that no other city in the U.S.—perhaps in the world, —can match. Birthplace of Al Hirt, Louis Armstrong, and Mahalia Jackson, wellspring of the blues and jazz, and home of Mardi Gras (North America's biggest party), the city's vitality, sophistication, architecture, and history have made it a must for any traveler, and for antiques lovers especially. New Orleans' culture is an alchemy of French, Spanish, African, and English influences, its history and architecture more related to the West Indies than any other place in North America. The number and quality of antiques in local shops reflect the fact that, as a port city with an international personality, it has maintained an active trade in home furnishings since the 18th century.

As evidenced in the 37,000 buildings listed on the National Register of Historic Places—more than any other U.S. city—Orleanians have treasured their past, including antiques. After Hurricane Katrina, most of the city's 200 antiques stores bounced back. Located in the fabled French Quarter, also known as Le Vieux Carré, a thriving

AT NEW ORLEANS' McKENDRICK-BREAUX HOUSE, A GREEK REVIVAL MANSION BUILT IN 1865, ANTIQUE FURNISHINGS AND WORK BY LOCAL ARTISTS CONVEY A SENSE OF TRADITION AND CONTINUITY.

THE MCKENDRICK-BREAUX HOUSE'S
CLASSIC NEW ORLEANS FAÇADE OPENS
TO A TROPICAL GARDEN, COMPLETELY
PRIVATE, BUT JUST STEPS AWAY FROM
MAGAZINE STREET ANTIQUES SHOPS.

120 blocks where many buildings date to the 1700s, Royal and Chartres (pronounced "charters") streets are prime antiquing territory. Royal Street has ten blocks of elegant shops, many of which present museum-quality furniture and decorative arts. On Chartres Street several blocks of shops contain items ranging from fine to shabby chic. Along Magazine Street, which begins in the Garden District, antiques shops extend along nearly 40 blocks.

In New Orleans, you will find things for every budget and taste: formal and country furniture, English, French, and Asian pieces, china and glassware, silver and jewelry, Art Deco statuary, Louisianan and American furniture, Civil War memorabilia, French culinary antiques, vintage clothing, and countless other things. There are also excellent conservators and restorers of furniture, textile, ceramics, silver, and other items. Local savant Macon Riddle is among those offering antiquing tours of the Crescent City.

That is one of New Orleans' nicknames, which describes the site at a bend in the Mississippi River that its founders chose in 1718. The other is "The Big Easy," which suits it very well. New Orleans has been called the country's most hedonistic city, and while this may or may not be true, it is a fact that the custom of brunch, Oysters Rockefeller, and Bananas Foster were invented here. It's hard to get a bad meal, or even a bad beignet. The music is as fine as the food, whether it's a jazz funeral, a gospel choir, a Second Linin' marching band, blues in a Bourbon Street club, Dixieland jazz at Preservation Hall, the Satchmo Summer Festival honoring native son Louis Armstrong in early August, or the New Orleans Jazz & Heritage Festival in late April/early May.

This is a very literary town, claiming among its writers Truman Capote and William Faulkner, with several literary festivals: the Tennessee Williams in March, the Saints and Sinners in May, and Words & Music in December. Other festivals include the Swamp Fest at the Audubon Zoo in November, the French Quarter festival in April, and the Voodoo Festival at Halloween. The mother of all festivals is, of course, Mardi Gras, or "Fat Tuesday;" held 47 days before Easter Sunday, its history in America dates to 1699.

New Orleans museum collections include one devoted to Mardi Gras at the Presbytere in the Jackson Square Landmark District. The Old U.S. Mint housing the Louisiana State Museum's New Orleans Jazz Collection and a collection of Arts & Crafts pottery is a few blocks away from the c.1745 Ursuline Convent, the oldest building in the Mississippi Valley, in the Faubourg Marigny, near the French Quarter. Other sites of interest here include the Ogden Museum of Southern Art, with its collection of 1,500 works by Audubon, Martin Johnson Heade, and others; the New Orleans Museum of Art with its glass and silver collections; the Confederate Museum; and the Museum of African American History. New Orleans' Faubourg Tremé, the oldest African American neighborhood in the U.S., traces ownership of homes by free blacks to 100 years before the Civil War.

New Orleans has been known for its house museums with period furnishings of surpassing quality: the 1858 Women's Opera Guild Home in the Garden District, the Pitot House Museum, the 1826 Beauregard-Keyes House, the rare 18th-century Creole-style Madame John's Legacy, the Creole-style Gallier townhouse, Longue Vue House and Gardens, artist Edgar Degas's house, the 19th-century Williams Residence, the 1832 Hermann-Grima House (the only Federal-style mansion in the French Quarter), and the Historic New Orleans Collection, a complex of five historic buildings at Royal and Toulouse streets. Other historic sites include the c.1797 Cabildo, where the 1803 Louisiana Purchase was signed; the Cathedral of St. Louis, King of France, the oldest continuously active Roman Catholic cathedral in the U.S.; and the c.1790 Le Petit Théâtre du Vieux Carré, the oldest continuously running community theater in the country.

Many New Orleans hotels, inns, and bed and breakfasts are located in historic buildings and furnished with an antiquer's sensibility. Their style and service reflect the city's sophistication. In the Garden District, near the Magazine Street shops, are Pontchartrain Hotel and the elegant McKendrick-Breaux House, a Greek Revival townhouse, along with Sully Mansion and the Grand Victorian Bed & Breakfast, both designed by local architect Thomas Sully. Favorites in the French Quarter, near the Royal and Chartres Street shops, are Soniat House, comprising three restored Creole townhouses, Hotel Maison de Ville and its Audubon Cottages, the Bienville House Hotel, and Hotel Provincial.

BEFORE YOU GO, visit
www.neworleanscvb.com
www.neworleansantiquedealers.com
www.neworleansonline.com/tours-attractions/shopping/antiquing.html
www.neworleansantiquing.com

FAVORITE LODGING:
The McKendrick-Breaux House
1474 Magazine Street
New Orleans, LA 70130
888-570-1700
www.mckendrick-breaux.com

Louisiana's Cajun Country

ention Cajun Country and the first thing that comes to mind are the sounds of rousing zydeco music and the taste of a zesty crawfish étouffée, enjoyed while sitting alongside a bayou, surrounded by trees dripping with Spanish moss. What's less well known is that Louisiana Cajun Country has more to offer than great music, food, and scenery—it also has very good antiquing. In keeping with the area's heritage, several dealers specialize in French furniture and decorative accessories. There are country finds, but this area also has its share of fine formal pieces. Shopping in a local antiques mall, an expert on Southern furniture found an 1870s Philadelphia pier table and hall tree, which are now in the Louisiana State Museum of Art in Baton Rouge. "Pieces like that had no business in a small town antiques mall," he said, "but there they were."

Acadiana's "antiquing capital" is the small town of Washington, population 1,000, on Bayou Courtableau, established in 1720 as a French trading post. This was one of Louisiana's earliest settlements, and for much of the 19th century, the largest inland port between St. Louis and New Orleans. With over 80% of its buildings on the National Register of Historic Places and over 100 antiques dealers, Washington, located on Louisiana's Zydeco Cajun Prairie Scenic Byway, is a great place to spend a weekend. One find in Washington is A French Farmhouse, where the emphasis is on French furnishings and textiles. Another is the Old School House Antique Mall, a 100-dealer center, where a museum-quality treasure awaited a savvy buyer. If you don't find the treasure you're seeking in Washington, nearby Lafayette and Breaux Bridge total about 20 shops, including malls and individual dealers who specialize in fine French antiques.

IN ANTEBELLUM WASHINGTON, LOUISIANA, AN EARLY-19TH-CENTURY FRENCH MARBIER CLOCK CHIMES AS GUESTS ENJOY BREAKFAST AT CRAWFORD HOUSE, A RESTORED STEAMBOAT PILOT'S HOME.

The word "Cajun" comes from "Acadian," referring to the French Catholics who were expelled from Acadia in Canada and given fertile land in the mid-18th-century Louisiana, a story told in Longfellow's poem "Evangeline." Cajun country is one of the culturally richest parts of the nation. In some small towns, like Cankton,

Vatican, and Ossun, French is still spoken. Festivals include Washington's catfish festival in March; Breaux Bridge's crawfish festival and Lake Charles' Contraband Days, both in May; Plaisance's zydeco festival in August; Lafayette's Festival Acadiens in September; and Church Point's Courir de Mardi Gras in February.

The lush landscape is enhanced by Creole architecture in plantation houses and backwater cottages. Washington's museums include the c.1829 Arlington Plantation; Magnolia Ridge Plantation's Gardens; Starvation Point, built in the late 1700s; and a small museum and tourist center with exhibits on the town's history. The historic village of Grand Coteau with its Cankton Plantation is a gem. Other area attractions are the Prairie Acadian Cultural Center and the Liberty Theater in Eunice, and, in Lafayette, the Acadian Village, the Acadian Cultural Center, and Vermilionville, a recreated bayou village of the 1800s. One of Louisiana's finest plantation museums, Melrose, is near Natchitoches, about two hours away.

Washington is some three hours drive west of New Orleans, with Baton Rouge situated between the two. Baton Rouge has a large number of good shops. If driving to Washington from New Orleans, the slower southern route, through Houma, passes through Atchafalaya Basin, one of the nation's largest undeveloped wetlands, and you can visit the Atchafalaya National Wildlife Refuge. Houma, Thibodaux, and New Iberia have enough shops to make this meandering route interesting. Also along the way are the Wetlands Acadian Cultural Center in Thibodaux, Arlington Plantation and Oaklawn Manor in Franklin, Le Beau Petit Musée in Jeanerette, and Shadows-on-the-Teche in New Iberia.

Washington's historic bed and breakfasts include the c.1825 Camilla Cove, furnished with Louisiana antiques; La Maison de Gabrielle, a c.1865 Acadian cottage; and Crawford House, a lovely restored 19th-century steamboat captain's house decorated with antiques, located just up the hill from Bayou Courtableau. No one can say, of course, how a Philadelphia treasure arrived here, but it may well have come up the Mississippi on a steamboat. Did another come with it? You just never know.

BEFORE YOU GO, visit
www.washingtonla.com
www.louisianacajun.com

FAVORITE LODGING:
The Crawford House Bed & Breakfast
331 East Carriere Street
Washington, LA 70589
337-826-5686
www.tinney.net/portraits/crawford.htm

Nashville, Tennessee, & the Heart of Country Antiques Show

F or lovers of country antiques, few shows have presented a more colorful array of American folk art, farmhouse furnishings, and 18th- and early-19th-century high country pieces than Nashville's Heart of Country Antiques Show. Started in the "Capital of Country Music" some 25 years ago, the show is now held at the Gaylord Opryland Hotel, adjacent the Grand Ole Opry, which presents three live performances a week. Altogether, it's a total immersion experience. Country music, country antiques, and country barbecue: Honey, pack the bags and gas the pickup.

Held on the Friday/Saturday/Sunday of the fourth weekend in February, Heart of Country attracts more than 200 dealers from all parts of the U.S. A sampling of their wares would include vivid quilts, tall case clocks, weather vanes, tavern signs, blanket chests in grain paint, yellowware, bandboxes, Sheraton country bureaus, step-down

GARTHOEFFNER GALLERY'S BOOTH AT NASHVILLE'S HEART OF COUNTRY ANTIQUES SHOW DISPLAYS AN ALBUM QUILT, BLANKET CHEST, AND THE DECORATIVE AND FOLK ART FOR WHICH THIS SHOW IS KNOWN.

Windsor chairs, and farmhouse tables. The show starts with a preview party on Thursday night, when early buyers scoop pieces up during cocktails. Special events include a show tour, lectures, and an evening on the town. As of this writing, the autumn Heart of Country Show has announced a move to Texas. (Check www.heartofcountry.com for information.)

To further entertain antiquers, Nashville has about 70 antiques shops and malls, many of them concentrated on Eighth Avenue South, which was the city's first antiquing district, and on 21st Avenue South. Along these streets are a range of dealers, with fine 18th- and 19th-century furniture, and antiques malls, with varied antiques, vintage items, and collectibles. Nashville's Friday/Saturday/Sunday flea market, considered among the best in the nation, is held at the Tennessee State Fairgrounds during the fourth weekend of each month, except December, when it falls on the third weekend. The event draws dealers and vendors from 30 states, and shoppers travel hundreds of miles to snag bargains on antiques, "antiques," collectibles, jewelry, arts and crafts, tools, housewares, and handcrafted items.

Nashville is more associated with country music than any other city in the U.S. Hopefuls and stars have been coming here since the 1930s, when a Nashville recording of singer/guitarist Jimmy Rodgers made him a national sensation. The Grand Ole Opry, which started broadcasting live concerts a mere five years after commercial radio began, is home to the world's longest-running live radio show, with performances every Tuesday, Friday, and Saturday night. The Country Music Hall of Fame focuses on the authentic 19th-century roots of this uniquely American music; its research collection includes recordings, artifacts, photography, video, and oral history, covering rock, jazz, blues, world, folk and bluegrass, as well as country music. The performing arts scene also includes ballet and symphony. For outdoor activities, there's Riverfront Park in the city and Radnor Lake State Natural Area not far away.

Among area historic sites are the Hermitage, Andrew Jackson's home, with period interiors, and Belmont Mansion, an opulent mid-19th-century Italianate mansion with antique furnishings and a staircase fit for Rhett and Scarlett. Other sites include the Tennessee State Museum, as well as the Cheekwood Botanical Garden and Museum of Art, a 1929 Georgian Revival mansion with collections of English and American decorative arts, including a comprehensive collection of Worcester porcelain and silver by Matthew Boulton and Hester Bateman. Nashville's Belle Meade, the "Queen of Tennessee Plantations," contains a Greek Revival mansion decorated with 19th-century antiques, a coin silver collection, and equine art and exhibits relating to the time when it was America's oldest and largest thoroughbred farm, breeding racehorses such as Iroquois, the first American-bred horse to win the English Derby.

Nashville traces its history to 1756, when a French fur trader carved out a trading post here. This led to the establishment of a fort. In 1775, the Cherokee Indians sold their claim to the land, opening the way for wider settlement. Nashville, on the bluffs of the Cumberland River, was founded in 1779 by a group of Virginians. In 1818, the first steamboat arrived, and it became a busy port. Recalling the area's early history are Mansker's Station Frontier Life Center in nearby Goodlettsville; Fort Nashborough on First Avenue in the city; and at Travellers Rest Plantation, a living-history museum with a c.1799 house and an annual festival in late October. Fort Negley, south of downtown, is where the Civil War Battle of Nashville took place. Built in 1862 with the help of 2,000 free African Americans, it was the largest Union fort west of Washington, D.C.

Nashville has six historic districts. Its landmarks include a full-scale 1897 replica of the Greek Parthenon and the Downtown Presbyterian Church, one of the nation's finest Egyptian Revival buildings. Jubilee Hall, a Victorian Gothic structure completed in 1876 and a National Historic Landmark, was the first permanent building erected for higher education of African Americans in the U.S. It is located on the campus of Fisk University, founded in 1866. Fisk's significant African art collection is exhibited at its Aaron Douglas Gallery. Historic streets include Printers Alley, located between 3rd and 4th streets, from Union to Church. Once home to Nashville's first publishing companies and an infamous red light district, it is now quiet by day but alive by night, with music clubs and restaurants housed in its historic buildings.

Among Nashville inns, the Timothy Demonbreun House, a 22-room Colonial Revival mansion just a mile south of downtown and Music Row, is a short walk from antiques stores. Recipient of a local preservation award, it is one of Nashville's most beautiful historic residences. Public and guest rooms are appointed with elegant furniture and period antiques. Other pleasures include private baths, Internet access, wonderful food, and gas fireplaces, ideal for basking in the satisfaction of a successful day's antiquing.

BEFORE YOU GO, visit
www.nashville.com
www.heartofcountry.com
www.nashvilleantiquedealers.com
www.nashvillelife.com/antiqueshops

FAVORITE LODGING:
The Timothy Demonbreun House
746 Benton Avenue
Nashville, TN 37204
615-383-0426
www.tdhouse.com

The World's Longest Yard Sale: from Kentucky to Alabama

T he event known as the Longest Yard Sale in the United States (and probably the world) is an outdoor extravaganza, which takes place from Thursday to Sunday on the first weekend in August and spans 450 miles in four states: Kentucky, Tennessee, Georgia, and Alabama. Stretched along U.S. Route 127, the Yard Sale starts (or ends, depending on your point of view) in Covington, Kentucky, just across the Ohio River from Cincinnati, and meanders like a long, languid sentence south through the Blue Grass State, passing midway between Lexington and Louisville and through Harrodsburg, and then through Tennessee, where it passes between Nashville and Knoxville, winds through Pall Mall, Jamestown, Allardt, Clarkrange, Crossville, Pikeville, Dunlap, and Whitwell, and continues to

THE SPIRAL STAIRCASE AT THE SHAKER VILLAGE OF PLEASANT HILL
IS A SOARING TRIBUTE TO THE 19TH-CENTURY CRAFTSMANSHIP OF THIS
RELIGIOUS SECT.

Chattanooga; there, briefly, it follows Route 27 (with which Route 127 should not be confused) and the Lookout Mountain Parkway, then flows into northwest Georgia, where it joins Highways 189 and 136 for short distances before joining 157, which leads to 48, which crosses into Alabama; once across that border, 48 changes its name to Route 117, and continues to Mentone, where it makes a left onto 89; this leads through DeSoto State Park, Fort Payne, and Dogtown, finally picking up Highway 176 into Gadsden, Alabama, the sale's southern terminus. The geographically challenged will be comforted to know that signs en route provide directions.

Though it's a truism that one person's trash is another's treasure, an astonishing amount of treasure awaits at this sale. Vendors—dealers and just plain folks—appear with all manner of antiques, vintage items, and collectibles, including countless country and shabby chic pieces, large and small. Craftspeople bring their wares, too: fruit preserves, wood- and ironwork, and quilts, to name only a few. Though typically vendors are not displaying museum-quality antique furniture, one can't be sure that a once-in-a-lifetime find will not turn up. In any case, for the dedicated antiquer, this is the roadshow to beat all roadshows.

The Yard Sale, started about 20 years ago, was the brainchild of a county executive, who wanted to lure travelers from the interstates to less-traveled roads. Buyers come in cars, trucks, and RVs. Route 127 is a two-lane road, and where vendors are scarce, traffic moves. However, in places where many vendors are concentrated in fields and front lawns, traffic is not only bumper-to-bumper, but drivers brake suddenly

when they spot something. There are places to park, and signs indicating where not to park—for instance, on residents' lawns. If you're in the mood to shop 'til you drop, wear comfortable shoes and bring cash. Some visitors do the whole route; others focus on one area, then depart for other activities.

By one count, more than 300 diversions are along the way, including myriad parks, recreational opportunities, historic sites, music, arts and crafts venues, and gorgeous scenery. Near Jamestown, in Fentress County, Tennessee, are the Sergeant Alvin C. York Grist Mill & Homeplace, dedicated to World War I's most decorated hero, and Big South Fork National River & Recreation Area, covering 120,000 acres of pristine wilderness with camping, hiking, fishing, and horseback riding. In the eastern part of Tennessee are the Chickamauga and

A SHAKER LADDERBACK CHAIR IS STORED ON A WALL RACK, AS IT WOULD HISTORICALLY HAVE BEEN IN SHAKER COMMUNITIES.

AT PLEASANT HILL IN HARRODSBURG, SHAKER BUILDINGS ACCOMMODATE OVERNIGHT GUESTS.

Chattanooga Civil War Battlefield Parks, Cherokee National Forest, Cumberland Gap Historic Park, the Davy Crockett Birthplace Historic Park, and Great Smoky Mountains National Park; in the middle of the state are the State and Agricultural Museums, Old Stone Fort Archeological Park, the Hohenwald Elephant Sanctuary, and the Natchez Trace Parkway. Northeast Alabama is home to Little River Canyon National Preserve, several lakes, and the Sequoyah and Cathedral Caverns. Constitution Village, a living-history museum with eight reconstructed Federal-period buildings, is in Huntsville, while Alabama's largest antebellum district and oldest house museum, the c.1819 Weeden House, are in Twickenham.

Antiquing detours off the Yard Sale route include Cincinnati, Ohio; Franklin, Lexington, and Louisville, Kentucky; Nashville, Knoxville, and Chattanooga, Tennessee; and Birmingham, Alabama, where the Antiques Dealers Association publishes an excellent guide (see www.bcvb.org). These cities contain hundreds of good antiques shops; some are mentioned in the listings section of this book. Several other noteworthy shows take place in this area. On the first Saturday/Sunday of June, the Shaker Village at Pleasant Hill sponsors its Antiques Show and Sale, presenting 75 dealers; it is one of several Harrodsburg shows held on this weekend. From March through December, the Historic Harrodsburg Antique & Collectible Show & Sale takes place on the last weekend of each month. In mid-March, there's a Friday/Saturday/Sunday Antiques & Garden Show in Lexington, Kentucky. And, on the third weekend of November, Friday/Saturday/Sunday antiques shows are held in Louisville, Kentucky, and Birmingham, Alabama.

You'll find lodging options along the Yard Sale route via links from its website (www.127sale.com). Accommodations near the southern endpoint of the sale include Bibb House in Huntsville, Alabama, and Mountain Grove at Cloudland B&B on Lookout Mountain, in Georgia, near Chattanooga. One standout midway on the sale route is Pleasant Hill Shaker Village in Harrodsburg, Kentucky, which people often use as a base when antiquing in Louisville and Lexington. An authentic 19th-century Shaker community, Pleasant Hill is one of the finest Shaker museums in the country, with glorious period architecture and an excellent restaurant. Its guest accommodations, not widely publicized, are wonderful, located in historic buildings and decorated with Shaker reproductions. After as much of the Yard Sale as you can handle, you might discover a newfound appreciation for the Shaker refrain "Tis a gift to be simple."

BEFORE YOU GO, visit
www.127sale.com
www.kentuckytourism.com
www.louisvilleantiquedealers.com
www.tnvacation.com
www.southeasttennessee.com
www.chattanoogacvb.com
www.touralabama.org
www.800alabama.com
www.bcvb.org/arts-antiques-guide.html

FAVORITE LODGING:
Shaker Village of Pleasant Hill
3501 Lexington Road
Harrodsburg, KY 40330
859-734-5411; 859-734-7278; 800-678-8946
www.shakervilleky.org

Midwest

Cincinnati, Ohio

I n the southwestern corner of Ohio, where the state borders Indiana and Kentucky, Cincinnati, on the banks of the Ohio River, is a diverse city with a rich cultural scene and a keen taste for antiques. The town Longfellow called "the Queen City of the West" possesses about 100 antiques stores. You'll find many of them in Cincinnati's Oakley/Oakley Square, Hyde Park/Hyde Park Square, and O'Byronville neighborhoods, which are a delightful mix of restaurants and cafés, boutiques, and galleries.

Because Ohio traces its beginnings to the late 1600s, and because its economy burgeoned in the late-19th and early-20th centuries, the state is a treasure-trove for antiques. You'll find early American, high country, and pieces in original paint, folk art, architectural elements, garden items, and Victorian, Mission, and Art Deco objects. Cincinnati also has many dealers who specialize in English, Continental, and

THE TUDOR-STYLE MARIEMONT INN'S RESTORED INTERIORS AND PERIOD FURNISHINGS ARE A TRIBUTE TO BEST WESTERN, WHICH OWNS THE HOTEL, A MEMBER OF HISTORIC HOTELS OF AMERICA.

Asian furniture, decorative arts, and fine art. The
Duck Creek Antique Mall, just east of Oakley
Square, about eight miles from downtown, is one of
the Midwest's best.

The American Art Pottery movement originated
in Cincinnati, with Rookwood, first made in 1880.
Ohio makers played a leading role in that movement,
which lasted through the mid-20th century, and
Ohio is still a good place to find pieces by Rookwood,
Roseville, Weller, Zanesville Stoneware, the widely
produced McCoy, and Clewell Metal Art.

Cincinnati is home to excellent antiques shows,
held in the Sharonville Convention Center. In mid-
October, the Friday/Saturday/Sunday Cincinnati
Antiques Festival brings over 40 nationally recognized dealers from 20 states, exhibiting American,
English, French, and Continental furniture and
accessories. The last weekend in February, the
Saturday/Sunday 20th Century Cincinnati Show is a
source for Art Deco, Streamline, Arts & Crafts,
mid-century modern, and Op/Pop pieces; the show's
emphasis is on classic forms from signature designers,
and it offers a range of items from investment-

AT THE MARIEMONT INN, A SPOT BY THE FIRE IS A
COZY PLACE TO UNWIND AFTER A DAY OF
ANTIQUING IN NEARBY CINCINNATI.

quality to funky and fun. The first weekends of May, July, August, September, and
October, the Tri-State Antiques Market, a Sunday show, is held at the fairgrounds in
Lawrenceburg, Indiana.

Cincinnati is also a hub for antiquing trips. Covington, Kentucky, one of the
end points of the World's Longest Yard Sale, is right across the Ohio River.
Waynesville and Lebanon, Ohio, with about 50 shops and malls, are just 30 miles
away, while Springfield is 84 miles to the north. Richmond, Indiana, and that state's
Antique Alley, is 67 miles away.

The Cincinnati Art Museum is known for Native American, Asian, African, and
African American Art, European Old Masters and decorative arts, British portrait
miniatures, American paintings, and decorative art, including Rookwood art pottery.
The Taft Museum of Art, in an 1820 Greek Revival mansion, has fine collections of
Chinese porcelains and European decorative arts. Other city museums include the
American Sign Museum; the Verdin Bell and Clock Museum; the American Classical
Music Hall of Fame; the National Underground Railroad Freedom Center; the Harriet
Beecher Stowe House; the German Heritage Museum, which traces the contributions

of German immigrants in Ohio; Skirball Museum at Hebrew Union College, which houses an interactive exhibit about the Holocaust; the William Howard Taft Historic Site; and the Contemporary Arts Center. The Cincinnati Museum Center complex is in the city's c.1933 Union Terminal, an Art Deco landmark; its ice cream parlor is walled in Rookwood tiles. The performing arts scene includes opera, ballet, symphony, theater, and other offerings.

For overnight stays, antiquers might want to check into the Mariemont Inn, 12 miles from downtown, near Mariemont. This Tudor-style hotel, built in 1923 as part of a planned community, is now part of the National Trust for Historic Preservation's Historic Hotels of America. Operated by Best Western, it offers their usual conveniences, along with carefully restored interiors and rooms with antique furnishings, four-poster and Victorian beds, imported rugs, and tapestries. From your window, you may hear one of the nation's only elected town criers. Clad in colonial garb, he calls residents to town meetings. He does not do wake-up calls, even for early-bird buying.

BEFORE YOU GO, visit
www.cincinnatiusa.com
www.artsinohio.com
www.cincinnatiantiquedealers.com
www.cincinnatiantiquesfestival.org
www.20thCenturyCincinnati.com
www.queencityshows.com

FAVORITE LODGING:
Best Western Mariemont Inn
6880 Wooster Pike
Cincinnati, OH 45227
513-271-2100; 800-678-8946
www.bestwestern.com
www.historichotels.org

Alton, Illinois,
& St. Charles, Missouri

he territory where two of North America's greatest rivers meet, the confluence of the Missouri and the Mississippi, near St. Louis, Missouri, is fertile ground for antiquing. In this area, first settled in the 18th century, two towns stand out. Alton, Illinois, located on the limestone bluffs on the Mississippi River, is home to more than 20 antiques dealers. Less than 40 minutes away, St. Charles, Missouri, on the Missouri River, has about ten shops. Between them, where a ferry makes regular crossings of the Mississippi, Grafton, Illinois, also has about ten shops.

As an antiques dealer in Alton once explained it, early settlers brought their family's antiques from the East; since then, collectors and dealers who have shopped nationally and internationally have added to that stockpile. Stores in Alton yield farmhouse finds, along with fine 18th- and 19th-century furniture, Victorian bibelots, and decorative accessories from Europe and Asia. Word has it that New England dealers and

decorators visit Alton because the cost of New England antiques, even with shipping, is lower there than in the East.

In St. Charles, you'll find Victorian and early-20th-century items, objects to lend élan to shabby chic and cottage interiors, and dealers specializing in coins, stamps, and military and architectural items. The first full weekend of every month except May, the outdoor Kane County Flea Market, held at the County Fairgrounds in St. Charles, typically has wicker pieces, kitchenware, textiles, garden items, country cupboards, and farm tables.

Prior to the Civil War, Missouri was a slave state and Illinois a free one. Alton was an active stop on the Underground Railroad, home to a Confederate prison, and, after the war, a settling place for African American farmers; this history is high-lighted in the town's museum. Besides antiquing,

PRAIRIE PEDDLER ANTIQUES IN ALTON, ILLINOIS, DISPLAYS NEW ENGLAND COUNTRY FURNITURE AND DECORATIVE ARTS.

activities include tours of Underground Railroad tunnels, downtown block parties, a heritage festival during the last weekend in September, and arts and crafts festivals. Alton's community theater, founded in 1934, is one of the oldest in Illinois. Outdoor offerings include free fishing clinics and guided prairie hikes in Gordon Moore Park, and exhibits about river ecology at the National Great Rivers Museum, a visitor center operated by the U.S. Army Corps of Engineers. In Grafton, a popular place to spot bald eagles is Pere Marquette State Park, Illinois' largest, where activities also include horseback riding, camping, fishing, and boating.

St. Charles, founded in 1769, was Missouri's first capital when it became a state in 1821. It boasts Missouri's first and largest historic district, a ten-block area with cobblestone streets, a trolley, gas lamps, and over 100 shops, boutiques, and restaurants. In the 19th century, German settlers came to this area, drawn by rumors that it resembled the Rhine Valley. St. Charles, the starting point for the Lewis and Clark expedition, is now the start of the 230-mile Katy Trail, a hiking and biking favorite. Seasonal activities include an Octoberfest, a Lewis and Clark Rendezvous, and a September Bluegrass Festival. Nearby, in Defiance, is the Daniel Boone Home

AGAINST A BACKDROP OF BOLD PATTERN AND COLOR, BLOSSOM ANTIQUES IN ST. CHARLES, MISSOURI, DISPLAYS A DELIGHTFUL MÉLANGE OF COTTAGE AND SHABBY CHIC FINDS—IRON BEDSTEADS, VARIED CHANDELIERS, WICKER CHAIRS, KITCHEN FURNISHINGS.

AT THE C.1880 JACKSON HOUSE, A BED AND BREAKFAST IN ALTON, ILLINOIS, A BEDROOM WITH PERIOD FURNISHINGS IS A HAVEN INVITING REPOSE.

and Boonesfield Village, an early-1800s living-history museum. Activities include recreation in town parks, and water parks popular with kids. This part of Missouri is a prime wine-growing area, and several local wineries offer tours.

For lodging in St. Charles, there's the c.1840 Boone's Lick Trail Inn. In Alton, two favorite places to stay are Jackson House, a c.1880 Victorian with a welcoming front porch and antique furnishings that have descended in the owner's family through four generations, and the Holly Hedges Guest House, an intimate c.1830 home evocatively decorated with period country antiques.

BEFORE YOU GO, visit
www.visitalton.com
www.historicstcharles.com
www.greatriverroad.com
www.kanecountyfleamarket.com

FAVORITE LODGINGS:

Holly Hedges Guest House
513 State Street
Alton, IL 62002
618-463-1103; 618-465-6114
www.illinoisbedandbreakfasts.com/holly.htm

Jackson House
1821 Seminary Street
Alton, IL 62002
618-462-1426; 800-462-1426
www.jacksonbb.com

Winnebago County, Illinois, & Rock County, Wisconsin

T he rolling landscape of northern Illinois and southern Wisconsin, called the Stateline area, is an antiquing oasis with more than 60 shops and multi-dealer malls and many other diversions within a 60-mile drive. In Winnebago County, Illinois, the towns of Rockford, Love's Park, Rockton, Pecatonica, Winnebago, and Roscoe contain over 35 antiques stores, two flea markets, and a semi-annual antiques show. In Rock County, Wisconsin, Janesville has about 12 shops, Elkhorn has eight shops and a good antiques show/flea market, and Beloit and Clinton each has a few shops. You'll find a mix of country, Victorian, and early-20th-century furnishings, many of which are evocative of small-town America, along with Scandinavian and other European pieces, quilts, and vintage linens.

In mid-May and mid-September, the Saturday/Sunday "Pec Thing" draws 500 dealers to the Pecatonica, Illinois, County Fairgrounds. From May through September, the Sunday Antiques & Flea Market (www.nlpromotionsllc.com) at Walworth County Fairgrounds in Elkhorn, Wisconsin, attracts 500 dealers. Both shows present furniture,

VICTORIAN ANTIQUES AT THE FOX RUN INN IN ROCKFORD, ILLINOIS, INCLUDE HEIRLOOMS THAT DESCENDED IN THE FAMILY OF ITS OWNER, WHOSE GREAT-GRANDFATHER BUILT THE HOUSE IN 1878.

glassware, pottery, linens, tools, farmhouse and decorative pieces, and art. Auctions include weekly (usually Sunday) sales at Rockford's West End Auction House; monthly outdoor auctions, usually on the third Saturday, at Rockford's Action Auctioneering; and area sales by Hack's Auction. In Roscoe, the Bargain Barn Antiques Mall holds a weekend flea market.

Here in America's heartland, town parks are havens for music festivals and concerts, farmers markets are a cornucopia of local products, and baseball teams recall a simpler time. In Rockford—with eight historic neighborhoods and a rich anti-slavery and immigrant history—attractions include an art museum and performing arts offerings; the 1871 Erlander Home, with Victorian furnishings and Rockford-made furniture; the c.1856–57 Italianate Bushnell Wheeler House and Graham Ginestra House; the 1865 Tinker Swiss Cottage Museum with Victorian interiors and gardens; an Ethnic Heritage Museum; Midway Village, a Victorian living-history museum with 24 buildings; the Anderson Japanese Gardens with 12 acres of gardens and traditional Sukiya buildings; and the Macktown Center with 150 acres of rare trees and shrubs. Rockford is known for its golf courses, and the Winnebago County Forest Preserve offers myriad other outdoor activities.

Rockton contains Illinois' largest collection of Greek Revival homes and an 1830s homestead museum located in its Macktown Forest Preserve. In Beloit, there's the Logan Museum of Anthropology, with pre-Columbian ceramics, Native American artifacts, ancient jewelry, and Paleolithic art; the 1857 Hanchett-Bartlett Homestead; the Milton House Museum, an 1844 hexagonal stagecoach inn and log cabin that was a stop on the Underground Railroad; and the c.1870 Tiffany Bridge, a rare five-arch stone structure.

One of Rockford's most charming places to stay is the c.1878 Fox Run Bed & Breakfast Inn. Its grand interiors feature honey oak woodwork, stained glass, and period carpets and wallpapers. Many of its antique furnishings were passed down in the owner's Rockford family, and represent what you might be fortunate enough to find when antiquing in Winnebago and Rock counties.

BEFORE YOU GO, visit
www.gorockford.com
www.oneregionfourrivers.com
www.rockton.ws
www.villageprofile.com/wisconsin/beloit/beloit2.html
www.winnebagocountyfair.com

FAVORITE LODGING:
Fox Run Bed & Breakfast Inn
2815 North Rockton Avenue
Rockford, IL 61103
815-963-8151
www.foxrunbedandbreakfast.com

Springfield, Waynesville, & Lebanon, Ohio

hio's first settlers were New Englanders, who arrived in the 18th century. Beginning in 1817, with the construction of the Erie Canal, a canal-river system opened Ohio to Eastern commerce, which included a steady influx of home furnishings. Maybe it's because of this history that Ohioans seem to have a particular affinity for antiques. From Cincinnati to Springfield, a distance of 84 miles, with Waynesville and Lebanon in between, there's some great antiques shopping.

The Springfield area contains an estimated 1,500 dealers, with more nearby in South Charleston, Harmony, Clifton, and Carlisle. Most do business in malls and multi-dealer shops. Two of the area's largest malls are the Heart of Ohio mall in Harmony, with some 650 dealers, and the AAA I-70 Mall in Springfield, with over 200. The American Antiquities Gallery, in Springfield, publishes *The American Antiquities Journal*, a magazine and guide to antiques in the Midwest.

At the Clark County Fairgrounds, southeast of Springfield, there's a mid-monthly Saturday/Sunday Antique Show and Flea Market. In May, July, and September, this

THE MILLWORK ON ITS GRACIOUS STAIRCASE, STAINED-GLASS WINDOWS, AND PERIOD FURNISHINGS TYPIFY THE TURN-OF-THE-CENTURY AMBIANCE AT THE HOUSTONIA BED AND BREAKFAST, A PRAIRIE VICTORIAN-STYLE INN, IN SOUTH CHARLESTON, OHIO.

becomes a Friday/Saturday/Sunday event, with 2,500 dealers presenting a vast variety of objects, from American period furniture to 1950s "Florida room" rattan, fine and folk art, and collectibles. An Antique Bottle and Fruit Jar Show and an Antique Gun, Weapon, and Tool show take place in November.

Waynesville, 36 miles south of Springfield, with about 25 shops, has been dubbed the "antiques capital of the Midwest." You'll find more stores nearby in Lebanon. These include malls, multi-dealer ventures, and individual dealer shops. These two towns are known for country finds, early-20th-century pieces, and collectibles. Lebanon, a former Shaker community with a pleasant village green, has two Saturday/Sunday antiques shows, the first in mid-January and the second on the first weekend of October.

Springfield's attractions include a museum with American and European art; a June/July arts festival; music and other performances; and Frank Lloyd Wright's c.1904 Prairie-style Wescott House museum. Waynesville holds an old-time music festival in late June, and the Ohio Sauerkraut Festival on the second weekend of October. Outdoor activities abound at Clifton Gorge, Glen Helen Nature Preserves, and John Bryan State Park.

For accommodations with historic ambiance, bed and breakfasts include Mill Pond Acre in Fairborn. In the Waynesville/Lebanon area, the Golden Lamb Inn is within walking distance of many shops, while the Hatfield Inn accommodates guests in a 1791 farmhouse. In South Charleston, favorites include the Victoria Green Plain Farm, a restored 1806 chinked-log cabin, and the c.1900 Houstonia Bed & Breakfast, a Prairie-Victorian with beautiful original woodwork, stained-glass windows, and period furnishings. Its amenities include an ample breakfast—exactly what you'll need before visiting 1,500 antiques dealers.

BEFORE YOU GO, visit
www.springfield-clarkcountyohio.info/antiquing.htm
www.springfield-clarkcountyohio.info/antique_show_flea_market.htm
www.waynesvilleohio.com
www.greenecountyohio.org

FAVORITE LODGING:
Houstonia Bed & Breakfast
25 East Mound Street
South Charleston, OH 45368
937-462-8855; 888-462-8855
www.houstonia.net

Indiana's Antique Alley

Richmond, Indiana, located in Wayne County, close to the Ohio border, and 73 miles from Indianapolis, is the hub of Indiana's Antique Alley. This area, which runs along Indianapolis Route 40 and extends north into Ohio's Darke County, is home to more than 900 dealers in shops, multi-dealer venues, and large malls, offering quality pieces at reasonable prices. A good first stop is the welcome center at I-70 near Richmond. Brochures listing and mapping shops are available locally and at www.visitrichmond.org.

Two antiquing routes network this area. One is a 75-mile loop along and north of Route 40 between Richmond and Knightstown, with about 40 antiques shops, nearly half of which are located in Centerville, Cambridge City, and Dublin. Indiana's largest antiques mall, featuring 500 dealers, is in Centerville, and the Carey Street Mall in Knightstown has 120 booths. The second route, with a like number of shops, leads north from Richmond to Portland, and across the Ohio border to Greenville, Arcanum, Englewood, Lewisburg, and Dunreith. South of Antique Alley, there are shops in Connorsville and Metamora, an 1838 canal town with seven antiques shops, a flea market, a historic gristmill, and a canal boat that traverses the nation's last wooden aqueduct.

IN HISTORIC CENTERVILLE, INDIANA, BRICK BUILDINGS WITH ARCH DETAILS ENHANCE THE STREETSCAPE AT THE LANTZ HOUSE INN.

As Indiana is "the Hoosier State," you'd expect to find Hoosier cabinets: They're here, along with farmhouse and country pieces, Victorian, Colonial Revival, Mission, Art Deco, and modern furnishings, primitives, trade signs, glassware, pottery, lighting, kitchen utensils, tools, paintings, silver, jewelry, and linens. Local farm auctions can be a good place to find things. Fairhaven, Ohio, 16 miles from Richmond, holds its Antiques Festival on the first weekend in June.

Route 40, the Historic National Road, built between 1828 and 1834, was the country's first federally funded interstate, stretching 824 miles from western Illinois to eastern

Maryland. Along this road, rural scenery includes an Amish community in Williamsburg and historic "pike towns" with 19th-century buildings. Richmond, founded in 1806 by North Carolina Quakers, contains four historic districts and cultural attractions; Gaar Mansion Museum, an 1876 Second Empire Victorian with period furnishings; and a 1902 railroad depot by Chicago architect Daniel Burnham. It also holds a place in the history of jazz: From the 1920s through the 1940s, Hoagy Carmichael, Tommy Dorsey, Jelly Roll Morton, Louis Armstrong, and others recorded here. Knightstown also has a large historic district. Centerville, the only town between Richmond and Terre Haute when the Historic National Road was built, is particularly well preserved and contains rare 19th-century row houses connected by archways; it hosts a quilt show the last weekend in August.

Other places to visit include the Museum of Overbeck Art Pottery in Cambridge City; the 1827 Levi Coffin House, where a Quaker abolitionist helped more than 2,000 fugitive slaves escape to freedom, in Fountain City; the museum home of "Hoosier poet" James Whitcomb Riley in Greenfield; the 1841 Huddleston Farmhouse Inn Museum in Mt. Auburn; and a classic car museum in Hagerstown. For a break, Ghyslain Chocolatier in Union City makes hand-decorated French confections that are sure to please. In Indianapolis, antiquers might be especially drawn to the Eiteljorg Museum of American and Indian Art and the 1865 Second-Empire Morris Butler House, featuring Victorian interior details and rare antique furnishings.

Choice lodgings with antique ambiance and modern creature comforts include the Philip W. Smith—Martha E. Perry Bed & Breakfast in Richmond. Other choices, in Centerville, are Denison House and the Historic Lantz House Inn, a brick townhouse with prize-winning gardens and antique furnishings.

One Antique Alley town is the village of Economy, population 200. Economy's a fine place, but, as of this writing, you won't find any antiques stores there.

BEFORE YOU GO, visit
www.in.gov/enjoyindiana
www.historiclandmarks.org
www.byways.org/browse/states/in
www.roadescape.com
www.visitrichmond.org
www.indianapolisantiquedealers.com

FAVORITE LODGING:
The Historic Lantz House Inn
214 West Main Street
Centerville, IN 47330
800-495-2689; 765-855-2936
www.lantzhouseinn.com

West Des Moines, Valley Junction, & Walnut, Iowa

Iowa's State Fair, held at the fairgrounds in Des Moines, the state capital, located in the center of southern Iowa, has been called the best in the country. The fair is not the only attraction here: For farmhouse finds, as well as late-19th- and early-20th-century furnishings, the area around Des Moines is one of the Midwest's best. Two top antiquing destinations are Valley Junction, part of West Des Moines, and Walnut, hailed as "Iowa's Antique City," 80 miles to the west. The drive between Valley Junction and Walnut passes through beautiful hilly countryside, with roadside wildflowers and fields in countless shades of green, dotted with red barns and white farmhouses.

Though locally advertised country auctions are a great way to find things and there are some single-dealer shops, the name of the game in this part of the country is the multi-dealer shop and the antiques mall. These can be vast: In Des Moines, the Brass Armadillo contains 450 antiques and collectible dealers, and Majestic Lion, with 150 dealers, presents one of the Midwest's largest collections of Victorian antiques. Des Moines also has individual dealer shops, one of which specializes in Mission furniture.

Valley Junction, part of West Des Moines, is rich antiquing territory, too, with over 30 individual shops and antiques malls. The emphasis is on Victorian to mid-20th-century items, but earlier items do turn up, as does country furniture in original surface. You'll also find folk art, glassware, primitives, stoneware, jewelry, advertising signs, toys, quilts, architectural and garden elements, stained-glass windows, and even vintage bicycles and French country furniture. The Antique Jamboree, a free event held on the second Sunday of June, August, and September along three blocks of Fifth Street in Valley Junction, draws more than 120 dealers offering a wide array of items including furniture, primitives, stoneware, quilts, and collectibles. Every Thursday, a farmers' market is held at the Heart of Iowa Marketplace on Fifth Street; on that evening, some antiques shops remain open later while others close earlier than usual.

Walnut has 15 shops, the majority being multi-dealer enterprises. The focus here is on late-19th- and early-20th century pieces—pressed oak chairs, glass-doored china cabinets, Eastlake tables, marble-topped dressers, slipper chairs, armoires, Colonial

Revival Duncan Phyfe—style dining tables, art pottery, vintage art, Depression glass, stoneware, Hoosier cabinets, quilts, and rustic items. Walnut holds two antiquing events. On the third weekend in June, a three-day Antiques Walk and Show attracts nearly 300 dealers; a Christmas Antique Walk takes place on the fourth weekend of November.

An impressive house museum is West Des Moines' Salisbury House, a 42-room Tudor mansion modeled on the King's House in Salisbury, England, with antique furnishings and art. Completed in 1928, it incorporates architectural elements imported from England, such as Elizabethan period rafters. The town's c.1850 Jordan House, once a station on the Underground Railroad, is a museum of local history.

In Des Moines, the performing arts scene includes opera, symphony, and theater. Visitors can tour Terrace Hill, the Iowa governor's residence, a National Historic Landmark built in 1869. The spectacular Second Empire mansion has ornate woodwork, a grand staircase, and stained-glass windows. Designed by W. W. Boyington, architect of the Chicago Water Tower, for Iowa's first millionaire, it was promptly dubbed the "Palace of the Prairie." The c.1877 Hoyt Sherman Place, known for its rococo plaster ceiling, showcases antique furnishings and a collection of 19th- and 20th-century art. Iowa's rural legacy is shown at Living History Farms, a 550-acre open-air museum with a Native American village, 1850 pioneer farm, 1875 frontier town, and agricultural exhibits. In August, the 11-day State Fair takes place at the Des Moines Fairgrounds. Recreational areas include Walnut Woods State Park, Four-Mile

AN IRON TESTER BED, REPRODUCTION 18TH-CENTURY SWEDISH GUSTAVIAN FURNITURE, AND
A LIVELY CORAL-AND-WHITE COLOR SCHEME DECORATE A GUEST ROOM AT BUTLER HOUSE ON
GRAND, A BED AND BREAKFAST IN DES MOINES, IOWA.

THE C.1923 TUDOR-STYLE BUTLER HOUSE ON GRAND IS NEAR THE DES MOINES ART CENTER AND GREENWOOD PARK, AND AN EASY DRIVE FROM WEST DES MOINES ANTIQUES STORES.

Greenway Trail, Jordan Creek Trail, Neal Smith Trail, Great Western Trail, and Bill Riley Bike Trail.

For stays in this area, a top choice is the lovely 1923 Tudor-style Butler House on Grand, a bed and breakfast across the street from the Des Moines Art Center and near Greenwood Park, with its rose garden, walking trails, swimming pool, playground, and pond. A designer show house in 1999, Butler House still showcases the work of area designers and artists. Its seven guest rooms are decorated with antiques in refined country style. Creature comforts include private bathrooms, cable television, and Internet access. Breakfast is served in an elegant dining room with a molded plaster ceiling and polished marble floor. In the living room, you can listen to music, play a parlor game, and admire the hand-carved Gothic Revival limestone fireplace. It may remind you of Salisbury House, or make you think of a special antique you might just have to have. As one antiques dealer's sign says, "Iowa—Fields of Opportunities."

BEFORE YOU GO, visit
www.iowatourism.org
www.destinationdesmoines.com
www.iowasantiquecity.com

FAVORITE LODGING:
Butler House on Grand
4507 Grand Avenue
Des Moines, IA 50312
515-255-4096; 866-455-4096
www.butlerhouseongrand.com

Madison &
the Wisconsin Dells

L ocated 60 miles north of Madison, Wisconsin Dells is the name of a town, and it's also the moniker of an area that is one of Wisconsin's major tourist destinations. The Wisconsin Dells is the self-proclaimed Water Park Capital of the World, with go-carting, drive-in theaters, a wax museum, the Bavarian Village complete with German glockenspiel, a museum of historic torture devices, and a Ripley's Believe It or Not Museum. It is also a gorgeous area, with scenic lakes, woods, farmland, and the Wisconsin River. Wollersheim, the state's oldest winery, a National Historic Site, is still a going concern in Prairie du Sac; it was started in the 1840s by Hungarian Count Agoston Haraszthy, who later went west with the gold rush and became a founder of the California wine industry. For mid-century modern, nothing beats Taliesin Preservation, Frank Lloyd Wright's 600-acre estate, Prairie-style

FLOOR-TO-CEILING WINDOWS FRAME AN EASTLAKE VICTORIAN BED IN A GUEST ROOM AT THE MANSION HILL INN, AN 1857 STONE GOTHIC REVIVAL MASTERPIECE IN MADISON, WISCONSIN. PERIOD FURNISHINGS ALSO INCLUDE A VICTORIAN ARMOIRE, DESK, AND CHAIR.

home and studio, in Spring Green, 48 miles west of Madison. Though it's unlikely any of Haraszthy's or Wright's furniture will turn up, you will find ample antiquing. In Madison, the state capital, and on excursions to area historic sites, you've the makings for a terrific antiquing weekend or vacation.

The town of Wisconsin Dells has a half dozen or so antiques stores, and more than 20 are in the nearby communities of Lake Delton, Mt. Horeb, Reedsburg, and Mauston. Many of the shops in the Dells area are malls and multi-dealer ventures of varying sizes. These offer varied antique and vintage furnishings, ranging from 19th-century country and primitive pieces to Victoriana and early-20th-century items. Funky finds such as gas station signs and shabby chic, Western, and rustic pieces enliven the mix.

Madison contains about 50 antiques shops, including malls, multi-dealer facilities, and individual dealer shops. Malls here can be of high quality, and some individual dealers present fine 18th- and 19th-century furniture and decorative arts. If mid-century Moderne inspires you, you'll find that, too. In mid-August, the Wisconsin Pottery Association Show and Sale features 50 dealers and a lecture series.

The Dells offers many outdoor activities at three state parks and on lakes and rivers, and some great hiking trails, including the Ice Age National Scenic Trail. There's golf on eight courses, fishing, canoeing, rides on amphibious craft, rock climbing, horseback riding, biking, ice skating, cross-country skiing, snowmobiling, and scenic tours by train and boat. In Baraboo, the International Crane Foundation's center is dedicated to these wonderful birds, and the Circus World Museum, a National Historic Landmark, is at the site of the original Ringling Brothers Circus Winter Quarters. The Studio and History Center, dedicated to the life and work of pioneering landscape photographer H. H. Bennett, is in the town of Wisconsin Dells. The Dells has an active summer music calendar, with gypsy, swing, folk, barbershop quartets, brass bands, Scottish pipes, and country music.

Madison is home to the State History Center, the Wisconsin Veterans Museum, the Overture Center for the Arts, and two art museums, as well as live theater, ballet, opera, symphony, and bluegrass performances, and a blues festival in August. About 40 to 60 minutes drive from Madison, southern Wisconsin is rich in historic sites. Old World Wisconsin, a living-history museum, is in Eagle, close to Milwaukee. Pendarvis Restoration, with an antique quilt collection, prairie landscape, lead mine, woodland gardens, and stone cottages built by immigrants from Cornwall, England, is located in Greenbush. On the Mississippi River, Villa Louis is in Prairie du Chien, and Stonefield Farm and the State Agricultural Museum are in Cassville.

The Dells area contains some 80 restaurants, and you can satisfy a sweet tooth at Goody Goody Gumdrop Candy Kitchens and Dell's First Fudge. Local micro-brewed beer, wine from Prairie du Sac, and Wisconsin cheeses add up to the perfect ingredients for a picnic. The region has no shortage of resorts, motels, hotels, camping sites, and bed and breakfasts.

Accommodations with an antique ambiance include Breese Way Bed and Breakfast, an Italianate mansion with antique furnishings, located in Portage, and Park View Bed and Breakfast, an 1895 Queen Anne house in Reedsburg. In Wisconsin Dells, two historic options stand out. One is the 1863 Historic Bennett House, once home of the landscape photographer. The other is the White Rose Inns, which comprises five c.1900 houses, appropriately appointed with antiques; it offers a swimming pool and hot tub a view of the Wisconsin River, lovely gardens, and high-speed wireless Internet access in all guest rooms. In Madison, Mansion Hill Inn, an 1857 stone Gothic Revival masterpiece, is a stunning restoration with leaded-glass windows, period wallpaper and carpets, and antique furnishings. Amenities include fireplaces, whirlpool baths, in-room phones and televisions with video and DVD players, and a civilized evening repast of hors d'oeuvres, dessert, and cordials—the perfect ending to a perfect day of antiquing.

BEFORE YOU GO, visit
www.travelwisconsin.com
www.dells.com
www.wisconsin.gov/state/core/visiting_wisconsin.html
www.wisconsinhistory.org
www.wistravel.com/wisconsinantiquessw.htm

FAVORITE LODGINGS:

Mansion Hill Inn
424 North Pinckney Street
Madison, WI 53703
608-255-3999; 800-798-9070
www.mansionhillinn.com

White Rose Inns
910 River Road
Wisconsin Dells, WI 53965
608-254-4724; 800-482-4724
www.thewhiterose.com

Marshall &
Michigan's Antique Alley

The part of Michigan known as the state's Antique Alley is located in its south-central region, in the area between Marshall and Coldwater at Route 69/27, and Monroe and LaSalle at Route 275, and including Ann Arbor, south of Route 94. In this 40-by-65-mile district, there are, by one estimate, more than 900 antiques dealers in malls and shops. The roads ribboning through small towns and farmland, and past several small lakes and ponds, are among the most historic in the state. Sections of I-94B through Marshall, M125 through Monroe, and US 12 through Clinton, Clinton Township, and Saline are designated Michigan Heritage Trails, and were significant in the state's early development. This antique alley has a wealth of picturesque scenery, small museums, farmers markets, and interesting villages to enjoy.

Marshall, located in the northwest corner of this district, has eight shops, housing about 70 dealers. Ann Arbor, in the northeast corner, has about 15. There are about 12 shops in Allen; five or six each in Tecumseh, Blissfield, and Clinton; and three or four each in Irish Hills, Saline, Adrian, Brooklyn, Britton, and Somerset Center. Coldwater, Manchester, Jasper, Morenci, Monroe, LaSalle, and Tekonsha each have one or two shops. These include single-dealer establishments with high-quality merchandise and multi-dealer enterprises. There are good country pieces, primitives, folk art, and furnishings from the high Victorian period through the mid-20th century.

OFFERED BY SUSAN SILVER
ANTIQUES, THIS C.1870 GOTHIC
REVIVAL OAK SIDE CABINET WAS
PROBABLY MADE IN SCOTLAND.

Among the best places in the Midwest to source period furniture and decorative accessories, from early Americana to Art Deco and 1950s modern, is the Ann Arbor Antique Market, held from April through November at the Washtenaw Farm Council Grounds. Dealers come from across the U.S. and Canada. Quality is good and prices are reasonable, particularly for pieces needing some TLC. Saturday/Sunday markets, featuring 350-450 dealers, are held on the third weekends of April and September. In other months, one-day indoor markets take place on the third Sunday, except in November, when it is the first Sunday of the month; these events draw some 250-350 dealers.

South-central Michigan is a popular recreational area, with hiking, biking, fishing, swimming, boating, cross-country skiing, and golf on 15 public courses. Cultural offerings include the Adrian Symphony Orchestra, music and live theater at the Croswell Opera House, and Lenawee County Historical Museum, all in Adrian; Southern

Michigan Railroad tours in Clinton; and the early-19th-century Walker Tavern Historical Complex in Onsted. Events include the weeklong Lenawee County Fair, Michigan's oldest, and the Lenawee County Heritage Festival, both held in August at the fairgrounds in Adrian.

Marshall contains a 14-block enclave of over 850 historic 19th-century buildings, one of the largest National Historic Landmark Districts in the country for a town of its size. With good restaurants, recreation areas, and over 70 antiques dealers, it's a delightful place. Its historic architecture includes the 1839 Greek Revival "Governor's Mansion," built in the hope that the state would place its capital here, and Honolulu House, a c.1860 Italianate mansion built by a chief justice of the Michigan Supreme Court who had been U.S. council to Hawaii. Listed on the National Register of Historic Places, and now the Historical Society museum, it features unique ceiling and wall murals.

Also along Michigan Heritage Trails in this area is Clinton Township, which in the 19th century was the most significant

A FLAG AND WICKER CHAIRS CREATE AN ALL-AMERICAN MOOD ON THE ROSE-ENTWINED PORCH OF THE ROSE HILL INN, A c.1860 ITALIANATE VILLA IN MARSHALL, MICHIGAN. WITHIN, ANTIQUE FURNISHINGS COMPLEMENT ORIGINAL ARCHITECTURAL DETAILS.

trading post west of Detroit. It has many preserved buildings, as does Monroe. Saline has a vibrant historical downtown with two museums—Curtiss Mansion and Rentschler Farm; the town's Michigan Avenue, historically called the Detroit and Chicago Road, was once a Native American trail.

For lodging, options in historic bed and breakfasts with antique furnishings include Briar Oaks Inn in Adrian, Vitosha Guest House in Ann Arbor, and the National House Inn, Michigan's oldest operating inn, in Marshall. For elegance and tranquility, a good choice is Marshall's Rose Hill Inn, an 1860 Italianate mansion, once the home of William Boyce, founder of the Boy Scouts. From its tall windows and welcoming porches, you can admire the views of the three-acre property, once owned by author James Fenimore Cooper. You can relax by fireplaces in two formal parlors and a cozy den, stroll in the garden, or enjoy the inn's tennis court and swimming pool. Rose Hill's six guest rooms, decorated in Victorian style with period antiques, vintage prints, lace curtains, and antique lighting, provide private baths and cable TV. Ample breakfasts are likely to sustain you through a morning's antiquing, and maybe longer, in Michigan's Antique Alley and along its Heritage Trails.

BEFORE YOU GO, visit
www.marshallmich.com
www.michigan.gov

FAVORITE LODGING:
Rose Hill Inn
1110 Verona Road
Marshall, MI 49068
269-789-1992; 877-767-3445
www.rose-hill-inn.com

West

Texas Hill Country

Round Top, Texas

East Texas

Denver & Colorado Springs, Colorado

Santa Fe, Albuquerque, Taos,
& New Mexico's Tribal Arts Shows

Glendale, Arizona

Texas Hill Country

T exas Hill Country, just west of Austin and San Antonio, is an antiquing destination you can return to again and again—for the pleasure of the landscape, the charm of the towns, and the finds that await. This 14,000-square-mile area deep in the heart of Texas welcomes five million visitors annually, but, even so, crowds are few. Settled in the mid-19th century, largely by German immigrants, one of some 37 ethnic groups that established Texas communities, farms, and ranches, the Hill Country is a place of rolling terrain, crystal lakes and rivers, fields thick with wildflowers, an active wine industry, and many wonderful antiques stores.

You'll find the greatest number and concentration of shops in New Braunfels, Boerne (pronounced BUR-nee), Fredericksburg, Kerrville, and Comfort. But because each Hill Country town possesses a unique character, and most have a designated National Historic District with at least one antiques shop, this is a fine area to explore. It's a source for country antiques and painted furniture, as well as high-style pieces, particularly from the 19th century.

In addition to individual shops and antiques malls, the Fredericksburg Trade Days antiques and collectibles show at Sunday Farm, held on weekends mid-month from June through December, is a fun place to shop for Texas primitives, shabby chic items, farm tools, and ranch furnishings.

The Hill Country's history creates a rich context for antiquing. In Comfort, for instance, the historic district comprises over 100 pre-1900 buildings, the most complete and authentic 19th-century downtown in Texas. It contains the only monument to the Union cause south of the Mason-Dixon line, erected in memory of German settlers killed because they opposed slavery and secession.

GUESTS AT SETTLER'S CROSSING IN FREDERICKSBURG, TEXAS, ARE TREATED TO TWO FINE COLLECTIONS: ACCOMMODATIONS ARE IN SEVEN RESTORED ANTIQUE HOUSES, INCLUDING THIS c.1865 *FACHEWORK* HOMESTEAD. INTERIORS SHOWCASE 18TH- AND 19TH-CENTURY AMERICAN COUNTRY ANTIQUES.

Bandera, with about ten shops, was founded in the mid-1800s as a cypress shingle camp and was the site of a Mormon colony; one of the oldest Polish communities in the U.S., it is a classic Western town, with rodeos twice a week during the summer.

Outdoor activities include horseback riding, fly-fishing, hunting in season, hiking, golf, country-and-western dances, festivals, swimming, camping, canoeing, kayaking, river tubing, rafting, nature walks, and birding. There are cattle ranches, butterfly ranches, the largest wildflower farm in the U.S., farm stands along country roads, and wineries that welcome visitors. Other attractions include museums—Kerrville's Cowboy Artists of America Museum and Fredericksburg's Fort Martin, Pioneer Village, and the National Museum of the Pacific War. Theater and musical performances enrich the local arts scene. Nearby, San Antonio and Austin also offer antiquing opportunities.

Texas is unique in having a directory of its antique inns: Historic Accommodations of Texas (HAT), a terrific source of information on lodgings around the state. One of the things that distinguishes Hill Country is the number of inns housed in vernacular folk structures, including dogtrot cabins and houses in the *fachework* building style German immigrants brought with them. These include the Gruene Homestead Inn, Meyer Bed and Breakfast on Cypress Creek, and several lodgings represented by the Gastehaus Schmidt reservation service. The area's premier historic accommodation is Settler's Crossing, a collection of seven impeccably restored antique buildings on a 35-acre estate just outside Fredericksburg. Furnished with 18th- and early-19th-century country antiques and folk art, these comfortable guesthouses are themselves collector's items. Offering a rare experience of America's past, they are a reminder that the West was won not just by cowboys, but by immigrants who sank roots in new soil and stuck with it.

BEFORE YOU GO, visit
www.hill-country-visitor.com
www.hat.org

FAVORITE LODGING:
Settler's Crossing
104 Settler's Crossing Road
Fredericksburg, TX 78624
830-997-2722; 800-874-1020
www.settlerscrossing.com

Round Top, Texas

L eave it to the Texans, who take pride in never doing anything in a small way, to transform a sleepy little town into the setting of one of America's block-buster antiques shows. In early April and early October every year, Round Top—population 850, give or take a few—swells with tens of thousands of antiquers who come for prime shopping. Started in the 1960s, the Original Round Top Antiques Fair, the area's oldest show to insist that only antiques be exhibited, is one of the most successful in the nation. Over the years, others have tailgated on its success. The best of the newer shows is the Marburger Farm Antique Show, launched nearly ten years ago.

One estimate places the total influx of dealers during the April and October Round Top shows at 2,500. Fact or Texas tall tale? It depends on how you count, but with all this antiquing, a stay in the area could extend for a week or more. The action in Round Top begins well before the weekend, with Marburger opening on Tuesday and the Original Round Top Fair on Thursday; both run through Saturday, though a few dealers might stay on until Sunday. This is a place where antiques dealers come from around the country to shop. If the two large shows aren't enough, area towns, including Bellville, Brenham, Columbus, Fayetteville, Flatonia, La Bahia, La Grange, Schulenburg, Shelby, and Warrenton, often hold special antiques and crafts events before and during the Round Top shows.

ANTIQUES AT HILLWOOD FARMS' BOOTH AT THE ORIGINAL ROUND TOP
ANTIQUES FAIR DISPLAYS EARLY-18TH-CENTURY AMERICAN AND ENGLISH
FURNISHINGS, INCLUDING A HALF-TESTER BED WITH EMBROIDERED HANGINGS.

At the Original Round Top Antiques Fair, some 400 American and European dealers exhibit everything from formal Continental furniture to country primitives in original paint, all of it antique. Quality is generally good, and items are not always inexpensive. In recent memory, a man spent $175,000 in less than three hours, dropping $75,000 on a single piece of German Black Forest furniture. A new addition to this show features Native American and Cowboy antiques, and art and artifacts of the Old West. Because this is Texas, some of the world's best barbeque is right on site, and the theme of the October show is Oktoberfest, in keeping with the town's German heritage. Emma Lee Turney, who founded the Round Top show, now manages a nearby Folk Art and Artisans Creative Market, featuring upscale traditional and contemporary crafts.

Down the road a piece, Marburger Farm hosts some 400 dealers from more than 30 states and several countries. Marburger is chock-a-block with items from all over the world and from diverse periods, including mid-20th-century. Top-quality antiques can also be found here. A sampling of merchandise would include American country furniture in original paint, Continental furniture, fine and folk art, ceramics, silver, china and glass, authentic Tiffany lamps, quilts and other textiles, African and Asian artifacts, Mexican *retablos*, garden urns, and statuary. Because of Texans' affinity for French furnishings, you might also see 150-year-old Baccarat chandeliers and bombé chests.

In addition to these major spring and fall shows, several smaller ones take place at Round Top's Big Red Barn during the year. These include a mid-January Winter Antique Show, a vintage garden and architecture show in late June, and an early-November Holiday Antiques Show, which includes seasonal decorations.

Those with the stamina and time-management skills to explore other activities will find plenty of historic and cultural attractions in and around tiny Round Top. Among these are a wonderful historic district; the McAshan Herb Gardens; the Henkel Square Museum Village of restored Anglo and German Texas farmhouses, furnished with antiques from the Faith Bybee collection; the Winedale Historical Center with its stage-coach stop and farmstead, restored and bequeathed to the University of Texas by Ima Hogg (whose River Oaks mansion and antiques collection form the core of Houston's Bayou Bend Collection); the Texas Pioneer Arts Foundation collection; the International Festival-Institute for music; and the University of Texas Shakespeare at Winedale program. Although Round Top's performing arts calendar does not always coincide with the show schedule, it's worth checking: http://music.utsa.edu and www.shakespeare-winedale.org.

Accommodations include Anderson's Round Top Inn, historic Texas buildings furnished with country antiques, located just off Round Top's historic square. Other options are Blisswood in Cat Springs and the Somewhere in Time Guest House in

Bellville. But with Houston about 90 miles to the east, and Austin 75 miles west, Round Top is within reasonable driving distance for lodging. Two good choices are the Ant Street Inn, located in Brenham, midway between Houston and Round Top, and the Governor's Mansion, one of Austin's most elegant inns. Wherever you hang your Stetson for the night, you're likely to feel satisfied with the buys you've lassoed at Round Top.

BEFORE YOU GO, visit
www.roundtop.org
www.roundtop.com
www.roundtoptexasantiques.com
www.roundtop-marburger.com
www.hat.org

FAVORITE LODGING:
Anderson's Round Top Inn
102 Bauer Rummel
Roundtop, TX 78954
979-249-5294; 877-738-6746
www.andersonsroundtopinn.com

A 19TH-CENTURY CUPBOARD IN
MUSTARD PAINT IS EVOCATIVE OF A
TEXAS HOMESTEAD.

East Texas

I
n 1931, the first oil well in Gladewater, Texas, came in, starting a boom that lasted some 40 years: The town still celebrates East Texas Gusher Days every April. Antiquing in this area, along Route 80, is a lot like celebrating a gusher. Fort Worth and Dallas are both terrific cities to shop for antiques, the latter recognized for its affinity for high style, and its deep pockets. (Midway between the two cities, Grapevine, Texas, is the new site of the September Friday/Saturday/ Sunday Heart of Country Antiques Show, formerly held in Nashville, Tennessee.) When Dallas residents go antiquing, they often head east, to Gladewater, Terrell, Forney, Canton, Mineola, Tyler, Longview, and as far away as Jefferson, 167 miles east, on Big Cypress Creek, a 19th-century river port for incoming goods from New Orleans.

All total, these towns east of Dallas boast more than 100 antiques stores. Forney, with about 20 shops, is a favorite for its quality and good prices. Gladewater, which has been called the "antiques capital of East Texas," also has about 20 shops, including large malls. Tyler contains more than 35 dealers, Longview and Jefferson about 20 each, Canton about 12, and ten in and around Terrell. They're easy to find: Malls and

A GUEST ROOM AT ROSELAND PLANTATION NEAR TYLER, TEXAS, CONTAINS A WHIMSICAL ARRAY OF COTTAGE-STYLE FURNISHINGS, INCLUDING A HAND-PAINTED VICTORIAN BED AND A WOODEN ROCKING HORSE.

THE LOVELY C.1854 NEOCLASSICAL-STYLE MAIN HOUSE AT ROSELAND
PLANTATION WAS ONCE THE CENTER OF A 3,000-ACRE COTTON ENTERPRISE.

individual and multi-dealer shops are along Route 80 and in brick shopfronts in manageable downtowns, some of the nicest 19th-century towns in the state.

East Texas's biggest antiquing event is Canton's First Monday Trade Days, located on Highway 64E and held on the Friday, Saturday, and Sunday preceding the first Monday of each month. Trade Days began in the 1850s, and took its name from the day the circuit judge arrived and townspeople conducted business in Canton's town square. This indoor/outdoor show attracts above 4,000 vendors with displays of antiques, vintage items, and recently minted arts and crafts. The finds here are terrific, and the food, ranging from barbeque to funnel cakes, is a treat. Among Texas antiquers, First Monday is a much-loved event.

Many of the objects available in East Texas arrived with the oil money early in the 20th century, so you'll come across both antiques and vintage items, ranging from fine 19th-century and earlier pieces to late-Victorian and 20th-century objects. Along with finer things, there are homestead and ranch finds, country furnishings, and pieces for shabby chic and cottage interiors. This being Texas, the Old West is ever present. One reason antiques shoppers favor this area is that prices are generally reasonable.

East Texas, with four national and five state forests, rivers, lakes, and piney woods, is a beautiful part of the state, with ample recreational activities. Among cultural events, Gladewater presents "opry" performances every Saturday night, and free gospel concerts on Friday. Rodeos are not an uncommon occurrence around here; Gladewater's Roundup Rodeo is in June. In Mineola, the Select Theater, considered the longest continuously running theater in Texas, presents movies and live productions. Tyler, known for its roses—30,000 bushes and 450 varieties in its public garden alone—celebrates its Rose Festival in October; in late March and early April, you can wander its azalea trails.

Historic sites include sawmills, iron furnaces, and early oil derricks. Several sites are related to the Civil War and to the area's large 19th-century African American population. Tyler boasts the Goodman Museum, a two-story 1859–1872 mansion with period furnishings. Its original Carnegie Library, built in 1904 and expanded in 1935 by the WPA, has exceptional original murals and an exhibit on Chinese immigrant pioneers. Jefferson is a jewel, called a "mini-Charleston," where you can take a steamboat ride on Lake Caddo or a backwater tour, or lounge in railroad magnate Jay Gould's 1861 private car. Marshall, with a few antiques stores, is an architecturally interesting town, with an Impressionist museum and a depot built in 1912 (still an Amtrak stop); its Starr Family State Historic Site contains the 1870 Italianate Maplecroft House, listed on the National Register of Historic Places and furnished with antiques, and Rosemont Cottage, a bed and breakfast.

In Jefferson, house tours are regularly given of several historic guest lodgings: Kennedy Manor, the Italianate Victorian House of the Seasons, the 1850s Excelsior House Hotel, and Twin Oaks Plantation, an antebellum sugar plantation and mansion. Jefferson's only waterfront lodging is Maison Bayou Bed and Breakfast, a replica of a 1850s Creole plantation. Other local lodgings of note include the Lott House in Gladewater.

For antiquers, one East Texas find is Roseland Plantation, an elegant 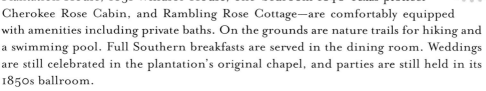 bed and breakfast near Tyler. Before the Civil War, it was a 3,000-acre cotton plantations; afterward, the owner deeded 2,800 acres to his 52 former slaves. Beautifully furnished with period antiques reflecting its heritage, Roseland Plantation's guest rooms—in its 1854 Hambrick Plantation House, 1851 Windsor House, one-bedroom 1848 Texas pioneer Cherokee Rose Cabin, and Rambling Rose Cottage—are comfortably equipped with amenities including private baths. On the grounds are nature trails for hiking and a swimming pool. Full Southern breakfasts are served in the dining room. Weddings are still celebrated in the plantation's original chapel, and parties are still held in its 1850s ballroom.

BEFORE YOU GO, visit
www.traveltex.com
www.tylertexas.com
www.gladewaterchamber.com
www.woodcountytx.com
www.forney-texas.com/biz-org/byantique.html
www.heartofcountry.com

FAVORITE LODGING:
Roseland Plantation
2601 State Hwy 64 West (6 miles from Tyler Airport)
Ben Wheeler, TX 75754
903-849-5553
www.roselandplantation.com

Denver & Colorado Springs, Colorado

D enver, Colorado, America's "Mile High City," at the base of the majestic Rocky Mountains, is the largest urban center within a 600-mile radius, a cultural and antiquing nexus in this part of the West. Surrounded by 120 miles of mountain range and almost 200 named peaks, Denver affords a view of the majestic Rockies from almost every street. It boasts 300 days of sun annually, the nation's largest urban park system, and 650 miles of paved bike trails. About 70 miles to the south, the town of Colorado Springs is an antiquing destination for Colorado residents and visitors.

Denver's Antique Row Business District contains 200 multi-dealer shops, large malls, and individual dealer enterprises, located in an 18-block stretch between numbers 200 and 2000 South Broadway. Known for its diversity and variety, this area has everything from Native American artifacts and New Mexican WPA furniture to signed Thonet chairs and French armoires. Many shops are open seven days a week. Antique Row holds sidewalk sales on the last weekend in June and the third weekend in November.

The annual Denver Antiques Show & Sale is usually held on the third weekend in April at the Wings Over the Rockies Air and Space Museum. This Friday/Saturday/Sunday event draws more than 30 dealers from the East, Midwest, and West, showing furniture, fine art, decorative arts, silver, jewelry, garden accessories, and other items.

At the Denver Merchandise Mart Expo Building, on the third weekends of March, July, and October, the Friday/Saturday/Sunday World Wide Antique Shows draw about 150 dealers from across the country. They bring furniture, decorative arts, mid- and early-20th-century items, folk art, Asian art and antiquities, glass, silver, ceramics, jewelry, art, posters, prints, textiles, books, maps, tribal art, and collectibles—enough variety for all price ranges. There are also smaller shows such as Pumpkin Pie Days in October and Strawberry Pie Days at Boulder Country Fairgrounds outside Denver.

An outdoor flea market is held every second Saturday of the month, from April through October, in the Ballpark neighborhood on Larimer Street between 21st and 22nd avenues. It features over 100 dealers with antiques and vintage furnishings, as well as new things.

Denver's most spectacular house museum is the former home of the "Unsinkable Molly Brown." Built in 1886 for a Colorado silver baron and once also the Governor's Mansion, its stunning interiors showcase high-style Victoriana. Other museums include the Colorado History Museum and the 1883 Byers-Evans Mansion, with period furnishings. The Denver Art Museum has a superb Native American collection, as well as pre-Columbian and Spanish colonial art; British, European, American, and Western art; and the collection of industrial designer and Bauhaus teacher Herbert Bayer. The Art and History Museums are located in the Golden Triangle Arts District, near more than 50 galleries and artist's studios, ballet and theater companies, restaurants, and specialty stores. Every first Friday of the month, Golden Triangle galleries stay open late, and free shuttles run to the open studios and galleries.

Denver's lower downtown Victorian historic district—LoDo—encompasses Union Station and the Oxford Hotel, and is connected to the performing arts complex via the 16th Street pedestrian mall. Over a mile in length, the mall brims with nightspots, restaurants, and microbreweries. The performing arts complex houses theater, dance, opera, and symphony performances. Other attractions include a large stock show and rodeo in January; the nation's largest Cinco de Mayo event and a Native American market and pow-wow in May; an Asian film festival in early June; and the Denver Film Festival in November. Fifteen miles west of Denver is the incomparable Red Rocks Amphitheatre, a huge arena carved out of gigantic boulders.

Some 70 miles south of Denver, Colorado Springs has over 30 antiques shops. Located on West Colorado Avenue, North and South Nevada, Broadway, and North Union Street, they include antiques malls and smaller establishments presenting a range of styles from European country pieces to Asian art, Native American artifacts, and decorative items evocative of the Old West. Six miles northwest is historic Manitou Springs, with a few shops, including places for cowboy and Native American antiques. The Friday/ Saturday/Sunday Pikes Peak Western Collectible Show draws 100 dealers of cowboy and Indian antiques and art, and is held on the last weekend in July at the Colorado Springs City Auditorium.

VICTORIAN ARCHITECTURAL DETAILS AND FURNISHINGS AT DENVER'S GREGORY INN BELIE THE FACT THAT THIS IS A NEW BUILDING PAINSTAKINGLY CRAFTED TO REPLICATE HISTORIC HOUSES IN ITS 1880S NEIGHBORHOOD, THE CITY'S OLDEST.

With skiing in winter and many summer recreational activities, including the Pikes Peak Marathon, held each August, this part of Colorado is a place for all seasons.

In the Colorado Springs area, Red Crags Bed and Breakfast Country Inn, and its sister property, the Bed and Breakfast at Historic OnaLedge, are two turn-of-the-century mansions listed on the National Register of Historic Places, where antique furnishings complement original architectural details. At Red Crags, you can enjoy the antique piano and fireplace in the parlor, bask near a rare cherry wood Eastlake fireplace while eating a gourmet breakfast, or admire the view of Pikes Peak from the solarium.

In Denver, an accommodation worth noting is the Gregory Inn. Near LoDo, it is a replica 1880s house that blends seamlessly into its Victorian streetscape in Curtis Park, Denver's earliest neighborhood. At this intimate, upscale bed and breakfast, Victorian architectural details and period-sensitive furnishings create a luxurious atmosphere. Guests are pampered with hearty food, plush seating and mattresses, working gas fireplaces in every room, whirlpool-jetted tubs in private marble and tile baths, and high-tech amenities including wireless Internet access. A short walk from shops, restaurants, and microbreweries, the Gregory Inn's hospitality extends beyond its doors with off-street parking and town car service at taxicab rates.

If you do travel between Denver and Colorado Springs, stop in Sedalia to see the 1926 Cherokee Ranch and Castle. Modeled after a historic Scottish castle, it features an extensive collection of art and antiques, and surrounded by 14,000 acres of open space, it offers spectacular views of the Front Range. For antiquers, this may be a peak Colorado experience.

BEFORE YOU GO, visit
www.colorado.com
www.denver.org
www.antiques-colorado.com
www.antique-row.com
www.denverantiquesshow.com
www.denvermart.com
www.ballparkmarket.com

FAVORITE LODGINGS:

Red Crags Bed & Breakfast Country Inn
302 El Paso Boulevard
Manitou Springs, CO 80829
719-685-1920; 800-721-2248
www.redcrags.com

The Gregory Inn
2500 Arapahoe Street
Denver, CO 80205
303-295-6570; 800-925-6570
www.gregoryinn.com

❄

Santa Fe, Albuquerque, Taos, & New Mexico's Tribal Arts Shows

T he antiquing scene in Santa Fe, Taos, and Albuquerque reflects the area's cultural sophistication, Native American traditions, and international influences. Located 70 miles southwest of Taos and 60 miles northeast of Albuquerque, Santa Fe is both an antiquing destination and a hub for antiquing in this area. At 7,000 feet above sea level, it is the highest of all of the U.S. state capitals. It is also the oldest. Its Palace of Governors, the oldest building in the U.S. still in continuous use, dates to 1610. By that time, Spanish galleons were already crossing the Pacific from the Far East, bearing Chinese ceramics, silks, and spices,

and unloading their cargo in Mexico. Goods traveled by mule train from Mexico City up the Camino Real (the Old King's Highway) to Santa Fe. The long interaction between distinct Anglo, Spanish, and Native American cultures makes Santa Fe, as locals say, "the City Different." Artists and photographers began arriving at the turn of the century, attracted by the Sangre de Cristo mountains, the crystalline air and quality of light, and the Pueblo Indian culture.

You'll find antiques shops in these three cities—Santa Fe contains more than 75, Albuquerque over 50, and Taos about 12 of high quality. The drive from Santa Fe to Taos passes Carson and Santa Fe National Forests, several Indian Reservations, and Rancho de Taos, which has many antiques shops. Between Santa Fe and Albuquerque, the small town of Bernalillo is an ideal stop for some antiquing.

NAVAJO RUGS AND POTTERY ARE AMONG THE ITEMS DISPLAYED AT SANTA FE'S HISTORIC INDIAN & WORLD TRIBAL ARTS SHOW, HELD IN MID-AUGUST.

AT TWILIGHT, THE COURTYARD AT THE INN OF THE FIVE GRACES IN SANTA
FE ASSUMES A TIMELESS QUALITY. ANTIQUES, SOURCED INTERNATIONALLY,
DECORATE ITS COLORFUL INTERIORS.

If tribal antiques interest you, August is the month to visit New Mexico: Santa Fe, Taos, and Albuquerque all hold antiques shows devoted to tribal art, with a large proportion of dealers exhibiting Native American art and artifacts. Albuquerque's Great Southwestern Antiques, Indian and Old West Show, a Friday/Saturday event, is held on the first weekend in August at the Lujan Center on the State Fairgrounds; it presents more than 190 dealers. Santa Fe's August antiques shows calendar begins with Fine Arts of the American West, a three-day show in early August with 65 dealers exhibiting antique works, photography, furniture, and decorative arts; days and dates change from year to year because the event is geared to the Native American calendar. In mid-August, the Historic Indian & World Tribal Arts Santa Fe show brings together 95 distinguished dealers from all over the U.S. and Canada for a Friday/Saturday/Sunday show at the Shellaberger Tennis Center at the College of Santa Fe. Also in mid-August is the Friday/Saturday/Sunday Antique Ethnographic Art Show at Albuquerque's Sweeney Center, with 175 dealers presenting a range of objects from Mexican jewelry to religious artifacts and Alaskan Indian items. The last of Santa Fe's August antiques shows is the three-day Antique Indian Art Show, devoted exclusively to pre-1940s Native American art and artifacts, with 175 dealers.

These antiquing events lead up to one of Santa Fe's largest events, the Indian Market, which showcases contemporary items by Native American artists and is the largest of its kind in the world. Numerous other Native American arts and crafts events are held throughout this area. A good source of information about them is the

Antique Tribal Art Dealers Association (www.atada.org). Semiannual American Indian Art Auctions are conducted by R. G. Munn in late March and late October in Albuquerque. The Tesuque Pueblo Flea Market, seven miles north of Santa Fe, features over 300 permanent vendors with antiques, Indian arts, crafts, and collectibles. Santa Fe's Spanish market is held on the last weekend in July. Check locally for days and hours.

Two Antiquities Shows, one in early July and the other on the last weekend in December, are held in Santa Fe's Sweeney Center. These Friday/Saturday/Sunday shows present about 60 dealers, with a mix of formal and eclectic items, including European, English, and American furniture, fine arts, silver, and decorative items.

Santa Fe is a beautiful town, with a main plaza dominated by an impressive cathedral and the Palace of the Governors. Its plaza is the setting for the city's Indian market, held daily. Many of the city's museums focus on Native American cultures and Spanish colonial heritage. There's the Southwestern History Museum in the Palace of the Governors and the Museum of Spanish Colonial Art, with the world's most comprehensive collection of its kind. The Museum of Indian Arts and Culture showcases traditional and contemporary Southwestern Indian pottery, jewelry, basketry, weaving, painting and sculpture. The Wheelwright Museum of the American Indian, in a building based on a traditional Navajo hogan, exhibits historic and contemporary art and craftwork from many Native American cultures. The Institute of American Indian Art features contemporary art by and about native people, including paintings, prints, sculpture, photography, pottery, jewelry, and beadwork. Santa Fe's Museum of International Folk Art presents a stunning array of ethnic arts from hundreds of cultures, one of the largest collections of folk art in the world. Its Museum of Fine Arts holds an extensive collection of Southwestern artists, including major pieces by Georgia O'Keeffe, and she is the sole focus of the Georgia O'Keeffe Museum. Not far from the city, El Rancho de las Golondrinas, once a stop on the Camino Real, is now a living-history museum on a 200-acre ranch.

The world-class Santa Fe Opera, which runs summer-long, is the town's most renowned performing arts entity, but you'll also find jazz, chamber music, symphony, dance, and a variety of other offerings. In early September, the city celebrates its Fiesta de Santa Fe. With more art galleries per square foot than any other city in the nation, Santa Fe is a paradise for art lovers.

Mountain and desert terrain, along with thousands of acres of National Forest and wilderness, provide opportunities for outdoor activities such as horseback riding, cross-country skiing, whitewater rafting, fishing, and golf on several award-winning courses. New Mexico's eight northern Indian pueblos welcome visitors and hold feast days and dances that are open to the public.

Several historic lodgings are especially reflective of this area's cultural traditions. In Taos, a favorite is the Mabel Dodge Luhan House, once the home of the wealthy heiress and her Pueblo Indian husband, who entertained D. H. Lawrence, Georgia O'Keeffe, and other leading cultural figures of the early 20th century. In Albuquerque, at the simple 200-year-old adobe Hacienda Antigua, Santa Fe style is showcased in Mexican, Spanish colonial, and Native American furnishings, and the Mauger Estate is an 1897 restored Queen Anne-style home. In Santa Fe, the Inn of the Five Graces is a 1938 adobe inn in one of the city's oldest barrios; its decor is a visually rich mix of furnishings sourced internationally. A few miles from town is the Bishop's Lodge Resort and Spa, with 111 guest rooms in adobe-style lodges; the resort contains a mid-19th-century chapel built by the first bishop of Santa Fe, the subject of Willa Cather's *Death Comes to the Archbishop*. You'll find modern amenities and creature comforts in all places, and varied expressions of Southwest style that may inspire local purchases.

BEFORE YOU GO, visit
www.newmexico.org
www.santafe.org
www.atada.org/calendar
www.cowboysandindiansnm.com
www.whitehawkshows.com
www.antiquities-shows.com
www.tribalantiqueshow.com

FAVORITE LODGING:
The Inn of the Five Graces
150 East De Vargas Street
Santa Fe, NM 87501
505-992-0957
www.fivegraces.com

THIS NICELY CRAFTED DOOR HANDLE GRACES A C.1800 PAINTED COUNTRY CUPBOARD.

Glendale, Arizona

I t's been said that the historic town of Glendale, Arizona, feels more like a Midwestern town than a Southwestern one. Its Old Town area, dating from 1892, is a place of red brick storefronts and sidewalks dotted with gaslights, and its focal point is Murphy Square, named after the man who built the first canals opening the area to agriculture. The Catlin Park neighborhood, listed on the National Register of Historic Places, is distinguished by 1920s–1940s Arts & Crafts bungalows along tree-shaded streets, where white picket fences line the sidewalks, green lawns are decorated with gazebos and fountains, and porches are graced with swings. The difference between Glendale and your average Midwestern town is that some of Glendale's tree shade comes from palms.

Glendale's manageable ten-block retail area, its shaded streets, and public art program (funded by a local sales tax) make it a nice place for strolling. About 100 antiques stores are located in the Old Town area, most of them on Glendale Avenue. You'll find more items tucked into specialty shops in Catlin Park. There's a fair amount of 1920s oak furniture and other vintage items, as well as objects evoking the Old West,

but this area also has antiques and decor items sourced internationally, especially from Asia. On the third Thursday of each month, and every Thursday in November, Old Town's stores extend their hours to 9 p.m. for Glendale's Gaslight Antique Walk. Area antiques shows include the Fairgrounds Antique Market in Phoenix, a Saturday/ Sunday event in mid-September; and the Scottsdale Fine Art & Antiques Show, a Saturday/Sunday event on the first weekend of March at Parada Hall in Scottsdale.

Glendale's Bell Road Corridor has many restaurants, and the city's sports complex is a dining and entertainment destination. Museums include the Bead Museum, displaying adornments from ancient and ethnic cultures, and the 1885 Historic Sahuaro Ranch, comprising 17 acres and 13 original buildings, with period 1920s furnishings, an art gallery, and gardens.

SOUTHWEST STYLE INCORPORATES A HAND-CARVED ARCHITECTURAL ELEMENT ABOVE THE MANTEL AND A WOODEN TRUNK AT THE c.1923 SPANISH COLONIAL-STYLE ROYAL PALMS HOTEL IN PHOENIX.

In Phoenix, nine miles away, the Phoenix Art Museum is the Southwest's largest, with extensive collections of American, Asian, European, Latin American, and Western art, and the interesting Thorne Miniature Rooms of Historic Design. The city's Heard Museum, Museum of History, and Museo Chicano explore Southwestern history and Native American and Mexican art, while the Pueblo Grande Museum teaches visitors about the area's first inhabitants, the Hohokum Indians. Phoenix's Pioneer Arizona Living History Museum focuses on Arizona territorial history from 1858-1912. There's an active performing arts scene, with theater, ballet, symphony, and other concerts. Heritage Square, the only remaining group of residential structures from the original town site of Phoenix, is a charming Victorian block of museums, shops, and restaurants. Nearby Scottsdale is known for art galleries and its evening First Friday Art Walk, held every month. Outside Scottsdale, Frank Lloyd Wright's winter home and studio, Taliesin West, is a museum and educational center dedicated to his work.

For recreation, the Phoenix area has Camelback Mountain, Papago Park, and the Sonora Desert, the nation's largest, home to the Sagauro cacti that grow nowhere else in the world. Nearby, you'll find a wealth of golf courses, other activities such as horseback riding, nature walks, and many natural and Native American sites.

Historic lodgings include Glendale's newly refurbished Gaslight Inn, within strolling distance of antiques shops. In Scottsdale, the Hermosa Inn, built by cowboy artist Lon Megargee, is a member of Historic Hotels of America. Another member of that group is the Royal Palms hotel in Phoenix. Comprising a c.1923 Spanish Colonial mansion, 117 stylish guest casitas and rooms, resort facilities, and a spa, the Royal Palms combines historic elegance with luxury amenities. If your idea of luxury is to enjoy a desert sunset on horseback, there's Rancho de los Cabelleros guest ranch, 45 miles from Glendale, in historic Wickenburg.

BEFORE YOU GO, visit
www.arizonaguide.com/glendale
www.visitglendale.com
www.historichotels.org

FAVORITE LODGINGS:

Royal Palms Resort and Spa
5200 East Camelback Road
Phoenix, AZ 85018
602-840-3610; 800-672-6011
www.royalpalmshotel.com

The Hermosa Inn
5532 North Palo Cristi Road
Scottsdale, AZ 85253
602-955-8614; 800-241-1210
www.hermosainn.com

Pacific Coast

The Los Angeles Area: Santa Monica,
Pasadena, & Orange

California's Monterey Peninsula

San Francisco, California

Sonoma County, California

Portland & Aurora, Oregon

Washington's Puget Sound

The Los Angeles Area: Santa Monica, Pasadena, & Orange

With its wealth of antiques shops, the internationally recognized Los Angeles Antiques Show, six other annual antiques shows, two major monthly flea markets, and many small flea markets, Los Angeles is a stellar antiquing destination. Because of its Hispanic heritage, role in the Arts & Crafts movement, and penchant for Modernism, this is a particularly good place to find those pieces. But, since dealers and residents have been bringing in varied furnishings for centuries, you can find almost anything here. Los Angeles is a city with a keen eye for style, whether it's high-end Continental, mid-century Moderne, or shabby chic. It has about 400 antiques stores, and it's wise to focus on particular antiquing neighborhoods. Beverly Hills has its share of shops. West Hollywood's design district is located along La Cienega Boulevard, south of Santa Monica Boulevard. South Robertson, La Brea, and Melrose avenues are dotted with shops. Nearby, Pasadena has over 60 shops, and Santa Monica more than 40. Just 30 miles southeast of L.A., the town of Orange, with over 50 shops, many of them on Glassell Street, is an antiquing destination mentioned by Hollywood set designers. Palm Springs, 100 miles east, has over 50 shops.

The Los Angeles Annual Antiques Show, sponsored by the Antiques Dealers Association of California, is known for its broad geographic scope, superb quality, and brilliant sense of design. Held during the last weekend in April, this Friday/Saturday/Sunday event draws 66 dealers from across the U.S., and from Canada, Europe, and Asia, with pieces sourced worldwide and dating from ancient times through the 20th century. The Pasadena Annual Antiques Show, usually held on the first full weekend in March, June, August, and December, draws 128 dealers with a wide range of furniture and decorative accessories, fine art, and jewelry. You'll find a similar mix, with over 80 dealers, at the Santa Monica Annual Antiques Show, normally held mid-month in January and April. The third weekend in February, the Dorothy Emerson Antiques Show draws 75 dealers, with decorative 18th- through mid-20th-century furnishings.

ARTS & CRAFTS STYLE AT THE CHANNEL ROAD INN IN SANTA MONICA, CALIFORNIA, INCLUDES A FIREPLACE WITH EARLY-20TH-CENTURY TILES BY PASADENA CERAMICIST ERNST BATCHELDER.

The city's two largest monthly flea markets are Pasadena's Rose Bowl Flea Market, with 2,000 vendors, held on the second Sunday, and the Santa Monica Antiques & Flea Market on the fourth Sunday. Smaller flea markets can draw up to 800 vendors. Every weekend, there's Peddler on the Roof on Saturday, atop a parking garage at 1423 North Gordon Street, and Melrose Trading Post on Sunday, at the corner of Fairfax and Melrose. Other monthly flea markets include two on the first Sunday (Pasadena City College Campus Flea Market at Colorado and Bonnie, and the Westside Antiques Show in Santa Monica); two on the third Sunday (Long Beach Veteran's Stadium and West Hollywood's Uni Flea), and one the fourth Sunday (Santa Monica Antiques & Flea Market, on Airport Avenue off of Bundy).

Los Angeles is a vibrant, varied town, and its attractions are many. The city is known culturally for its fine symphony, theater, dance, and other offerings. The Los Angeles County Museum of Art has extensive collections of furniture, decorative arts, and art from America, Europe, Asia, and the Middle East. The J. Paul Getty Museum collections include architecture and room elements, furniture, decorative arts, paintings, sculpture, photography, jewelry, antiquities, and illuminated manuscripts. The

Huntington Library, Art Collections, and Botanical Gardens, in San Marino, is known for American, British, and French art, while the Norton Simon Museum in Pasadena showcases European, American, and Asian paintings and sculpture. Smaller museums  are UCLA's Fowler Museum, with art from Africa, Asia, the Pacific, and the Americas; the UCLA Armand Hammer Museum of Art, with works by European and American masters; the Museum of Latin American Art; the Pacific Asia Museum; the California African American Museum; the Autry National Center Museum of the West; and the Fashion Institute Design Museum. Several museums are devoted to contemporary art and to the entertainment industry.

In the L.A. area, historic bed and breakfasts are few and far between, but you can snag a coveted view of the Pacific at the c.1912 Channel Road Inn Bed and Breakfast in Santa Monica. The inn's location near the Santa Monica Boulevard bus line makes it easy to reach antiques shops on La Cienega Boulevard, and guests can use its bicycles, rollerblade on the boardwalk, stroll to Santa Monica pier and the beach, and walk to restaurants. Guest rooms feature fireplaces and/or private decks, TVs with video players, data ports, and private baths. Arts & Crafts interior detailing and Victorian, Arts & Crafts, and Colonial Revival furnishings offer inspiration for antiquing. With the ocean just a few blocks away, a day of antiquing along Montana Avenue in Santa Monica is like a day at the beach.

BEFORE YOU GO, visit
www.lacvb.com
www.antiquedealersca.com
www.losangelesantiqueshow.com
www.bustamante-shows.com
www.goodridgeguides.com/fleamarketusa
www.fleamarketguide.com
www.keysfleamarket.com
www.peddlerontheroof.com

FAVORITE LODGING:
Channel Road Inn Bed and Breakfast
219 West Channel Road
Santa Monica, CA 90402
310-459-1920
www.channelroadinn.com

California's Monterey Peninsula

he Pacific coast between Los Angeles and San Francisco is more than a scenic wonder; it also contains some prime towns for antiquing. The Monterey Peninsula, a small rocky fist thrust into the Pacific south of San Francisco, delivers a lot of variety for its modest acreage. The towns of Carmel, Monterey, and Pacific Grove, just minutes from one another, contain about 40 antiques shops. The pleasures of the peninsula include fine wining and dining, listening to the surf as you drift off to sleep, and exploring the beach and tide pools between the rocks. The scenery is spectacular—one reason that the area is favored by painters. At daybreak, the rocky shoreline is veiled in fog, which dissipates, revealing the Pacific's sparkling blue expanse, as the sun rises in the sky.

In Pacific Grove, California, an 1860s Chippendale Revival bed, part of the collection at the c.1899 Martine Inn, offers ocean views.

The town of Monterey is best known for Cannery Row, made famous by novelist John Steinbeck. Its wharf, aquarium, and once rough and raucous canneries are now a tourist destination, and it has several antiques malls. Carmel-by-the-Sea is a polished, upscale community, with an English sensibility and an artistic flair, where art galleries mix happily with high-end antiques stores in the area around Ocean, Lincoln, Dolores, Mission, and 7th streets. Pebble Beach is more focused on golf than antiques, at least in terms of its shopping opportunities.

Pacific Grove, which began in the late-19th century as a Methodist tent camp and is proud of its turn-of-the-century architectural treasures, has a few shops and malls, many of them on Lighthouse Avenue. These shops present a range from shabby chic to American and European antiques. Pacific Grove's Antiques and Collectibles Fair, which draws about 100 vendors, is a Friday/Saturday/Sunday event held in mid-July.

At the end of July, the funky fishing community of Moss Landing, about 20 miles north, holds its Antiques Street Fair with 200 dealers from all over the West Coast. In the Monterey area, the biggest collectible may be classic cars. Historic automobile races are held in mid-August, and the Monterey Sports Car Championship, part of the American Le Mans series, takes place in mid-October. In August, classic car auctions are held here by Bonhams & Butterfields and by Christie's.

Late summer is a good time to visit the peninsula, but you can't go wrong at any time. It's wise to check the weather: Strong seasonal rains sometimes wash out coastal roads north of Los Angeles. Between Monterey and Los Angeles, Cambria and Morro Bay are favorite antiquing stops. One required stop is the 165-room Hearst Castle in San Simeon, now a museum. Built over a period of nearly 28 years for publishing tycoon William Randolph Hearst, it is opulently furnished with Spanish and Italian antiques and art. Between Monterey and San Francisco, on Highway 1, Santa Cruz, Aptos, and Soquel Village are good antiquing towns.

One of the best ways to enjoy the peninsula's Pacific views is to drive along Ocean View Boulevard or walk the four-mile recreational trail that begins at Cannery Row, skirts the edge of Pacific Grove, and ends at Asilomar State Beach, on the tip of the peninsula. Not far away, near Lighthouse Avenue, are Point Piños Lighthouse, established in 1855 and the oldest in continuous operation on the West Coast, and Pacific Grove's Monarch Butterfly Sanctuary. Every year, thousands of Monarch butterflies find their way to Pacific Grove's pine and eucalyptus groves. Their arrival is greeted by parades of children, wearing painted wings; from October through March, at midday, when the sun has warmed their wings, the Monarchs take flight. Other area performances include theater and music events: The famed Monterey Jazz Festival, in mid-September, is the longest-running event of its kind in the world. An active schedule of festivals includes wine and food fests: The Garlic Festival, held in Gilroy in late July, is 40 miles northeast. The peninsula's recreational opportunities include playing golf on several courses and watching the NCGA Amateur Golf Championships in Pebble Beach in mid-August.

The Monterey Peninsula is home to some fine inns. The most interesting, from an antiquer's standpoint, is the Martine Inn, in Pacific Grove. Built in 1899, this Victorian-Mediterranean Revival mansion overlooking the ocean was meticulously restored to period. The harmony of interior architecture and decoration is a visual delight. Interiors feature Honduran mahogany woodwork, claw-foot tubs, brass fixtures, marble sinks, Victorian paint colors and period appointments. What's most stunning here are the museum-quality antique furnishings decorating the inn's 25 rooms. Each reflects a different period, from Empire to Art Deco. Furnishings include a mahogany bedroom suite exhibited at the 1893 Chicago World's Fair, Hollywood costume designer Edith Head's bedroom suite, ruby-glass lamps with fringed shades, English porcelain coal bins, humidor nightstands, and early California landscape art. The garage houses a collection of vintage MGs.

With a staff on call 24/7, the Martine Inn recreates the gracious lifestyle of the well-to-do of the early 20th century. Ocean views, posh bathrooms, wood-burning fireplaces, a billiard room, fresh fruit and roses in silver vases, fine linens, gourmet breakfasts served on antique china, and hot hors d'oeuvres in the evenings are only a few of the amenities designed to revive even the weariest antiquer.

BEFORE YOU GO, visit
www.montereyinfo.org
www.pacificgrove.org
www.monterey.com
www.bestofcal.com
www.antiquedealersca.com
www.oldtowneorange.net/directoryofshops.htm

FAVORITE LODGING:
The Martine Inn
255 Oceanview Boulevard
Pacific Grove, CA 93950
831-373-3388; 800-852-5588
www.martineinn.com

San Francisco, California

C alifornia's "City by the Bay" is known among serious antiques collectors—not for the Golden Gate, but for the golden opportunities that await in antiques shops in the Jackson Square and Sacramento Street sections of town, and in late October, when dealers nationwide come for the San Francisco Antiques Show, one of the country's best. The members of the San Francisco Antiques Dealers Association represent some of the city's highest quality shops, and notable auction houses include Bonhams & Butterfields. But the city has many dealers representing a wide variety of items. With more than 600 antiques dealers listed in San Francisco proper and neighboring communities, such as Berkeley, this area could occupy a year of antiquing weekends.

San Francisco's Jackson Street, in the city's North Beach area, offers some 20 high-quality shops. In late March, the area holds its Jackson Square Promenade, a Thursday-through-Saturday event. Sacramento Street is home to the city's design center and also to many antiques shops. The San Francisco Antique and Design Mall alone features 200 dealers. Among the city's many flea markets is one held on Thursdays, at Market and Hyde Streets. Elsewhere in the Bay Area, visitors will find concentrations of good antiques stores in Berkeley, Oakland, Freemont, and Menlo Park.

A REMINDER OF THE GILDED AGE, SAN FRANCISCO'S ARCHBISHOP'S MANSION IS A 1904 SECOND EMPIRE MASTERPIECE LOCATED NEAR THE CITY'S HISTORIC ALAMO SQUARE PARK.

North of Berkeley, San Anselmo, on Route 101, has 20 or more shops. For antiquing day trips from San Francisco, there's Sonoma County to the north and Santa Cruz, Aptos, and Soquel Village, on Highway 1, about 70 miles south.

The nationally renowned San Francisco Fall Antiques Show is held during the last weekend in October at the Festival Pavilion of the Fort Mason Center. It draws 70 dealers from across the U.S. and Europe. They offer exceptional antiques of

THE TOSCA GUEST ROOM AT ARCHBISHOP'S MANSION FEATURES COFFERED CEILINGS, ORNATE WOODWORK, A WORKING FIREPLACE, AND POSH VICTORIAN FURNISHINGS.

many styles and periods, including American, English, Continental, and Asian furniture, rugs, silver, porcelain, glass, and fine art. This Thursday-through-Sunday event begins with a preview gala on Wednesday evening.

Two Friday/Saturday/Sunday antiques shows, each drawing 60 dealers with a wide range of 18th-, 19th-, and early-20th-century furniture and accessories, take place in late August and in early April at the Fort Mason Center. On the first weekends of June and December, an Art Deco-60s Show brings 200 dealers to the Concourse Exhibition Center.

San Francisco's Pacific Rim orientation makes it a particularly good place to find Asian antiques. The Arts of Pacific Asia show, held on the first weekend in February, features 80 of the world's top dealers who exhibit mainland and Pacific Asian artifacts and antiques, dating back as far as 2,000 years. Internationalism is also the theme of mid-February's Friday/Saturday/Sunday Tribal, Folk, & Textile Arts Show, which draws 90 dealers displaying objects from Africa, Oceania, and the Americas.

After a day's antiquing, visitors can take in world-class performances of opera, symphony orchestra, ballet, or theater. Located in Golden Gate Park are the city's Asian Art Museum, with one of the world's finest collections, and the M. H. de Young Museum, known for its collections of art and artifacts from Africa, Oceania, New Guinea, and the Americas, textiles, American painting, sculpture, and decorative arts. There's also a Craft & Folk Art Museum, the Frank Lloyd Wright–designed Circle

Gallery, Bernard Maybeck's Palace of Fine Arts, Ghirardelli Square, and the 1890s Ferry Building Marketplace. Another great part of town is the gallery-rich SoMa area (south of Market Street), home to the celebrated San Francisco Museum of Modern Art, Sony's Metreon (an urban theme park), a Jewish museum, and a Mexican museum.

Architecturally, San Francisco is diverse, but it is best known for its many Victorian houses, dubbed "Painted Ladies." Many are located around historic Alamo Square, near one of San Francisco's best small hotels, the Archbishop's Mansion. Just minutes from antiquing areas and performing arts venues, the French Second Empire mansion, built in 1904 for the city's second Roman Catholic Archbishop, Patrick Riordan, is a featured stop on tours of historic buildings, sponsored by the city library. At the Archbishop's Mansion, elegant redwood woodwork and a three-story mahogany staircase set the stage for antique furnishings evoking a French chateau of the late-19th century. The mansion's appointments include a chandelier used in the 1939 film *Gone With the Wind,* a gilded mirror that belonged to Mary Todd Lincoln, and a baby grand player piano once owned by Noel Coward. Guest room names and decor take their inspiration from opera, the most opulent of art forms. There are fireplaces in some guest suites, breakfast delivered to your room, evening receptions in the parlor, and a few complimentary hours with a "Golden Gate Greeter," a guide who leads guests in an exploration of some of the city's neighborhoods.

You may not leave your heart in San Francisco, but, if you're an antiquer, chances are you'll leave with your wallet a few ounces lighter.

BEFORE YOU GO, visit
www.sfvisitor.org
www.antiquedealercsa.com
www.sanfranciscoantiquedealers.com
www.sffas.org
www.bustamante-shows.com
www.caskeylees.com
www.artdecosale.com

FAVORITE LODGING:
The Archbishop's Mansion
1000 Fulton Street
San Francisco, CA 94117
415-563-7872; 800-543-5820
www.thearchbishopsmansion.com

Sonoma County, California

S onoma County, 35 miles north of San Francisco, is well known for its beautiful scenery, majestic old-growth redwood trees, thriving arts scene, gourmet restaurants, and, of course, wineries. From its 58-mile coastline, up the Sonoma Valley, inland to the Russian River, and beyond, Sonoma County is studded with vibrant towns. The picturesque town of Sonoma, first settled in 1823, is where Franciscan fathers planted the area's first grapes. The area continues its agricultural tradition, with the growing of grapes and with wonderful artisan food products, such as breads, cheeses, olives, and olive oils—the makings of a great picnic to take along while you explore the county's antiques stores. Sonoma County is a bonanza for antiquers, with hundreds of dealers in several areas.

MEADOW GREEN WALLS AND WHITE COTTON CUTWORK BED HANGINGS SET THE STAGE FOR A VINTAGE APPLIQUÉD TULIP QUILT AT THE INN AT OCCIDENTAL, CALIFORNIA.

One route to follow is the Antique Row stretching eight miles along Highway 116, between arts-oriented Sebastopol in western Sonoma County and Cotati (where the visitor center serves up an introduction to wine country). By one count, Antique Row contains 90 dealers. Variously accommodated in old schoolhouses, barns, and Victorian houses, their merchandise represents what has descended in California families and what has been brought in, from formal to country furniture, to early-20th-century radios, milk glass lamps, and vintage fruit crates. On the western end of the Row, the town of Sebastopol contains several antiques shops as well as a large group enterprise, the Antique Society, with 70 dealers.

Farther north, situated between the Alexander, Dry Creek, and Russian River Valleys, Healdsburg, a charming turn-of-the-century town with a Spanish-style square, contains a number of antiques collectives and shops, totaling some 100 dealers. Nearby are more than 70 wineries and Lake Sonoma, a popular spot for recreation. In the past, antiques-related events in Healdsburg have included monthly auctions and two summer fairs. There are also a variety of performing arts events and a museum showcasing local history.

Petaluma, the southernmost town in Sonoma County, is a riverfront Victorian gem with a well-preserved historic district, and a rich vein for antiquers. Dozens of stores dot Kentucky, Petaluma, Western, and Washington streets, and in late April and September, there are outdoor antiques fairs. Walking tours are popular here, as are arts fairs and festivals, and activities along the river. The restored adobe rancho in Petaluma's Adobe State Historic Park gives visitors an appreciation of early life in California. Performances and clubs create a lively cultural scene.

Santa Rosa and Freestone have some antiques shops, too, as does Duncans Mills on the Russian River, Bodega, located five miles inland, and Cloverdale, the county's northernmost town.

Non-antiquers won't be bored here. Along the Russian River, resort towns nestle among majestic redwood trees, and there's hiking, swimming, fishing, canoeing, and kayaking. In Guerneville, annual events include the Russian River Blues and Jazz Festivals; north of town, Armstrong Redwood State Reserve encompasses 700 acres containing many old-growth redwoods. In Santa Rosa, attractions include horticultur-alist Luther Burbank's home and gardens, the Burbank Center for the Performing Arts, and four museums, including one devoted to modern art and one to Charles M. Schulz, creator of the Peanuts cartoon strip. In western Sonoma County are Burbank's Gold Ridge Farm, a butterfly farm, seasonal festivals, and farmers markets. One of the American Le Mans car races takes place in Sonoma in July.

Sonoma County is known for its wonderful small inns. The Inn at Occidental is the undisputed lodging of choice for lovers of Americana. The c.1876 inn, snug in a stand of redwoods eight miles from Sebastopol, is decorated in a sophisticated country mélange of folk art and antiques: hand-sewn quilts, country beds and

THE TIME-WORN WICKER FURNITURE GRACING THE PORCH OF THE INN AT OCCIDENTAL IS A PERFECT PLACE TO ENJOY THE WANING AFTERNOON AND REFLECT ON THE DAY'S ANTIQUING IN SONOMA COUNTY.

bureaus, tramp art, toy wooden horses and rocking cows, waterfowl decoys, circus gear, and original art work. Fireplaces, enveloping sofas, and plush carpets tempt guests to relax and enjoy the eye candy that surrounds them. After dinner at a nearby gourmet restaurant, guests can pull up a vintage wicker chair on the porch, sip one of Sonoma County's best wines, and savor the triumph of the day's purchases. But be forewarned: Wine tasting and antiquing, when combined, can result in a serious case of buyer's remorse.

BEFORE YOU GO, visit
www.visitcalifornia.com
www.sonomacounty.com
www.sonoma.com/thingstodo/antiques/listings.html
www.antiquedealersca.com

FAVORITE LODGING:
Inn at Occidental
3657 Church Street
Occidental, CA 95465
707-874-1047
www.innatoccidental.com

Portland & Aurora, Oregon

T he fact that Oregon has no sales tax is just one reason to shop for antiques here. Portland and neighboring Aurora are both good antiquing towns, and Portland is home to the Northwest's largest antiques show. The city's Antique Row, located in its southeast section and known as Sellwood, is a 12-block area with 50 varied shops. Sellwood's antiques malls are temples of shabby chic, collectibles, early-20th-century, and more upscale items. For exotic Far Eastern furniture, explore Asia America. Besides Sellwood, Portland's Pearl District, known for its galleries, shops, and restaurants, contains several Asian antiques galleries and carpet dealers.

A GRACIOUS PARLOR AT THE LION AND THE ROSE VICTORIAN BED & BREAKFAST IN PORTLAND, OREGON, RECALLS THAT PERIOD.

Places to source architectural antiques and hardware include Rejuvenation Hardware, started 30 years ago, in the Grand Avenue Historic District, and the 1874 House in Sellwood. Frederick Squire Antiques has fine European items.

In mid-July and again at the end of October, Portland's Expo Center is the site of the Northwest's largest antiques and collectibles show. Called America's Largest Antique and Collectible Sale, it presents some 1,800 dealers displaying furniture, art glass, vintage advertising, toys, china, Western and Native American items, textiles, jewelry, kitchenware, tools, and memorabilia. On a smaller scale, the indoor Saturday/Sunday Fantastic Flea Market at 19340 SE Stark features 150 vendors.

For day trips, antiquers often head south to Aurora, a mere 25 miles away. Founded in 1857 by a Protestant German sect, its historic ambiance is enhanced by many antiques stores. Most are located on Main Street and along Highway 99E, which passes through town. Some shops to investigate are Aurora Antiques & Décor, where American and

A VINTAGE METAL BEDSTEAD, PERIOD CHANDELIER, AND WICKER CHAIR DECORATE A GUEST ROOM AT THE LION AND THE ROSE, A GLORIOUS QUEEN ANNE MANSION ON A TREE-LINED STREET.

French furniture and fine art date from 1850 to 1950; Aurora Depot Antiques with 19th- and 20th-century English and American lighting, including oil lamps; and the Antique Colony, for Mission furniture, Hoosier cupboards, and the ventilated cupboards commonly known as "pie safes."

Portland is a sublimely manageable city, an area of 13 by 26 blocks spread over gentle hills along the Willamette River. Regularly voted one of the country's most livable cities, Portland gets an average of 32 inches of rainfall a year. In fact, it is one of America's "greenest" cities: When the U.S. failed to sign the international Kyoto Treaty, Portland decided to implement environmental improvements on its own. It boasts many miles of bicycling and nature trails, 200 parks and wildlife refuges, public rhododendron and rose gardens, a classical Chinese garden, a Japanese garden covering over five acres, and the spectacular Hoyt Arboretum. The city's scale and ambiance mean it's an ideal place for strolling and bicycling. An especially pleasant amenity is its many sidewalk drinking fountains.

Some of the best restaurants in the Pacific Northwest and a myriad of arts venues are located here. The Portland Art Museum, the oldest in the Northwest, has fine collections spanning 35 centuries. The city's symphony, and ballet and opera companies are excellent. There are concerts of all types and an active theater scene. Places to explore include the arty Hawthorne district; Burnside Street's Saturday (and Sunday) Market, which features some 300 craftspeople and artists; and Powell's City of Books, three floors of new and used books occupying an entire city block, a source of out-of-print books about antique furniture, decorative arts, and collectibles. Outside the city, wineries welcome visitors, and Mount Hood, 60 miles away, offers skiing nearly ten months of the year. Seasonal events include a rose festival in June and beer festivals, highlighting local microbreweries.

Vintage hotels include the c.1912 Benson on Broadway, worth a visit even if you're staying elsewhere. The Lion and the Rose, a bed and breakfast in the Irvington neighborhood, is one of the best ways to experience one of the most livable neighborhoods in this most livable of cities. A designated Portland landmark listed on the National Register of Historic Places, this majestic 1906 Queen Anne mansion, on a tree-lined street a few blocks from restaurants, shops, and public transportation, has a welcoming wraparound porch and octagonal turret, and restored interiors with fine architectural details. Its five guest rooms, each with its own bath, showcase Edwardian, Eastlake, and Colonial Revival furnishings, including antique armoires, marble-topped dressers, and period carpets. Guests are pampered with amenities such as Jacuzzis and claw-foot tubs in private baths, cable TV, off-street parking, hors d'oeuvres in the parlor, and candlelight breakfasts.

As you explore Portland's neighborhoods and antiques stores, you may revel in such small pleasures as a drink from a sidewalk fountain, cycling and strolling on city trails, and relaxing in Washington Park. Environmentally speaking, time-honored customs like those, along with time-honored furnishings, may be proof positive that what's old can be new again.

BEFORE YOU GO, visit
www.travelportland.com
www.all-oregon.com/shopping/antiques.htm

FAVORITE LODGING:
Lion and the Rose Victorian Bed & Breakfast
1810 NE 15th Avenue
Portland, OR 97212
503-287-9245; 800-955-1647
www.lionrose.com

Washington's Puget Sound

A long Washington's Puget Sound, from Tacoma and the Kitsap Peninsula, north to Seattle and nearby Snohomish, and up to La Conner, the antiquing route takes in lovely small towns and two vibrant cities. The coastline is glorious, with a rich heritage of logging, milling, and fishing, and plenty of places and ways to enjoy its natural beauties, both on the land and on the water.

Tacoma and nearby Lakewood have about 45 shops between them. Tacoma's Antique Row is along Broadway Avenue; Pacific Avenue also has some shops. The city's antiquing events include an outdoor Antique & Craft Fair on the third weekend in August and an Antiques Show and Sale, drawing 500 dealers, held on the last weekend in September. This arts-minded city has an outstanding public sculpture program, the Tacoma Art Museum, and an active performing arts scene.

BUILT IN 1889, CHINABERRY HILL INN IN TACOMA, WASHINGTON, FEATURES PERIOD INTERIORS, VIEWS OF COMMENCEMENT BAY, AND ONE OF THE EARLIEST EXAMPLES OF LANDSCAPE GARDENING IN THE NORTHWEST.

THE QUEEN-ANNE STYLE WHITE SWAN GUEST HOUSE IN MOUNT VERNON, WASHINGTON, IS SET ON THE SKAGIT RIVER AMID ACRES OF FARMLAND.

Nearby, on the Kitsap Peninsula, nearly every small town has at least one antiques store. Port Gamble, the only company-owned mill town in Puget Sound, and a National Historic Site, has several antiques shops and a Sunday outdoor Antiques Market from May through October. Kitsap Peninsula events in August include a Renaissance Fair in Gig Harbor, Chief Seattle Days Indian Festival in Susquamish, and the Kitsap County Fair and Rodeo in Bremerton.

In Seattle, there are more than 120 antiques shops offering American, English, Continental, and Asian furniture, decorative arts, fine art, and Native American art and artifacts. Antiquing districts are located downtown under the Viaduct, on First Avenue around Pike Place Market, and in Pioneer Square. Museums include the Seattle Art Museum, with collections of European and American paintings and decorative arts, African art, and Northwest Coast Native American art; the Frye Art Museum, with 19th- to 21st-century representational art; the Asian Art Museum; and the Wing Luke Asian Museum. Dance, theater, opera, symphony, and other performances run all year long.

Snohomish, 15 miles northeast of Seattle, dubbed the "antiques capital of the Northwest," is one of the places Seattle residents talk about when they talk about antiquing. Founded in 1859, its downtown is listed on the National Register of Historic Places, and residential areas are a delightful mix of Victorian and Arts & Crafts homes. Snohomish has some 24 antiques stores, including several malls, the largest of which houses about 175 dealers. The majority are located along First Street. Shops feature a range of antiques and vintage furnishings, primitives and country furniture, Native American artifacts, and decorative accessories, including art glass and pottery. There's a February Antiques Sale and an Art and Antiques Walk on the second Saturday of April. Historic sites include Blackman's House Museum and Old Snohomish Village, with late-19th- and early-20th-century buildings and exhibits. Nearby, Edmonds has about six antiques shops.

Fifty miles north of Snohomish, La Conner, a waterfront town listed on the National Register of Historic Places, has several antiques shops. There are more nearby in Ferndale, Bellingham, and Centralia, which boast the state's largest antiques mall. Visitors to La Conner can enjoy nature trails, whale watching around the San Juan

Islands, the Quilt Museum with an annual festival in August, the historic Gaches Mansion, art galleries; and the Museum of Northwestern Art. Seasonal events include spring poetry and tulip festivals, a fall classic car and yacht show, and, in winter, a chance to herald arriving snow geese and trumpeter swans. You can also take a ferry to Whidbey Island or Bainbridge Island.

Several lodgings hold special attraction for antiquers. Choices include Pillows & Platters Bed and Breakfast in Snohomish, and Mildred's Bed and Breakfast in Seattle. On the Kitsap Peninsula, there's Old Glencove Hotel in Gig Harbor and the Brauer Cove Guest House, Murphy House, or the Green Cat Bed and Breakfast in Poulsbo. Near La Conner, the White Swan Guest House, a rural Queen Anne on the Skagit River, has a stylish "granny's farmhouse" ambiance. (As in granny's day, the guest rooms all have baths down the hall rather than en suite.) Its interiors are comfortable, colorful, and decorated with period antiques. This, and the owner's interest in antique textiles and samplers, makes the White Swan popular among visitors to La Conner's Quilt Museum. In Tacoma's Historic District, Chinaberry Hill inn is an 1889 Victorian with views of the bay and one of the earliest examples of landscape gardening in the Northwest. Pampering here includes guest room fireplaces, private baths with Jacuzzis, and "serious coffee." Chinaberry Hill's period furnishings, perfectly in keeping with its fine interior woodwork, art glass chandeliers, and other appointments, have inspired many an aspiring antiquer.

BEFORE YOU GO, visit
www.experiencewashington.com
www.traveltacoma.com
www.visitkitsap.com
www.seeseattle.org
www.cityofsnohomish.com
www.snohomish.org

FAVORITE LODGINGS:

Chinaberry Hill
302 Tacoma Avenue North
Tacoma, WA 98403
253-272-1282
www.chinaberryhill.com

The White Swan Guest House
Bed and Breakfast
15872 Moore Road
Mount Vernon, WA 98273
360-445-6805
www.thewhiteswan.com

Antiquing Venues

PART ONE: NEW ENGLAND

Down East Maine

Belfast

Belfast Antiques and Books
96 Miller St.
207-338-5239
Continental & American furniture, accessories, architecturals.

Kendrick's Antiques
213 Northport Ave.
207-338-1356
Formal & country furniture.

Blue Hill

Belchers Antiques
232 Ellsworth Rd. (across from Blue Hill Fairgrounds)
207-374-3751
Country furnishings, accessories, folk art, nautical, advertising, toys.

Blue Hill Antiques
8 Water St.
207-374-8825
European & American fine & country furniture, decorative items.

Emerson's Antiques
33 Water St.
207-374-5140
18th- & early-19th-c. American furniture, decorative arts.

Liros Gallery
14 Parker Point Rd.
207-374-5370; 800-287-5370
www.lirosgallery.com
Fine paintings, watercolors, prints, maps. Russian objects.

Steven J. Rowe Antiques
138 Main St.
207-374-3811;
603-382-4618 (winter)
Classical & country furniture, paintings, folk art, architecturals.

Ellsworth

Old Creamery Antiques
13 Hancock St.
207-667-0522
35+ dealers.

The Big Chicken Barn
Rt. 1 (halfway betw. Bucksport & Ellsworth)
207-667-7308
www.bigchickenbarn.com
From 19th-c. armoires to books on Zen.

Searsport

Down East Auctions & Antiques
328 E. Main St. (Rt. 1)
207-548-2393
Victorian furniture, accessories, ephemera, architecturals.

Gaul's Antiques
64 W. Main St.
207-548-0232
Early pattern & Victorian art glass, porcelains, transferware.

Primrose Farm Antiques
384 E. Main St.
207-548-6019
Country furnishings, glass, folk art, mochaware, Shaker smalls.

Pumpkin Patch Antiques Center
15 W. Main St.
207-548-6047
18th- & 19th-c. paintings, country furniture, folk art, nautical, Native American, Victoriana.

Sedgewick

Burton W. Pearl Antiques
Rt. 1
207-359-2102
Early American furniture, accessories, redware, pewter.

Sedgwick Antiques
Rt. 172
207-359-8834
Furnishings, decorative items.

Thomas Hinchcliffe Antiques
26 Cradle Knolls Lane (West Sedgwick)
207-326-9411
Country furniture in original paint, prints, rugs, quilts, boat models.

Other

Eagull Gallery
E. Main St.
Stonington
207-367-5508
18th- & early-19th-c. American & West Indian furniture, decorative arts, fine art.

Old Cove Antiques
Rt. 15
Sargentville
207-359-2031
Formal & country furniture in original paint, accessories, fine & folk art, marine items, decoys.

Vermont's Champlain Valley & Quebec's Eastern Townships

QUEBEC

Eastman

Antiquités Le Vieux Presbytère
547, rue Principale
450-297-9962
Quebec pine furniture, 1850-1900.

Antiquités Rosalie
336, rue Principale
450-297-4475
Rustic & hardwood Quebec furniture, glassware, dishes, art, etchings, textiles, folk art, lamps.

North Hatley

Emporium North Hatley
100, rue Principale
819-842-4233
Art, small furnishings, decorative items.

Jean Drapeau & G. Funkenberg
900 Massawippi St.
819-842-2725
Quebec furniture & folk art.

Other

Antiquités Gélineau
247, Chemin Granby
Bromont
450-534-2414
Victorian & rustic furniture, smalls.

Décor 1900
335, Chemin McDonald
Hatley (Ville et Canton)
819-562-8698
Victorian & rustic furniture, glassware, dishes, small objects.

Galerie Relais des Arts
5, rue River
Stanbridge East
514-249-5837
Art objects, small furnishings, decorative items.

VERMONT (NORTHWESTERN)

Burlington

Architectural Salvage Warehouse
53 Main St.
802-658-5011
www.architecturalsalvagevt.com
Architecturals: doors, stained glass,
mantels, lighting, ironwork, columns,
plumbing, garden items.

Burlington Center for Antiques
3093 Shelburne Rd.
802-985-4911
Multi-dealer mall: furniture, decorative
items, glassware, china, silver, jewelry.

Colin and Elizabeth Ducolon Antiques
41 University Terrace
802-863-1497
Rural painted furnishings &
 accessories, flint glass, textiles.

Whistle Stop Antiques
208 Flynn Ave.
802-863-1168
Glassware & collectibles.

Middlebury

BeJeweled
4 Frog Hollow Alley
802-388-2799
Jewelry, collectibles, pottery, vintage
clothing, accessories, buttons, lace.

Bix Antiques
Rt. 116 (2 mi. north of Middlebury
Antique Center)
802-388-2277
Country & Victorian furniture, china,
linens, woodenware, tools.

Vergennes

**Kennedy Brothers Factory
Marketplace Antiques Center**
Rt. 22A (off Rt. 7)
802-877-2975
Jewelry, pottery, small furnishings,
ephemera, picture frames.

Stone Block Antiques
219 Main St.
802-877-3359
Furniture, collectibles, glassware,
art from the early-19th c. on.

Other

Back Chamber at the Wayfarm
3593 Rt. 2
North Hero
802-372-4347
American country furniture &
accessories; early- to mid-20th-c.
furnishings.

Ethan Allen Antique Shop
262 Eagle Mountain Harbor Rd.
Milton
802-863-3764
Early American furnishings.

Middlebury Antique Center
Rt. 7 (at Rt. 116)
East Middlebury
802-388-6229
Multi-dealer shop: country & other
furniture, accessories.

Shelburne Village Antiques
Rt. 7 (on The Green)
Shelburne
802-985-1447
Early New England furniture, folk art,
watercolors, ceramics, incl. redware,
tin, toleware, quilts, rugs.

Mid-Coast Maine

Bath

Brick Store Antiques
143 Front St.
207-443-2790
Country, Victorian, & decorative pieces
(some with old paint or gilt), china,
glassware, paintings.

Drake's Antiques
660 Berry's Mills Rd.
207-443-2349; 207-443-8098
Early American & European decorative
arts, incl. glass, ceramics, silver,
lighting, textiles.

Front Street Antiques & Books
190-192 Front St.
207-443-8098
Multi-dealer shop.

New England Antiques
180 Front St.
207-442-8000
Country & formal furniture, quilts,
hooked rugs, fine linens, china,
decorative accessories.

Camden

Downshire House
49 Bayview St.
207-236-9016
Longcase clocks, wall regulators,
barometers, some furniture.

Suffolk Gallery
47 Bayview St.
207-236-8868
European & American furniture &
accessories, paintings, English silver,
ceramics.

Ten High Street Antiques
10 High St. (Rt. 1, north of Camden)
207-236-2770
American period & country furniture,
paintings, accessories.

Damariscotta

Another Season
930 Biscay Rd.
207-563-1056
American furniture in original surface
& 18th- & 19th-c. accessories.

Damarine Antiques
263 Bristol Rd.
207-563-3949
Period American formal & country
furniture, accessories, pottery, art.

Newcastle

Jewett-Berdan Antiques
15 Hopkins Hill Rd.
207-563-3682
Folk art, painted furniture, hooked
rugs, portraits, architecturals.

Merndale Antiques
283 Mills Rd. (Rt. 215)
207-563-1086
18th- & 19th-c. American country
furniture, accessories, fine & folk art,
beds, quilts, sleds, wagons.

Portland

Mulberry Cottage
45 Western Ave.
207-775-5011
English, Irish, & Continental furniture
& accessories.

Portland Antiques & Fine Art
223 Commercial St.
207-773-7052; 800-896-8824
www.portlandantiques.com
18th- & 19th-c. American furniture
& accessories. Folk, fine, & marine art,
nautical items, architecturals.

Rockland

Bruce Gamage Jr. Antiques
467 Main St.
207-594-4963
www.gamageantiques.com
American period furniture, art, & rugs.

Liberty Tree Antiques
S. Main St.
207-594-5561
American country furnishings in
original paint, folk art.

Rockland Antiques Market Place
25 Rankin St.
207-596-9972
100+ dealers: from country furniture to
Native American artifacts, jewelry.

Thomaston

Anchor Farm Antiques
364 Main St.
207-354-8859
Silver, estate jewelry, china, tools.

David C. Morey American Antiques
161 Main St.
207-354-6033
17th- & 18th-c. American furniture,
glass, pottery, textiles.

Ross Levett Antiques
187 Main St.
207-354-6227
American, European, Asian, & Islamic
objects, ancient to 20th c.

**Thomaston Place Auction
Galleries/Kaja Veilleux**
51 Atlantic Hwy. (Rt. 1)
207-354-8141; 800-924-1032
www.thomastonauction.com

Wiscasset

Avalon Antiques Market
536 Bath Rd.
207-882-4029
Country pieces, decorative items, Arts
& Crafts furnishings, china, silver,
glass, lighting.

Blythe House Antiques
161 Main St. (Rt.1)
207-882-1280; 207-882-4188
Multi-dealer shop: Federal period
& country pieces.

**Debra Elizabeth Schaffer Antiques &
Interiors**
19 Fort Hill St.
207-882-8145
18th- & 19th-c. furniture in old
surface, samplers, theorems, textiles,
silhouettes, hooked rugs.

Dennis Raleigh Antiques
64 Main St.
207-882-7821
www.dennisraleighantiques.com
19th-c. country furnishings, folk art,
hooked rugs, fine art.

Drake's Antiques
660 Berry's Mills Rd.
207-443-2349; 207-443-8098
Period English & American decorative
arts, ceramics, glass, lighting, textiles,
silver.

Jeremiah Dalton House Antiques
Corner, Fort Hill & Bradbury Sts.
207-882-9475
Formal & country furniture, Chinese
export & English ceramics, nautical
items, art.

Margaret B. Ofslager
Main St. (at Summer St.)
207-882-6082
Painted furniture, 19th-c. accessories,
hooked rugs.

Marston House Antiques
Main St. (at Middle St.)
207-882-6010
www.marstonhouse.com
18th- & 19th-c. furniture in as-found
surface, textiles, folk art, ironstone,
yellowware, French pottery.

Part of the Past
37 Water St., S.
207-882-7908
www.goantiques.com/members/partof
thepast
Early country furniture, folk art, rugs,
iron, books, prints, nautical, scientific,
& sporting items, toys.

Patricia Stauble Antiques
Corner, Pleasant & Main Sts.
207-882-6341
18th- & 19th-c. American furniture &
high country, art, pottery, folk art,
rugs, quilts, nautical items.

Priscilla Hutchinson Antiques
62 Pleasant St.
207-882-4200
18th- & 19th-c. furniture in original
surface, folk art, paintings, rugs,
weathervanes, theorems.

Robert Snyder & Judy Wilson Antiques
72 Main St.
207-882-4255
Painted furniture, hooked rugs, paintings, folk art, trade signs, accessories.

Water Street Antiques
51B Water St.
207-882-9700
Multi-dealer shop: period American
country furnishings, nautical items.

Other

Nobleboro Antique Exchange
104 Rt. 1
Nobleboro
207-563-6800
18th- & 19th-c. furniture & country
pieces. Accessories, incl. glass, china,
Oriental porcelain.

The Priscilla Antiques
685 Winslows Mills Rd.
Waldoboro
207-832-0683
Country furniture & accessories,
quilts, rugs, dolls, art, estate jewelry,
silver, early lighting.

Southern Vermont:
Manchester & Dorset

Bennington

Clifford L. Buisch Antiques
307 N. Main St.
802-442-2612
English, French, Italian, American
Federal & Neoclassical furniture, fine
art, accessories.

The Antique Center at Camelot Village
60 West Rd.
802-447-0039
120 dealers: furnishings, collectibles.

Dorset

Hersom and Co. Estate Sales
239 Cheney Rd.
802-867-9800

Judd & Peg Gregory Antiques
802-325-2400 (by appt.)
17th- & early-19th-c. American &
English furniture, decorative arts,
ceramics, art.

Marie Miller Antique Quilts
1489 Rt. 30
802-867-5969
19th- & early-20th-c. quilts.

Jamaica

Fiske & Freeman Antiques
Rt. 155
802-259-2579
Period formal & high country furniture
in original finish, fine & decorative art.

Old Corkers Antiques
Rts. 30 & 100
802-874-4172
Country furniture & collectibles.
Angling & sporting items.

The Painted Cottage
Rts. 30 & 100
802-874-4200
Painted cottage furniture, accessories
for house & garden.

Manchester

Brewster's Antiques
152 Bonnet St. (Rt. 30)
802-362-1579
Estate jewelry, glassware, art.

Comollo Antiques and Auction
4686 Main St.
802-362-7188
American & European furnishings
& fine art.

Judy Pascal
145 Elm St.
802-362-2004
Country, cottage, & shabby chic
home furnishings.

Mark Reinfurt-Equinox Antiques
5036 Historic Main St.
802-362-3540
www.equinoxantiques.com
Fine early American, Irish-English,
& French furniture, decorative arts,
paintings.

Newfane

Jack Winner Antiques
Rt. 30
802-365-7215
Chinese period furniture, accessories.

Schommer Antiques
Rt. 30
802-365-7777
Furniture (mostly 19th-c.), accessories, paintings, china, glass, table settings.

Townshend

Riverdale Antiques and Collectibles
Rt. 30
802-365-4616
65+ dealers: furnishings & collectibles.

Townshend Auction Gallery
129 Riverdale Rd.
802-365-4388
www.townshendauctions.com

Warlé Antiques
Rt. 35
802-365-4339
European, American, & Oriental furnishings: porcelain, faience, glass, art, books, lamps.

Other

Country Gallery Antiques
Rt. 315
Rupert
802-362-1125
Scandinavian furniture, rugs, lighting, yellowware, needlepoint.

Drury House Antiques
Rt. 100 (at Markham Lane)
Weston
802-824-4395
Clocks, furniture, lamps, porcelain, bottles, advertising.

Newell Hill Farm Antiques
378 Newell Hill Rd.
West Wardsboro
802-896-6264
Furniture & smalls: stoneware, chamber sets, transferware, from mid-19th c. on.

Wigren-Barlow Antiques
29 Pleasant St.
Woodstock
802-457-2453
19th-c. English & American furniture, fireplace & garden items, desks, brass, silver, clocks, china.

New Hampshire Antiques Week

Manchester

From Out of the Woods Co-op
465 Mast Rd.
603-624-8668
80+ dealers: furnishings, all periods.

Mark & Marjorie Allen Antiques
300 Bedford St., Ste. 421
603-672-8989
www.antiquedelft.com
American period & high country furniture & accessories. Delft, paintings, needlework, brass.

Paul D. Sullivan
P.O. Box 3773
603-669-8886 (by appt.)
Pre-1850 formal & country furnishings.

Resser-Thorner Antiques
5 Kennard Rd.
603-669-7677
18th-, 19th-, & 20th-c. art & furnishings, New Hampshire material, historical Americana.

Three Corners: Cape Ann, Massachusetts; Coastal New Hampshire; & Southern Maine

MAINE

Kennebunk

Cattails Antiques
154 Port Rd.
207-967-3824
Country furniture, accessories, folk art, paintings, nautical, Shaker items, hooked rugs, textiles.

Old Fort Antiques
Old Fort Ave.
207-967-5353
www.oldfortinn.com
Country furniture, primitives, tin, advertising items.

Wells

Antiques "R" Us
1690 Post Rd.
207-646-4391
Country furniture, Oriental rugs, architectural & garden items, trade signs, Quimper ceramics.

Corey Daniels Antiques and Art
2208 Post Rd. (Rt. 1)
207-646-5301
Vintage to modern furniture, decorative objects, garden items, photography.

MacDougall-Gionet Antiques
2104 Post Rd.
207-646-3531
www.macdougall-gionet.com
Country & formal early American, English, Continental furniture, period accessories.

R. Jorgensen Antiques
502 Post Rd. (Rt. 1)
207-646-9444
www.jorgensen.com
17th-, 18th-, & early-19th-c. furniture, accessories.

Wells Union Antiques
1755 Post Rd.
207-646-4551
American & European furniture, 19th-c. frames, lamps, decorative accessories, architectural, garden.

York

Betsey Telford's Rocky Mountain Quilts
130 York St.
800-762-5940
www.rockymountainquilts.com
1780-1940 quilts. Launders & restores quilts & hooked rugs.

Bob Withington Antiques
611 Rt. 1
207-363-1155
European & American furniture & accessories, garden ornaments.

York Antiques Gallery
746 Rt. 1 North
207-363-5002
www.yorkantiquesgallery.com
Multi-dealer shop: furniture & accessories, Americana, incl. country, decorative, garden.

Other

Marie Plummer & John Philbrick
35 Old County Rd.
North Berwick
207-676-8662
17th- & 18th-c. early American furniture & accessories.

MASSACHUSETTS

Essex

APH Waller & Sons Antiques
140 Main St. (Rt. 133)
978-768-6269
Oriental items, bronzes, art, ceramics, Continental furniture.

Brick House Antiques
166 Main St.
978-768-6617
Furniture, collectibles, textiles, porcelain, paintings.

Ellen Neily Antiques
157 Main St.
978-768-6436
American & Continental furniture, paintings, China trade objects, decorative accessories.

Friendship Antiques
55 John Wise Ave. (Rt. 133)
978-768-7334
Period furniture, rugs, paintings, china, silver, glass.

Joshua's Corner
2 Southern Ave.
978-768-7716
Country furniture in original paint, decorative accessories, New England redware, textiles.

L. A. Landry Antiques
164 Main St.
978-768-6233
Continental & other furniture, porcelain, Chinese screens, chests, decorative arts.

R. C. Coviello
155 Main St.
978-768-7365
18th-, 19th-, & 20th-c. furniture &
decorative arts.

South Essex Antiques
166 Eastern Ave. (Rt. 133)
978-768-6373
European, American, & Asian
furnishings, textiles, paintings, china,
decorative accessories.

Newburyport

Paul and Linda DeCoste
288 Merrimack St.
978-462-2138
18th- & 19th-c. furniture &
accessories, folk art, nautical,
scientific & medical instruments.

Peter H. Eaton Antiques
39 State St.
978-465-2754
17th- & 18th-c. New England furniture,
most pieces in original condition.

Other

Colette Donovan
98 River Rd.
Merrimacport
978-346-0614
Early American country furniture,
textiles, lighting, baskets,
hearth items.

Interiors with Provenance
114 Elm St.
Amesbury
978-388-2732
www.interiorswithprovenance.com
Furnishings, Oriental rugs, textiles, art.

NEW HAMPSHIRE

NH Rt. 4/Northwood

Coveway Antique Center
603-942-7500
30 dealers: period country & formal
furniture, accessories, art pottery,
porcelain, glass, militaria.

Evans & Wright at the Eagle
603-942-5020
Country furniture, textiles, Civil War
items, Maxfield Parrish prints.

Fern Eldridge & Friends
603-942-5602
30 dealers: 18th- & 19th-c. formal
& country furnishings, folk art,
Shaker items.

Lakeview Antique Center
603-942-8460
60 dealers: furniture, glass, silver,
jewelry, watches, toys, dolls, trains,
radios, advertising.

Parker-French Antique Center
603-942-8852
135 dealers: jewelry, silver, primitives,
glass, china, paper, memorabilia,
garden items.

R. S. Butler's Trading Co.
603-942-8210
Country & formal furniture,
accessories.

Town Pump Antiques
603-942-5515
Group shop: country & formal
furnishings, lighting, art, glass, linens,
books, tools, clocks.

Wonderful Things Antiques
603-942-8832
18th- & 19th-c. country & formal
furniture, jewelry, tall clocks.

NH Rt. 4/Other

Austin's Antiques
114 Dover Rd. (Rt. 4)
Chichester
603-798-3116
50+ dealers: American country &
primitive furnishings.

Portsmouth

**Antiquarium/Sharon Platt & Hollis
Brodrick**
25 Ceres St.
603-427-1690
18th- & early-19th-c. American
furniture in original surface, early
artifacts & decorative arts.

Ed Weissman Antiques
110 Chapel St.
603-431-7575
www.edweissmanantiques.com
Pre-1840 American furniture, 19th-
& 20th-c. art, fine brass, American
& European accessories.

M. S. Carter
175 Market St.
603-436-1781
Early-19th-c. country furniture
& accessories, folk art, antique
woodworking tools.

Northeast Auctions
93 Pleasant St.
603-433-8400
www.northeastauctions.com

Other

Peter Sawyer
17 Court St.
Exeter
603-772-5279
www.petersawyerantiques.com
American clocks, 18th- & 19th-c.
furniture, New England pieces in
original condition, fine & folk art.

RJG Antiques
Rye
603-433-1770 (by appt.)
www.rjgantiques.com
18th- & early-19th-c. American
furniture in original surface,
accessories, folk art, decoys.

The Wingate Collection
94 Portsmouth Ave. (Rt. 108)
Stratham
603-778-4849
French Canadian & American country
furnishings.

Brimfield, Massachusetts & Connecticut's Quiet Corner

CONNECTICUT

Putnam

Antiques Marketplace
109 Main St.
860-928-0442
200+ dealers: furniture, kitchenware,
sterling, glass, silver, collectibles.

Antiques Unlimited
91 Main St.
860-963-2599
Furniture, decorative items.

Little Museum Co.
75-83 Main St.
860-928-2534
English & French furniture &
decorative accessories.

Palace Antiques
130 Main St.
860-963-1124
Furnishings, collectibles.

Other

Brooklyn Restoration Supply
12 Gorman Rd.
Brooklyn
860-774-6759
18th- & 19th-c. architectural items:
mantels, doors, hardware, stone sinks,
boards, beams.

MASSACHUSETTS

Sturbridge

Antique Center of Sturbridge
426 Main St.
508-347-5150
10 dealers: assortment of items from furniture to clocks.

Showcase Antique Center
Rt. 20
508-347-7190
Decorative items, glass, china, toys.

Sturbridge Antique Shops
200 Charlton Rd.
508-347-2744
60 dealers: furniture, art, glass, china, toys, yellowware, pewter, baskets.

The Berkshires

MASSACHUSETTS

Great Barrington

Berkshire Home & Antiques
107 Stockbridge Rd. (Rt. 7)
413-644-9262
18th- & 19th-c. French country furniture, architectural & garden items, bath & kitchen furnishings.

Coffman's Antiques Market
Jennifer House Commons
Stockbridge Rd. (Rt. 7)
413-528-9282
www.coffmansantiques.com
100 dealers: 18th- to early-20th-c. furniture & accessories.

Corashire Antiques
Belcher Sq. (Corner, Rts. 7 & 23)
413-528-0014
Shaker & American country furniture & accessories.

Country Dining Room Antiques
178 Main St. (Rt. 7)
413-528-5050
www.countrydiningroomantiq.com
18th-, 19th-, & early-20th-c. dining furniture, decorative accessories, china, silver, glassware, etc.

Elise Abrams Antiques
11 Stockbridge Rd. (Rt. 7)
413-528-3201
www.eliseabrams.com
18th- to early-20th-c. dining furniture & accessories: porcelain, stemware, paintings, glassware.

Great Barrington Antiques Center
962 Main St. (Rt. 7)
413-644-8848
Multi-dealer mall: primitive to Moderne furnishings, paintings, prints, lighting, ceramics, decorative items.

P. W. Vintage Lighting
2 State Rd. (Rt. 7 at the bridge)
413-644-9150
www.pwvintagelighting.com

The Emporium Antique Center
319 Main St. (Rt. 7)
413-528-1660
20+ dealers: early-19th- to mid-20th-c. furniture, accessories.

The Farmhouse
635 S. Main St.
413-528-6452
Country furnishings, mostly 19th c.

Lee

Henry B. Holt
125 Golden Hill
413-243-3184
19th- & early-20th-c. American paintings.

Rose Cottage Antiques
40 Main St.
413-243-6336
19th- & 20th-c. items: formal & country furniture, china, glass, silver, jewelry, linens, kitchenware.

Sheffield

Bradford Galleries
Rt. 7
413-229-6667
www.bradfordauctions.com

Corner House Antiques
Rt. 7
413-229-6627
www.americanantiquewicker.com
19th- & early-20th-c. American wicker & bamboo furniture.

Cupboards & Roses Antiques
296 S. Main St. (Rt. 7)
413-229-3070
www.cupboardsandroses.com
18th- & 19th-c. painted furniture from Scandinavia & Europe.

Darr Antiques
Rt. 7
413-229-7773
Formal 18th- & 19th-c. English & American furniture & accessories.

Frederick Hatfield Antiques
99 S. Main St. (Rt. 7)
413-229-7986
Silver, paintings, prints, small furnishings.

Good & Hutchinson & Associates
Rt. 7
413-229-8832; 413-258-4555
18th- & 19th-c. American, English, & Continental furniture, art, Chinese export, brass, lamps.

Hill House Antiques
276 S. Undermountain Rd. (Rt. 41)
413-229-2374
www.hillhouseantiques.com
Arts & Crafts & Mission furniture, art pottery & tiles, metalwork, textiles, lighting, accessories.

Kuttner Antiques
576 Sheffield Plain (Rt. 7)
413-229-2955
American & English 18th- & early-19th-c. formal & country furniture & accessories, paintings, porcelain.

Le Trianon
1854 N. Main St. (Rt. 7)
413-528-0775
www.letrianonantiques.com
17th- to early-19th-c. English & Continental furnishings, paintings, tapestries, carpets.

Painted Porch Antiques
102 S. Main St. (Rt. 7)
413-229-2700
www.paintedporch.com
18th- to early-20th-c. French, English, & Canadian country furnishings.

Samuel Herrup Antiques
Rt. 7
413-229-0424
Late-17th- to early-19th-c. American furniture, folk art, American & European decorative arts.

Susan Silver Antiques
Rt. 7
413-229-8169
www.susansilverantiques.com
Formal 18th- & 19th-c. English & Continental furniture & decorative accessories, library furniture.

White Oak Antiques
755A N. Main St. (Rt. 7)
413-229-7765
18th- & 19th-c. American & English formal & country furniture, art & decorative accessories, ceramics.

South Egremont

Elliott and Grace Snyder
37 Undermountain Rd. (Rt. 41)
413-528-3581
18th- & early-19th-c. American furniture, painted pieces, folk art, rugs, needlework, pottery, art.

Geffner/Schatzky Antiques
Rt. 23 (town center)
413-528-0057
Furnishings, incl. garden & architectural items, jewelry.

Williamstown

LiAsia Gallery
31 Spring St.
800-790-0711
www.liasia.com
Chinese furniture, art & architecturals, Buddha statues.

The Library Antiques
70 Spring St.
800-294-4798
www.libraryantiques.com
Furniture, lighting, jewelry, art, books.

Other

Nora's Estate Goods
446 Tyler St.
Pittsfield
413-499-0927
Furniture, china, glassware, books,
linens, collectibles.

Sawyer Antiques
1 Depot St.
West Stockbridge
413-232-7062; 413-443-5908
www.sawyerantiques.com
Early American formal & country
furniture, accessories.

New York

Hillsdale Barn Antiques
10394 Rt. 22
Hillsdale
518-325-1357
www.hillsdalebarnantiques.com
American country furniture, painted
pieces, folk art, rugs, quilts, stoneware
& baskets, 18th c. on.

Meissner's Auction
Rts. 20 & 22
New Lebanon
518-766-5002
www.meissnersauction.com

Connecticut's Litchfield Hills

Bantam

Black Swan Antiques
725 Bantam Rd. (Rt. 202)
860-567-4429
17th- through 19th-c. English &
European furniture & accessories.

Canterbury Antiques
710 Bantam Rd. (Rt. 202)
860-567-8130
18th- & 19th-c. English & European
country & formal furniture, china,
Staffordshire, decorative items.

725 Bantam Rd. (Rt. 202)
Judy Hornby Antiques
860-567-8130
17th- to the 19th-c. French furniture,
lamps, accessories.
Le Parc Interiors
860-567-9613
1770s to 1960s traditional, country,
Art Deco furniture, decorative art from
France & Hungary.
Linsley Antiques
860-567-4245; 800-572-2360
English period furnishings, tables,
armoires, Welsh dressers, chairs.

Old Carriage Shop Antiques
920 Bantam Rd. (Rt. 202)
860-567-3234
20+ dealers: furniture & decorative
items: rugs, lighting, tablewares.

Toll House Antiques
38 Old Turnpike Rd.
860-567-3130
Country furniture, clocks, primitives,
baskets, woodenware, stoneware,
yellowware.

Kent

Company Store Antiques
Rt. 7 North
860-927-3430
Country & formal furnishings, folk
art, paintings, silver, tools, French
enamelware, clocks, jewelry.

Pauline's Place
79 N. Main St. (Rt. 7)
860-927-4475
Jewelry: Georgian, Victorian,
Art Nouveau, Edwardian, Art Deco,
Art Retro, Tiffany, Cartier.

Litchfield

Bradford House Antiques
33 West St.
860-567-0951
Period jewelry, silver, fine art,
decorative pieces, porcelain.

Jeffrey Tillou Antiques
39 West St.
860-567-9693
18th- & 19th-c. American furniture, paintings, folk art, decorative accessories.

Les Plaisirs de la Maison
Corner, West & Meadow Sts.
860-567-2555
18th- to 20th-c. French country
furnishings, paintings, prints, lighting,
copper, brass, pottery.

Roberta's Antiques
Rt. 202
860-567-4041
Rustic, country & formal furniture,
period firearms, glass, sterling,
pottery, decorative items.

Newtown

**McGeorgi's Antiques and
Consignments**
129 S. Main St.
203-270-9101
Furniture, glass, linens, paintings,
books, jewelry, rugs, collectibles.

Newtown Country Mill
160 Sugar St. (Rt. 302)
203-270-3441
Country primitives, furniture, folk art,
prints, lighting, tin, rugs.

Norfolk

Joseph Stannard Antiques
Station Place
860-542-5212
17th- to early-20th-c. French furniture,
decorative accessories, garden items.

Morrison & Coker Antiques
24 Rt. 44
860-542-5782
17th- to 19th-c. European
& English furnishings, art, tapestries,
screens, mirrors.

Salisbury

John Spencer Antiques
92 Canaan Rd. (Rt. 44)
860-435-1090; 860-435-1099
www.johnspencerantiques.com
18th- & early-19th-c. fine American
furniture, decorative objects, paintings,
mostly Federal period.

Passports
15 Academy St.
860-435-8855
19th- & early-20th-c. country furniture
from around the world, 19th-c. garden
ornaments.

Ragamont House Antiques
8 Main St.
860-435-8895
18th- & 19th-c. fine European &
English furniture & decorative arts,
paintings, porcelain, silver.

Woodbury

Abrash Galleries
40 Main St., N.
203-263-7847
Persian, Indian, Chinese,
& Turkish rugs.

Antiques On Main
255 Main St., S.
203-263-3233
18th- & 19th-c. furniture,
country accessories.

Antiques on the Green
6 Green Circle (North Green)
203-263-3045
Late-17th- to early-20th-c. furniture,
glass, silver, china, accessories.

Art Pappas Antiques
266 Washington Rd.
203-266-0374
18th- & 19th-c. American furniture,
accessories, architecturals: doors,
mantels, flooring, paneling.

Authantiques
480 Main St., S.
203-266-9121
18th- & 19th-c. English, French,
Canadian, & American folk art,
furnishings, accessories, lighting.

B. Bourgeois Antiques
270 Main St., S. (Rt. 6)
203-263-7770
18th- & 19th-c. French furnishings,
lighting, wine accessories, period &
contemporary art.

Black Pearl Antiques & Fine Arts
161 Main St., S.
203-266-0299
American, English, Continental, &
Oriental furniture, paintings, sculpture,
decorative items.

Country Loft Antiques
557 Main St., S. (Rt. 6)
203-266-4500
18th- & 19th-c. European furniture,
art, decorative objects, faience.

David Dunton Antiques
Rt. 132 (off Rt. 47)
203-263-5355
American Federal period formal
furnishing. Late-18th- & early-19th-c.
American, English, & French
accessories & paintings.

Eleish-Van Breams Antiques
487 Main St., S. (Rt. 6)
203-263-7030
18th- & 19th-c. Scandinavian &
northern European furnishings,
decorative & garden accessories.

G. Sergeant Antiques
88 Main St., N. (Rt. 6)
203-266-4177
17th-, 18th-. & 19th-c. English
Continental & American furnishings
& accessories.

Galpin Brook Antiques & Rugs
745 Main St., N. (Rt. 6)
203-263-6658
Formal & country 18th- & 19th-c.
English & Continental furnishings,
decorative accessories, rugs.

Hitchcock House/David Schorsch
244 Main St., S. (Rt. 6)
203-263-3131
18th- & 19th-c. American furniture,
folk art, Shaker objects.

Ile de France
289 Main St., S. (Rt. 6)
860-868-4321
French antiques, emphasis on kitchen,
wine, & decorative accessories.

Jennings and Rohn Antiques
289 Main St., S. (Rt. 6)
203-263-3775
16th- to 20th-c. decorative European
furniture, lighting, accessories, Old
Master paintings, drawings.

Joel Einhorn Antiques
452 Main St., S. (Rt. 6)
203-266-9090
American formal & country furniture,
clocks, decorative arts, toys, nautical
art, maps.

Madeline West Antiques
737 Main St., S. (Rt. 6)
203-266-4606
18th-, 19th-, & early-20th-c.
porcelains, furniture, art.

Main St. Antiques Center
113 Main St., S. (Rt. 6)
203-263-0046
40+ dealers: English, Continental,
& American furniture, decorative
& fine arts, silver, glass, china.

Mill House Antiques
1068 Main St., N. (Rt. 6)
203-263-3446
Formal & country English & French
furniture, incl. Welsh dressers.

Monique Shay Antiques
920 Main St., S. (Rt. 6)
203-263-3186
Canadian country painted & natural
pine furnishings.

Thomas Schwenke Antiques
50 Main St., N. (Rt. 6)
203-266-0303
1785-1820 formal American furniture,
Federal replicas.

Tucker Frey /Robert S. Walin
451 Main St., S. (Rt. 6)
203-263-5404
18th- & 19th-c. American high country

furnishings, accessories, fireplace
utensils, folk & fine art.

Wayne Pratt Antiques
346 Main St., S. (Rt. 6)
203-263-5676
18th- & 19th-c. American furniture,
emphasis on original condition.

West Country Antiques
Rt. 47 (1½ mi. from Main St.)
203-263-5741
19th-c. French country furniture
& decorative accessories.

Winsor Antiques
289 Main St., S. (Rt. 6)
203-263-7017
English & French country furniture,
early English pottery, naive & folk art,
original & painted surfaces.

Woodbury Antiques & Fine Art
473 Main St., S. (Rt. 6)
860-210-8105
18th- & 19th-c. American, British,
& Continental furnishings & decorative
accessories.

Woodbury Guild
319 Main St., S. (Rt. 6)
203-263-4828
18th- to early-20th-c. American
& European furnishings, American
clocks, bronzes.

Other

Bittersweet Shop
Rt. 7 (Junction, Rt. 55)
Gaylordsville
860-354-1727
14 dealers: country & formal furniture,
paintings, quilts.

Blast From The Past
25 Church St.
New Milford
860-354-3517
1890s-1950s: furniture, kitchenware,
ephemera, jewelry, pottery, Christmas
collectibles.

Charles M. Haver
3 Southbury Rd. (Rts. 67 & 317)
Roxbury
860-354-1031
Americana, country furniture, lighting,
hooked rugs, baskets, accessories.

Dawn Hill Antiques
11 Main St.
New Preston
860-868-0066
18th- & 19th-c. Swedish & French
painted furniture, decorative & garden
items, transferware, quilts.

Cape Cod & Nantucket, Massachusetts

Brewster

B. D. Hutchinson Time Flies
1274 Long Pond Rd.
508-896-6395
Watches & clocks.

Kingsland Manor
440 Mass. Rt. 6A
508-385-9741
www.kingslandmanor.com
Victorian & old cane furniture china,
silver, decorative items.

Chatham

Chatham Antiques
1409 Mass. Rt. 28
508-945-1660
Early American furniture, clocks, art,
china, pewter, silver, glass.

Kahn Antiques
582 Main St.
508-945-6450
www.kahnfineantiques.com
17th- to 19th-c. furniture, folk art,
militaria, fine art, porcelain, glass,
silver, nautical items.

Cotuit

Cotuit Antiques
4404 Mass. Rt. 28
508-420-1234
Furniture, pottery, glass, collectibles.

Sow's Ear Antique Company
4698 Mass. Rt. 28
508-428-4931
18th- & 19th-c. furniture, rugs, folk art, baskets, decoys, vases, silver.

Dennis

Antiques Center of Cape Cod
243 Mass. Rt. 6A
508-385-6400
www.antiquecenterofcapecod
250+ dealers: diverse items.

Red Lion Antiques
601 Mass. Rt. 6A
508-385-4783
15+ dealers: variety incl. clocks, china, silver, collectibles.

Falmouth

Red Barn Antiques
681 West Falmouth Hwy.
(West Falmouth)
508-548-4440
18th-c. furniture, rugs, paintings.

The Antiquarium
204 Palmer Ave.
508-548-1755
American & European furniture, china, glass.

Provincetown

Provincetown Antiques
136 Commercial St.
508-487-5555
Furniture, textiles, stained-glass windows, art pottery, maps, prints.

West End Trading Co.
146 Commercial St.
508-487-2327
Vintage & new home goods.

Sandwich

Antique Center at Sandwich Village
131 Rt. 6A
508-833-3600
100 dealers: varied furnishings.

Paul Madden Antiques
146 Old Main St.
508-888-6434 (by appt.)
www.paulmaddenantiques.com
Nantucket baskets, ship baskets, marine items.

Sandwich Auction House
15 Tupper Rd.
508-888-1926
www.sandwichauction.com

The Weather Store
146 Main St.
508-888-1200; 800-646-1203
www.theweatherstore.com
Weather instruments & books, compasses, marine items, maps.

West Barnstable

Decoys Unlimited Americana Auctions
2320 Main St.
508-362-2766
Bird carvings, folk art, decoys, baseball memorabilia.

Maps of Antiquity
1022 Mass. Rt. 6A
508-362-7169
www.mapsofantiquity.com
19th-c. & earlier world & New England maps, railroad maps, coastal charts.

West Harwich

Diamond Antiques
103 Main St.
508-432-0634
American paintings.

Harwich Antiques Center
10 Mass. Rte. 28
508-432-4220
130+ dealers: furniture, paintings, decoys, tools, quilts & linens, silver, glass, china, majolica.

Yarmouthport

Constance Goff Antiques
161 Mass. Rt. 6A
508-362-9540;
508-362-5300 (winter)
19th-c. furniture & accessories: rugs, lamps, jewelry, silver, ceramics, incl. flow blue.

Suzanne Courcier/Robert Wilkins
240 Main St.
508-362-5420 (by appt.)
18th- & early-19th-c. American furniture, folk art, accessories.

Other

Countryside Antiques
6 Lewis Rd.
East Orleans
508-240-0525
English, Irish, & Scandinavian furniture, accessories.

Crocker Farm
1210 Race Lane
Marstons Mills
508-428-3326 (by appt.)
Primitives, folk art, vintage children's pieces.

Eldred's Auction Gallery
1483 Rt. 6A
East Dennis
508-385-3116
www.eldreds.com

Horsefeathers Antiques
454 Mass. Rt. 6A
East Sandwich
508-888-5298
Linens, china teacups, valentines, vintage christening gowns.

Marketplace
61 Main St.
Bourne
508-759-2114
Furniture, glassware, collectibles.

Mashpee Antiques
Mashpee Rotary
Mashpee
508-539-0000
Furnishings, glassware.

Pleasant Bay Antiques
540 Mass. Rt. 28
South Orleans
508-255-0930
Early American furnishings.

Pocasset Exchange
710 County Rd.
Pocasset
508-563-2224
Vintage jewelry, linens, glass, china, furnishings.

Stanley Wheelock
870 Main St.
Osterville
508-420-3170
American, English, & Continental furniture, decorative items, china, glass, fine prints.

Nantucket

Antiques Depot
14 Easy St.
508-228-1287
American & European furnishings, incl. export china, marine paintings, folk art, decoys.

English Trunk Show Co.
8 Washington St.
508-228-4199
www.englishtrunkshowco.com
English furniture & decorative items: linens, transferware, boxes, tea caddies, botanicals, garden.

European Traditions Antiques
12 Straight Wharf
508-325-8976
www.europeantraditionsantiques.com
English & Irish cottage & formal furniture, accessories.

International Rugs of Distinction
P.O. Box 1392
508-360-9002 (by appt.)
www.internationalrugs.biz
Oriental & other carpets.

Island Antiques & Auction House
5 Miacomet Ave.
508-325-5053
Furniture, paintings, collectibles. Also, estate sales.

Janice Aldridge
6 Coffin St.
508-228-6673
Period engravings & 17th- to 20th-c.
European furniture & accessories.

Nina Hellman Marine Antiques
48 Centre St.
508-228-4677
www.nauticalnantucket.com
Scrimshaw, folk art, paintings,
prints, whaling & other nautical items,
books, manuscripts.

Rafael Osona Auctioneer
P.O. Box 2607
508-228-3942
www.rafaelosonaauction.com

Sylvia Antiques
6 Rays Court
508-228-0960
www.sylviaantiques.com
American furniture, nautical items,
porcelain, paintings, decoys, ivory.

Tonkin of Nantucket Warehouse
5 Teasdale Circle
508-228-5523
www.tonkin-of-nantucket.com
English & American formal & country
furnishings & accessories.

Val Maitino Antiques
31 N. Liberty St.
508-228-2747
www.valmaitinoantiques.com
American & English furniture,
decorative & nautical items.

The Connecticut Coast

Centerbrook

Antiques at Rue 154
61 Main St.
860-767-0626
European furniture, decorative items,
paintings, 1820-1940.

Brush Factory Antiques
33 Deep River Rd.
860-767-0845
30+ dealers: furnishings, collectibles.

Chester

One of a Kind Antiques
21 Main St.
860-526-9736
18th- to 20th-c. furniture, art, silver,
china, jewelry, sculpture.

William L. Schaeffer Photographs
41 Main St.
860-526-3870
19th- & 20th-c. vintage American
& European photographs.

Clinton

Clinton Antique Center
78 E. Main St. (Rt. 1)
860-669-3839
85+ dealers: furnishings, collectibles.

**Miriam Green Antiquarian Book Shop
& Gallery**
88 E. Main St. (Rt. 1)
860-664-4200
Rare books, decorative arts.

New London

New England Antique Center
227 Bank St.
860-444-8922
Furniture & decorative items.

New London Antiques Center
123 Bank St.
860-444-7598
80 dealers: furniture, decorative
items, collectibles.

Old Lyme

Antiques Associates
11 Halls Rd.
860-691-3378
American art, furnishings, jewelry,
silver, mid-20th-c. items.

Oriental Rugs
23 Lyme St.
860-434-1167
www.orientalrugsltd.com
Oriental carpets; conservation,
washing, restoration.

The Cooley Gallery
25 Lyme St.
860-434-8807
www.cooleygallery.com
American paintings, 1850-1920.

Old Saybrook

Atrium Antiques
1450 Boston Post Rd.
860-434-4049
18th- to 20th-c. European & American
furnishings, art, lighting, porcelain,
glass, jewelry, mirrors.

Old Saybrook Antiques Center
756 Middlesex Turnpike
860-388-1600
100+ dealers: variety of furnishings,
1800s to Art Deco.

Saybrook Antiques Village
345 Middlesex Turnpike
860-388-0689
Quilts, furniture, books, collectibles.

Stephen & Carol Huber
40 Ferry Rd.
860-388-6809 (by appt.)
Samplers, needlework pictures,
silk embroideries, school girl art.

Other

Antique Puzzles
31 Bogue Lane
East Haddam
860-873-3093
19th- & 20th-c. handcrafted wooden
jigsaw puzzles.

Bonsal-Douglas Antiques
1 Essex Sq.
Essex
860-345-3441
Fine art, early European furniture,
decorative items.

Fred Giampietro
153½ Bradley St.
New Haven
203-787-3851
www.fredgiampietro.com
American painted furniture, folk art,
sculpture, paintings, carousel & cigar
store figures.

New Canaan Antiques
12 Burtis Ave.
New Canaan
203-972-1938
Early American furniture, English
ceramics, brass.

On Consignment
77 Wall St.
Madison
203-245-7012
Furniture, silver, china.

River Wind Antique Shop
68 Main St.
Deep River
860-526-3047
Quilts, furniture, collectibles.

T. F. Vanderbeck Antiques
32 Town St.
Hadlyme
860-526-3770
Decorative furnishings & accessories.

Part Two: Mid-Atlantic

New York's Hudson Valley

Beacon

Dickenson's Antiques
440 Main St.
845-838-1643
1800s-1900s furniture & decorative
accessories, rugs, art.

Early Everything
468-470 Main St.
845-838-3014
19th- & 20th-c. furnishings.

Simply Country
184 Main St.
845-838-1599
Early-20th-c. furniture, decorative
objects, dishes, curio cabinets.

Hudson

A. Sutter Antiques
556 Warren St.
518-822-0729
www.sutterantiques.com
Biedermeier, Empire, & Art Deco
furniture, decorative objects,
architecturals, garden items.

Ad Lib Antiques & Interiors
522 Warren St.
518-822-6522
www.adlibantiques.com
18th- to 20th-c. formal & rustic French
furniture, lighting, decorative arts.

**Alain Pioton Antiques/Hudson
Antiques Center**
536 Warren St.
518-828-9920
www.alainpiotonantiques.com
18th- to 20th-c. French formal &
country furniture, accessories, fine art,
plus a multi-dealer shop.

Angelika Westerhoff
606 Warren St.
518-828-3606
www.angelikawesterhofantiques.com
18th- & 19th-c. Continental, Asian, &
American art & decorative furnishings, from Louis XVI to Shaker.

Armory Art & Antique Gallery
51 N. 5th St. (at State St.)
518-822-1477
Multi-dealer mall: 18th- to 20th-c.
furniture & accessories.

Eustace & Zamus Antiques
513 Warren St.
518-822-9200
www.ezantiques.com
18th- to 20th-c. country & formal
American furniture, decorative arts.

Gottlieb Gallery
524 Warren St.
518-822-1761
www.gottliebgalleryhudson.com
Continental & Neoclassical furniture,
lighting, mirrors, art, decorative items.

Historical Materialism
601 Warren St.
518-671-6151
www.historicalmaterialism.com
19th- to mid-20th-c. formal & informal
furniture. Cast iron & decorative items.

Hitchcock & Eve Fine Art
624 Warren St.
518-822-0106
www.hitchcock&eve.com
Art & artifacts from Asia, Africa, &
Middle East. American paintings.

Howard Dawson Antiques
529 Warren St.
518-822-9775
www.howarddawsonantiques.com
18th- to mid-20th-c. European
furniture, lighting, decorative
items, garden.

Hudson House Antiques
738 Warren St.
518-822-1226
www.hudsonhouseantiques.com
19th-c. furnishings & accessories,
Empire through Renaissance & Gothic
Revivals to Eastlake.

Kendon
508 Warren St.
518-822-8627
www.kendonantiques.com
18th- & 19th-c. American formal &
country furniture, paintings, prints,
folk art, collectibles, vintage toys.

Keystone
746-748 Warren St.
518-822-1019
www.godmanskeystone.com
Furniture, lighting, architecturals,
garden, bath & kitchen items,
claw foot tubs, farmhouse sinks.

Mark McDonald
555 Warren St.
518-828-6320
www.markmcdonald.biz
20th-c. Moderne furniture, lighting,
art glass, accessories.

Peter Jung Fine Art
512 Warren St.
518-828-2698
www.peterjungfineart.com
19th- to 20th-c. American & European
paintings, some furniture.

Relics Antiques
528 Warren St.
518-828-4247
www.relicsantiques.com
18th- to 20th-c. French & American
furniture, lighting, decorative &
garden items.

Tallents Hardy
536 Warren St.
518-822-1860
www.tallents-hardy.com
16th-c. to present day art, furniture,
decorative accessories.

Van Den Akker Antiques
547 Warren St.
518-822-1177
www.vandenakkerantiques.com
18th- to 20th-c. European furnishings,
incl. Amsterdam School, Art Deco.

Red Hook

Annex Antiques Center
23 E. Market St.
845-758-2843
Early-19th- to 20th-c. items,
kitchenware, textiles, country.

Cider Mill Antiques
5 Cherry St.
845-758-2599
www.cidermillantiques.com
Country furniture, yellowware, textiles,
pantry boxes.

Red Hook Antique Center
7531 N. Broadway
845-758-2223
www.redhookantiquescenter.com
12 dealers: from country primitives to
1950s furnishings, decorative items.

Rhinebeck

Asher House Antiques
6380 Mill St.
845-876-1794
www.asherhouse.com
18th-c. to 1930s English, French
& Continental furniture, decorative
accessories.

Beekman Arms Antique Market & Gallery
5387 Mill St. (at Beekman Sq.)
845-876-3477
30+ dealers: furnishings, decorative arts, collectibles.

Rhinebeck Antiques Center
7 W. Market St.
845-876-5555
30+ dealers: furnishings, collectibles.

Other

Copake Auction
266 Rt. 7A
Copake
518-329-1142
www.copakeauction.com

Maren Dunn Antique to Modern
75 Coolidge Hill Rd.
Diamond Point
518-828-9996
www.marendunn.com
Early-19th to mid-20th-c. European & American furniture & decorative items, lighting, art.

Central New York: Bouckville & Madison

Bouckville

Allen's Emporium
Rts. 20 & 12B
315-893-7270
Furniture, art, decorative accessories.

Bittersweet Bazaar
Rt. 20
315-893-7229; 315-893-7573
18th- & 19th-c. furniture & country wares from Europe & America.

Bouckville Antique Corner Store
6723 Rt. 20
315-893-7172
1800s to 1900s furniture & decorative accessories.

Cider House Antiques
6769 Rt. 20
315-893-7579
20 dealers: Americana, primitives, decorative objects.

The Cobblestone Store
Rts. 20 & 46
315-893-7670
Primitive & country furniture, tools, ephemera, linens, ironstone, china.

The Depot Antique Gallery
Rt. 20
315-893-7676
Furniture & decorative objects, incl. Mission & Arts & Crafts, lighting, collectibles, musical instruments.

Madison

Antique Pavilion
6783 Rt. 20
315-893-7411; 315-339-0794
7 dealers: variety of items incl. furniture, glassware, silver, toys, early-19th-c. to 1950.

Cottage Rose Antiques
3317 Maple Ave.
315-893-1786
Multi-dealer shop: furniture, toys, collectibles from the early 20th c.

Grasshopper Antiques
Rt. 20
315-893-7664
Furniture, art, & objets d'art, bronzes, sculpture, architecturals, African tribal art, Americana.

Other

Sangerfield Antique Exchange
7674 Rt. 20
Sangerfield
315-841-8984
18th- to 19th-c. country decorative arts, Americana.

New York City & Antiques Week

Brooklyn

Antique Room
412-416 Atlantic Ave.
718-875-7084
www.antiqueroom.com
19th- & 20th-c. American & English Victorian furnishings.

Circa Antiques
377 Atlantic Ave.
718-596-1866
www.circaantiquesltd.com
19th-c. American & Continental furniture, art, decorative accessories.

Moon River Chattel
62 Grand St.
718-388-1121
19th- & early-20th-c. furniture, lighting, linens, architecturals, garden items.

Silk Road Antiques
313 Atlantic Ave.
718-802-9500
www.silkroadartandantiques.com
19th-c. Chinese furniture, Asian art & decorative arts.

Manhattan

Abe's Antiques
815 Broadway
212-260-6424
19th-c. French furniture & decorative accessories.

Abraham Moheban & Son
139 E. 57th St.
212-758-3900; 800-247-0001
European & Oriental carpets.

Charles Isaacs Photographs
25 W. 54th St.
212-957-3238
www.charlesisaacs.com
Vintage 19th- & 20th-c. masterworks of photography.

Christie's (auctions)
20 Rockefeller Plaza
212-636-2230
www.christies.com

Connors Rosato Gallery
39 Great Jones St.
212-473-0377
www.michaelconnorsantiques.com
18th- & 19th-c. West Indian colonial furniture, related decorative accessories, fine art.

Cora Ginsburg
19 E. 74th St.
212-744-1352
www.coraginsburg.com
17th- to 20th-c. textiles, decorations, needlework, costumes.

Doyle New York (auctions)
175 E. 87th St.
212-427-2730
www.doylenewyork.com

Eileen Lane Antiques
150 Thompson St.
212-475-2988
www.eileenlane.com
Swedish furniture & lighting, incl. Biedermeier & Art Deco.

Far Eastern Antiques & Art
799 Broadway (at 11th St.)
212-460-5030
Asian furniture, ceramics, lacquer, baskets, 200 BC to 20th c.

Hirschl & Adler Galleries
21 E. 70th St.
212-535-8810
www.hirschl&adler.com
18th-c. to present American & European prints, paintings, watercolors, drawings, sculpture.

Historical Design
306 E. 61st St.
212-593-4528
www.historicaldesign.com
Furniture, metalwork, silver, art pottery, glass, jewelry, sculpture, paintings, 1870 to present.

Jerome Jacalone Antiques
1144 Second Ave.
212-838-9118
English, French, & Italian furniture, decorative & fine art.

John Rosselli International
523 E. 73rd St.
212-772-2137
www.johnroselliantiques.com
European & American furniture,
decorative accessories, painted
finishes, blue & white ceramics.

Judith and James Milne
506 E. 74th St., 2nd fl.
212-472-0107
www.milneantiques.com
American folk art, country furniture,
garden accessories.

Karl Kemp & Associates, Antiques
36 E. 10th St.
212-254-1877
www.karlkemp.com
19th- to 20th-c. Empire, Biedermeier,
French Art Deco, & 1950s
Scandinavian furnishings.

Kelter-Malcé Antiques
74 Jane St.
212-675-7380
American folk art, painted furniture,
textiles, game boards, trade signs.

Laura Fisher Antique Quilts
1050 Second Ave., Gallery #84
212-838-2596
www.laurafisherquilts.com
Quilts, Americana, rugs, folk art.

Leigh Keno American Antiques
127 E. 69th St.
212-734-2381
www.leighkeno.com
Late-17th- to early-19th-c. American
furniture, paintings, decorative arts.

Macklowe Gallery
667 Madison Ave.
212-644-6400
www.macklowegallery.com
French Art Nouveau & Art Deco
furniture, lighting, lithos, bronzes,
ceramics, glass, Tiffany lamps.

Marcy Burns American Indian Arts
525 E. 72nd St., 26G
212-439-9257 (by appt.)
American Indian basketry, pottery,
textiles, jewelry from Taxco, Mexico.

Manhattan Art & Antiques Center
1050 Second Ave.
212-355-4400
www.the-maac.com
104 dealers: period furnishings from
America, Europe, & Asia. African art.

Ralph M. Chait Galleries
724 Fifth Ave., 10th fl.
212-758-0937
www.rmchait.com
Chinese art, porcelain, jade, sculpture,
ceramics, silver, Indian colonial silver.

Safani Gallery
980 Madison Ave.
212-570-6360
www.safani.com
Art of Egypt, Greece, Rome, Near East,
from the 5th millennium BC to 6th c. AD.

Sidney Gecker American Folk Art
226 W. 21st St.
212-929-8769
18th- & 19th-c. furniture, paintings,
slip decorated pottery, chalkware,
fraktur, weathervanes, carvings.

Sotheby's (auctions)
1334 York Ave.
212-606-7000
www.sothebys.com

Swann Galleries (auctions)
104 E. 25th St.
212-254-4710
www.swanngalleries.com

The Old Print Shop
150 Lexington Ave.
212-683-3950
www.oldprintshop.com
1750-1950 American prints, drawings,
maps, watercolors.

The Showplace
40 W. 25th St.
212-633-6010
www.nyshowplace.com
135+ dealers: wide variety.

Throckmorton Fine Art
145 E. 57th St., 3rd fl.
212-223-1059
www.throckmorton-nyc.com
Pre-Columbian sculpture, textiles,
Chinese jade, ceramics, tribal art,
vintage photography.

Tom Thomas
318 E. 59th St.
212-688-6100
European furniture, decorative arts,
lighting, glass, ceramics, 1930s–40s.

White Trash
304 E. 5th St.
212-598-5956
Thrift store with 20th-c. furnishings,
especially 1940s to '70s.

Woodard & Greenstein American Antiques
506 E. 74th St.
212-988-2906
www.woodardweave.com
Americana, country furniture, folk art,
decorative accessories, rugs, textiles,
quilts, architecturals.

The Hamptons

Amagansett

Balasses House
Main St. & Hedges Lane
631-267-3032
Dining tables, chests of drawers,
painted furniture, lighting.

Decorum Antiques & Accessories
248 Main St.
631-267-4040
French 18th- & 19th-c. country
furniture, silver, porcelain, glass, etc.

Nellies of Amagansett
230 Main St.
631-267-1000
American pottery, quilts, glassware,
fine & painted furniture, garden items.

Bridgehampton

Amy Perlin Antiques
2462 Main St.
631-537-6161
www.amyperlinantiques.com
From Roman antiquities to mid-20th-c.
furnishings.

**Barbara Trujillo Antiques;
Kelter-Malcé Antiques; Kinnanman
& Ramaekers Antiques**
2466 Main St.
631-537-3838
Period American country furniture,
folk art, Native Indian art & jewelry,
paintings, china, pottery, glass,
advertising art, early photography.

Chez Soi at Frederick P. Victoria & Son
2426 Montauk Hwy.
631-537-0496
www.chezsoi.us
Furniture & accessories, 1880-1940.

Denton & Gardner
2491 Main St.
631-537-4796
www.dentongardner.com
19th- & 20th-c. French, English, &
American art & furnishings.

English Country Antiques
26 Snake Hollow Rd.
631-537-0606; 631-204-0428
www.ecantiques.com
French, English, & Chinese furniture,
ceramics, lighting, decorative objects.

Gray Gardens
17 Montauk Hwy.
631-537-4848
18th- to 20th-c. furnishings & decoration,
lamps, mirrors, fine art, garden items.

Hampton Briggs Antiques
2462 Main St.
631-537-6286
Asian art & furnishings from China,
Thailand, Burma, Japan.

Laurin Copen Antiques
1703 Montauk Hwy.
631-537-2802
www.laurincopenantiques.com
18th-, 19th-, & 20th-c. indoor &
outdoor furniture, art, decorative
items, lighting.

The American Wing
2415 Montauk Hwy.
631-537-3319
www.theamericanwing.com
American & Continental furniture
& accessories incl. rattan & bamboo,
architecturals, garden items, toys.

Easthampton

Huntting House Antiques
Red Horse Plaza, shop #12
74 Montauk Hwy.
631-907-9616
18th- & 19th-c. English & French
furnishings.

**Jay Moorhead Antiques/Jack's Place
at Baiting Hollow Green**
26 Montauk Hwy.
631-324-6819
Furniture, prints, paintings, pottery,
glass, china, mirrors, rugs, quilts,
dolls, brass, copper.

Lars Bolander
Red Horse Plaza
74 Montauk Hwy.
631-329-3400
18th- & 19th-c. English, French,
& Scandinavian furniture & accessories.

The Grand Acquisitor
12 Pantigo Rd. (off Main St.)
631-324-7272
Textiles, lace, bed & table
linens, furniture, silver, jewelry,
decorative items.

Victory Garden
63 Main St.
631-324-7800
Country French furniture, faience,
accessories, architecturals, garden.

Yard Sale East Hampton
66 Newtown Lane
631-324-7048
From flea market finds to fine antiques,
outdoor furniture, wicker, pottery.

Sag Harbor

Around Again
1 Long Wharf
631-725-4067
Art Deco to mid-20th-c . indoor &
outdoor furniture, art, lighting,
decorative objects.

Bagley Home
34 Main St.
631-725-3553
Vintage industrial lighting, primitives,
French silver, linens.

Bella Casa
4 Bay St.
631-725- 6176
www.bellacasa.com
18th- & 19th-c. Italian ceramics, outdoor furnishings, linens, paintings,
lighting.

Christy's Building Art Center
3 Madison St.
631-725-7000
18th- & 19th-c. Continental & English
furniture, art, decorative & garden
items.

Miyamoto Japanese Antiques
75 Washington St.
631-725-1533
Folk textiles, tansu chests, ikebana
baskets, screens, lacquerware, tables.

Sage Street Antiques
Sage St. (off Rt. 114)
631-725-4036
Country furnishings, kitchen items,
linens, prints, fireplace equipment,
mirrors, lamps.

Southampton

Another Time
765 Hill St.
631-283-6542; 631-283-6223.
19th- & 20th-c. furniture, decorative
accessories: china, pottery, prints,
dolls, trains, toys.

Collette Designer Resale
89 Jobs Lane &10 Main St.
631-204-9511; 631- 283-1867
Consignments. Main St.: home
furnishings. Job's Lane: clothing.

Old Town Crossing
46 Main St.
631-283-7740
English, French, & Continental
furnishings, lamps, silver, china.

Second Chance
45 Main St.
631-283-2988
Sterling, china, crystal, small
furniture, linens, jewelry.

1708 House
25 Hampton Rd.
631-287-3859
www.1708house.com
Early-19th- to early-20th-c. English,
French, & American furniture
& period accessories.

Other

Good Ground Antique Center
52 W. Montauk Hwy.
Hampton Bays
631-728-6300
Furniture, mirrors, ceramics, art,
silver, glassware, linens, lamps.

Gustavo Olivieri Antiques
720 Montauk Hwy.
Watermill
631-726-1100
20th-c. European designer furniture &
accessories, Murano glass, chandeliers.

Lambertville & Hunterdon County, New Jersey; New Hope & Bucks County, Pennsylvania

NEW JERSEY

Frenchtown

Brooks Antiques
24 Bridge St.
908-996-7161
Primitives, folk art, country furnishings, incl. pieces in original surface,
spongeware & yellowware.

Revelations Sacred Antiquities
43A Bridge St.
908-797-7550
Rare 15th- to 19th-c. European
religious paintings, sculptures.

Lambertville

America Antiques & Design
5 S. Main St.
609-397-6966
www.americadesigns.com
19th- & 20th-c. artifacts, furniture, art,
architectural iron, garden items.

Antique Center/People's Store
28 N. Union St.
609-397-9808
Art, furniture, silver, decorative arts,
clothing, books, lighting.

Bridge Street Antiques
65 Lincoln Rd.
609-397-1643
Victorian furnishings, accessories,
jewelry, collectibles.

Broadmoor Antiques
6 N. Union St.
609-397-8802
www.rossiart.com
10 dealers: decorative objects, art.

G. Evans Ltd. Antiques
8 Bridge St.
609-397-4411
www.gevansltdantiques.com
Furniture, lighting, accessories,
porcelain, glass, fireplace items.

Golden Nugget Flea Market
1850 River Rd.
609-397-0811
www.gnmarket.com
300+ dealers: vintage & antique
furnishings, collectibles, art.

James Curran Antiques
202 N. Union St. (Corner, Elm St.)
609-397-1543
www.curranantiques.com
17th-c. to Edwardian English &
American furnishings, art, objects.

Jim's Antiques
6 Bridge St.
609-397-7700
Formal European & American
furniture, art, decorative items.

June's Antiques
36 Coryell St.
609-397-1359
English, French, & American textiles,
sterling, china, mirrors, art, furniture.

Lovrinc Antiques
15 N. Union St.
609-397-8600
18th- to early-19th-c. American &
English furniture & accessories.

Mix Gallery
17 S. Main St.
609-773-0777
www.mixgallery.com
1800-1960 furnishings, folk art, high
country, Moderne. 20th-c. designer
handbags, accessories.

Peter Wallace
3 Lambert Lane
609-397-4914
Engravings, prints, paintings,
ceramics, country, formal & Raj
furniture; lighting; objets d'art.

Rago Arts and Auctions
333 N. Main St.
609-397-9374
www.ragoarts.com

The Sitting Room Antiques
12 Church St.
609-773-0022
18th- to 20th-c. European & American
furniture, lighting, accessories.

PENNSYLVANIA

New Hope

A Stage in Time
12 W. Bridge St.
215-862-6120
www.astageintime.com
Early-20th-c. Arts & Crafts furniture,
lighting, pottery.

Cockamamie's
6 W. Bridge St.
215-862-5454
www.cockamamies.com
Art Deco furniture, lighting, collectibles,
memorabilia, glass, barware.

Ferry Hill Antiques
15 N. Main St.
215-862-5335
www.ferryhill.com
Small furnishings, art, lamps,
Staffordshire, transferware, tea sets,
Oriental pottery, Limoges.

Gardner's Antiques
6148 Lower York Rd. (Rt. 202S)
215-794-8616; 215-794-7759
www.gardnersantiques.com
Formal to country French furniture
& decorative items.

Hobensack & Keller
57 Old York Rd.
215-862-2406
Furniture, decorative objects, art,
18th-c. to present.

Ingham Springs Antiques Gallery
6319 Lower York Rd. (Rt. 202)
215-862-2145; 215-862-9751
American, English, & Continental
furniture, accessories, paintings,
incl. New Hope Impressionists.

Legacy Antiques
6642 State Hwy. 179
215-862-6310
www.legacyantiquesinc.com
English & European furnishings,
clocks, mirrors, lighting, art,
copper, ceramics.

Olde Hope Antiques
2878 Creamery Rd.
215-297-0200
Primitive & country furnishings, folk art.

Rice's Sale & Country Market
6326 Greenhill Rd.
215-297-5993
www.ricesmarket.com
700 vendors (outdoors): some antiques
& vintage items, Amish farm products.

Other

Artefact Architectural Antiques
Rt. 263 (¼ mi. south of Rt. 313)
Furlong
215-794-8790
www.artefactantiques.com
Architecturals: mantels, doors,
windows, lighting, garden items.

Bucks County Antique Gallery
8 Skyline Dr.
Chalfont
215-997-3227
Consignment store with many periods
& types of furniture, decorative items.

Olde Mill Flea Market
Bellevue Ave. (betw. Hulmeville &
Trenton Rds.)
Hulmeville
215-757-1777
www.antiquesoldmill.com
Furnishings, collectibles.

Roger D. Winter Antiques
Solebury
215-794-5926 (by appt.)
18th- & early-19th-c. American
& English furniture, incl. formal
& country dining room furniture.

Trading Post Antiques
532 Durham Rd.
Wrightstown
215-579-1020
Furnishings & collectibles.

Philadelphia, Pennsylvania

Alfred Bullard
1604 Pine St.
215-735-1879
1700-1840 English furniture
& accessories.

Antiques Markets of Chestnut Hill
7928 & 8139 Germantown Ave.
215-248-5190
Multi-dealer shop: furnishings,
decorative objects.

Architectural Antiques Exchange
715 N. 2nd St.
215-922-3669
Architectural items.

Bob Berman Mission Oak
136 N. 2nd St.
215-733-0707
Arts & Crafts furnishings.

Charles A. Whitaker Auction
7105 Emlen St.
215-844-8788

Classic Lighting Emporium
62 N. 2nd St.
215-625-9552
www.classic-lighting.com
Lighting, incl. prisms, globes, shades,
hard-to-find parts.

Elle Shushan
1600 Arch St., Ste. 1603
267-514-2033
www.portraitminiatures.com
18th-& early-19th-c. portrait miniatures.

Francis J. Purcell
251 N. 3rd St.
215-574-0700
www.francisjpurcell.com
Period English, American, French,
& Russian furniture, decorative
pieces, mantels.

Freeman's 200 Auction House
1808 Chestnut St.
215-563-9275
www.freemansauction.com

George T. Hobe Antiques
8407 Germantown Ave.
215-247-5733
1800 to 1950s American & English
art, ceramics.

Harry A. Eberhardt & Son
2010 Walnut St.
215-568-4144
19th-c. American & Continental
objects: ceramics, lamps, ivory, jade,
glass, Oriental furniture.

Jeffrey L. Biber
1030 Pine St.
215-574-3633
18th- to 19th-c. silver, hollowware, &
flatware, primarily made in New York
& Philadelphia.

John Alexander
10 W. Gravers Lane
215-242-0741
British fine art, furniture, decorative
objects, 1860-1920.

Kohn & Kohn Antiques
1112 Pine St.
215-923-0432
18th- & 19th-c. European & American
furniture, art, stained-glass windows.

M. Finkel & Daughter
936 Pine St.
215-627-7797
www.samplings.com
17th- to 19th-c. needlework, samplers,
furniture, decorative accessories.

Mode Moderne
159 N. 3rd St.
215-627-0299
www.modemoderne.com
Mid-century Moderne furniture,
lighting, pottery.

Newman Galleries
1625 Walnut St.
215-563-1779
www.newmangalleries1865.com
Early-20th-c. American art, 19th-c.
American & European paintings.

Niederkorn Antique Silver
2005 Locust St.
215-567-2606
Napkin rings, frames, tea balls, desk
accessories, baby gifts. Jensen,
Spratling, Tiffany.

The Schwarz Gallery
1806 Chestnut St.
215-563-4887
www.schwarzgallery.com
American & European paintings, incl.
Philadelphia artists: Eakins, Peto,
Carles, Peale family.

Adamstown & Lancaster County, Pennsylvania

Adamstown

Adamstown Antique Mall
94 Lancaster Ave.
717-484-0464
Furnishings from around the world.

Clock Tower Antique Center
Rt. 272
717-484-2757
www.stoudtburg.com
10+ dealers: international wares.

Heritage Antiques
Rt. 272
2750 N. Reading Rd.
717-484-4646
68 dealers: furnishings, collectibles.

Oley Valley Architectural Antiques
2453 N. Reading Rd.
717-335-3585
Victorian furniture, doors, stained-glass
windows, mantels, wall units, bars.

Pine Hills Antiques Mall
144 Furlow Rd. (off intersection
of Rts. 272 & 222)
717-484-6313
100+ dealers: decorative items,
collectibles, glass, 50's kitchenware.

The Country French Collection
Rt. 272
717-484-0200
www.countryfrenchantiques.com
French furniture, decorative items.

Denver

Adams Antiques
2400 N. Reading Rd.
717-335-3116
www.adamsantiques.com
Country, Victorian, & other furnishings,
accessories, glassware, art pottery.

Antiques at The Black Horse
2222 N. Reading Rd. (Rt. 272)
717-335-3300
www.blackhorselodge.com
300 dealers: North American
& European furniture, decorative
items, collectibles.

European Pine Antiques
52 Hill Rd.
717-335-3408
Furniture from Ireland, England, France,
Holland, & Germany, 1850–1920.

Lancaster

RevChi's Antiques & Collectibles
324 N. Queen St.
717-509-8497
18th- & 19th-c. furniture, artwork,
glass, china, books, porcelain.

Then & Again Antiques
318 N. Queen St.
717-390-2780
Furniture, collectibles, decorative items.

Reinholds

Alternative Furnishings
2664 N. Reading Rd. (Rt. 272)
717-484-2225
www.alternativefurnishings.com
Furniture, decorative objects, garden.

General Heath's Antiques
Rt. 272
717-484-1300
50 dealers: furniture, decorative items,
pottery, jewelry.

Shupp's Grove Antique Market
607 Willow St. (off Rt. 897 South)
717-484-4115
Furnishings, collectibles, art.

Other

Garthoeffner Gallery
122 E. Main St.
Lititz
717-627-7998
Americana, country & Pennsylvania
furniture, folk art, quilts, rugs, textiles,
other decorative objects. Rare toys.

Mulberry Street Heritage Antiques
2 Deborah Dr.
Leola
717-656-4772
19th-c. country furnishings
& decorative items, stoneware,
baskets, Native American items.

The Brandywine Valley & Wilmington, Delaware

DELAWARE

Newcastle

Lauren Lynch Antiques
1 E. 2nd St.
302-328-5576
Furniture, Asian pieces, linens, art,
decorative items, books, collectibles.

Oak Knoll Books
310 Delaware St.
302-328-7232
www.oakknoll.com
Books about books; collecting,
papermaking, binding, printing.

Raven's Nest
204 Delaware St.
302-325-2510
Collectibles, jewelry, home décor.

Wilmington

Brickhouse Antiques
100 South Rd.
302-762-8900
Country furniture, 1800s to present.

East Coast Antiques and Architecturals
802 Naamans Rd.
302-475-7266
1890-1930 Mission furniture, American art, pottery, glassware.

Merrill's Antiques
100 Northern Ave.
302-994-1765
Collectibles, figurines, decorative items.

Ronald C. Bauman
5722 Kennett Pike
302-655-4466
18th- & 19th-c. American furniture, tall case clocks, decorative arts.

Other

Academy Street Antiques
501 Pine St.
Laurel
302-875-1111
Consigned 18th- & 19th-c. furnishings, glass, china, textiles.

Mid-Atlantic Auctions and Appraisals
P.O. Box 4365
Greenville
302-633-9470
www.mid-atlantic.com

PENNSYLVANIA

Chadds Ford

Brandywine River Antiques Market
878 Baltimore Pike
610-388-2000
35 dealers: 19th- & 20th-c. furniture, Victoriana, primitives, textiles, paintings, lamps, clocks, stoneware, collectibles, smalls.

Pennsbury-Chadds Ford Antique Mall
640 E. Baltimore Pike
610-388-1620
100+ dealers: furnishings, silver, jewelry, glass, ceramics, textiles, art, incl. signed Wyeth prints.

R. M. Worth Antiques
810 Baltimore Pike
610-388-4040
18th- & 19th-c. American furniture, paintings, decorative arts, porcelain.

Exton

Ball & Ball
463 Lincoln Hwy.
610-363-7330
www.ball&ball.com
Hardware, lighting, period furniture, hearth items. Reproduction hardware.

John W. Bunker & Son
431 E. Lincoln Hwy.
610-363-7436
18th- & 19th-c. country & formal furniture.

Malvern

Olivier Fleury Antiquities de France
57 W. Lancaster Ave.
610-722-5900
www.ofleury.com
18th- & 19th-c. country French furnishings.

The Olde General Store
2447 Yellow Springs Rd.
610-647-8968
18th- & 19th-c. items, decoys, folk art, nautical items, stoneware, Native & Latin American artifacts.

Van Tassel/Baumann American Antiques
690 Sugartown Rd.
610-647-3339
18th- & early-19th-c. furniture & accessories, incl. early schoolgirl needlework.

West Chester

County Seat Antiques & Consignments
41 W. Gay St.
610-696-0584
Furniture, decorative accessories.

H. L. Chalfant Antiques
1352 Paoli Pike
610-696-1862
www.antiques&fineart.com/chalfant
17th- to early-19th-c. American furnishings, folk art, paintings, weathervanes.

Monroe Coldren Antiques
723 E. Virginia Ave.
610-692-5651
www.monroecoldren.com
Architecturals, lighting, hearth equipment, candlesticks, hardware, furniture, 1720-1890.

Other

Antiques and Images at Avondale
902 Gap Newport Pike (Rt. 41)
Avondale
610-268-0226
www.antiques&images.com
18th- & 19th-c. Delaware Valley furniture, Quimper, stoneware, classic cameras, advertising photography.

H. D. Wilder Antiques
2027 Ridge Rd.
Elverson
610-469-9774
Pre-1850 furniture, incl. old painted finishes, pre-1950 bird decoys.

Irvin and Dolores Boyd Antiques
509 Bethlehem Pike
Ft. Washington
215-646-5126
www.boydsantiques.com
American period & country furniture.

Philip H. Bradley Antiques
1101 E. Lancaster Ave.
Downingtown
610-269-0427
18th- & 19th-c. American furniture & accessories.

Stevens Antiques
446 & 627 Lancaster Ave.
Frazer
610-644-8294; 610-644-8282
www.stevensantiques.com
19th- & 20th-c. American, English, & Continental furniture, lighting, accessories.

Annapolis & Maryland's Eastern Shore

Annapolis

Annapolis Furniture Co.
238 West St.
410-295-7463
www.annapolisfurniture.com
Irish furnishings, rustic & distressed styling. Imports from other countries.

Dawson Gallery
44 Maryland Ave.
410-269-1299
19th- & early-20th-c. oil & watercolor paintings.

Evergreen Antiques, Art and Accessories
69 Maryland Ave.
410-216-9067
Furniture, art, silver, jewelry, linens, vintage clothing, glass, pottery, bottles.

Hobson's Choice Antiques
58 Maryland Ave.
410-280-2206
18th- & 19th-c. furniture, silver, brass, Chinese export & other porcelain, nautical items, trains.

Natalie Silitch Folk Art Crafts & Antiques
2114 Renard Court
410-266-9311
www.nataliesilitch.com
Furniture & decorative accessories, incl. holiday items.

Ron Snyder Antiques
2011 West St. (Rt. 450)
410-266-5452
18th- & early-19th-c. furniture & accessories, emphasis on the American Federal period.

Merry Walk Antiques
706 Melrose St.
410-268-6233
www.merrywalk.com
Old French faience, textiles, needlework, painted country pieces, garden
& wall decoration.

Centreville

Aileen Minor Antiques
208 S. Liberty St.
410-758-1489
www.aileenminor.com
18th- & 19th-c. American furniture,
paintings, accessories, garden.

Gary E. Young Antiques
128 S. Commerce St.
410-758-2132
English & Irish period furniture,
decoration, portrait miniatures.

Easton

Camelot Antiques
7871 Ocean Gateway
410-820-4396
18th- & 19th-c. furniture, art glass,
clocks, decoys, silver, ceramics, incl.
majolica, Quimper, Chinese.

Easton Maritime Antiques
27 S. Harrison St.
410-763-8843
Nautical art & implements.

North Bend Galleries
28220 St. Michael's Rd.
410-820-6085
Furniture, art, toys, trains, folk art,
country, primitives, pottery, silver,
clocks, ephemera, military items.

St. Michaels

Coco & Co.
209 S. Talbot St.
866-696-2626
www.cocoandcompany.com
Vintage & period furnishings,
decorative accents.

Galerie Française
405 S. Talbot St.
410-745-6329
www.judithsummers.com
1899-1950 European posters.

Gatsby's Collection
1007 S. Talbot St.
410-745-3700
www.gatsbyscollection.com
Decorative furnishings, lighting.

3 Krazy Ladies
104 N. Talbot St.
410-745-0497
www.3krazyladies.com
Shabby chic furnishings,
decorative accessories.

Other

AAA Antiques Mall
2659 Annapolis Rd. (Rts. 175E & 295)
Hanover
410-551-4101
www.aaaantiquesmallmd.com
400+ dealers: furniture, decorative
items, collectibles, textiles, lighting,
pottery, china, glass.

Americana Antiques
111 S. Morris St.
Oxford
410-226-5677; 410-226-5677
www.americanaantiques.net
18th- to early-19th-c. American
furniture, accessories, paintings,
folk art, carousel figures.

Chesapeake Antique Center
Rt. 301
Queenstown
410-827- 6640
www.chesapeakeantiques.com
70+ dealers: period American, English,
& European furnishings, art, books.

Denton Station Antiques Mall
24690 Meeting House Rd.
Denton
410-479-2200
www.dentonstation.com
100+ dealers: furniture, decorative
items, collectibles. Monthly auction.

Firehouse Antiques Center
102 N. Main St.
Galena
410-648-5639
American country furniture,
decoys, quilts, Oriental rugs, folk art,
related accessories.

Jones' Antiques
518 High St.
Cambridge
410-228-1752
Decorative items, china, brass,
silver, collectibles.

Washington, D.C.;
Kensington, Maryland;
& Alexandria, Virginia

MARYLAND

Kensington

Acanthus Antiques
4132 Howard Ave.
301-530-9600
www.acanthusantiques.com
17th- to 20th-c. American, English,
& European furniture, paintings,
decorative accessories, silver.

Chelsea & Co.
4116 Howard Ave.
301-897-8886
www.chelsea-antiques.com
Furniture & accessories from England,
Europe, Asia. Vintage costume jewelry.

Gonzales Antiques
4130 Howard Ave.
301-564-5940
19th-c. to Art Deco Continental
furniture, paintings, bronzes, objets
d'art, lighting.

Hunters & Gatherers
4229 Howard Ave.
301-896-0348
European furnishings, Moretti glass,
Fortuny lighting, decorator textiles.

Huret Antiques
4106 Howard Ave.
301-530-7551
www.huretantiques.com
18th-, 19th-, & 20th-c. French
furniture & accessories.

Jill & Company
3744 Howard Ave.
301-946-7464
Early 1800s-1940s Americana, folk art,
quilts, country furniture.

La Belle Epoque
4088-A Howard Ave.
301-530-1183
www.lbeantiques.com
19th- to early-20th-c. French &
European furniture & accessories,
incl. country pieces.

Onslow Square Antiques
4125-4131 Howard Ave.
301-530-9393
www.onslowsq.com
Formal & country English &
Continental furniture, stained glass,
architecturals, garden items.

Osiris Books
3746 Howard Ave.
301-962-7462
Home library items: book cases,
desks, lecterns, lighting, books.

Sally Shaffer Interiors
3742 Howard Ave.
301-933-3750
American country & cottage-style
furniture & accessories, ironstone
pottery, toleware.

Sparrows
4115 Howard Ave.
888-800-1235
www.sparrows.com
18th- to early-20th-c. formal & country
French furniture, lighting, ironwork,
faience, majolica, art.

Split Personality Antiques
3760 Howard Ave.
301-942-4440
Oak furniture, Art Deco, art pottery.

The Great British Pine Mine
4144 Howard Ave.
301-493-2565
www.pinemine.com
English & European pine furniture.

VIRGINIA

Alexandria

French Country Antiques
1000 King St.
703-548-8563
18th- & 19th-c. French furniture,
pottery, glassware, linens. French
& American paintings.

Golden Rhodes
1305 King St.
703-535-5560
www.goldenrhodes.com
19th-c. furnishings & mirrors.

James Wilhoit Antiques
277 S. Washington St.
703-683-6595
www.jameswilhoit.com
18th- & 19th-c. American & English
furniture & accessories, art, porcelain,
glass, silver.

Silverman Galleries
110 N. Saint Asaph
703-836-5363
www.silvermangalleries.com
18th- & 19th-c. furniture, jewelry,
silver, paintings, accessories.

Spurgeon-Lewis Antiques
112 N. Columbus St.
703-548-4917
18th- to mid-19th-c. American furniture; chandeliers, paintings, mirrors,
prints, silver. Old Paris porcelain,
1770-1870.

Studio Antiques and Fine Art
524 N. Washington St.
703-548-5188
www.studioantiques.net
18th- to 19th-c. English & American
furniture & accessories, tea caddies,
19th-c. paintings.

Sumpter Priddy III
601 S. Washington St.
703-299-0800
www.sumpterpriddy.com
17th- to early-19th-c. American &
Southern formal & country furniture &
accessories, incl. folk art, tall clocks.

The Antique Guild
113 N. Fairfax St.
703-836-1048
www.theantiqueguild.net
19th- & early-20th-c. jewelry: Art
Deco, gold stick pins, Victorian lockets,
brooches, silver.

Washington Square Antiques
425 & 689 S. Washington St.
703-836-1020
www.washingtonsquareantiques.com
18th-, 19th-, & select 20th-c. English
& American furniture, fine art,
decorative accessories.

WASHINGTON, D.C.

Adam A. Weschler Auctions
909 E St., NW
202-628-1281; 800-331-1430
www.weschlers.com

Adams Davidson Galleries
2727 29th St., NW, Ste. 504
202-965-3800
19th- & 20th-c. American paintings
& drawings.

Antiques on the Hill
701 North Carolina Ave., SE
202-543-1819
Vintage bric-a-brac, incl. textiles,
 silver, toys, art, jewelry.

Brass Knob Architectural Antiques
2311 18th St., NW
& 2329 Champlain St., NW
202-332-3370;
202-256-0587 (warehouse)
www.thebrassknob.com
Doors, doorknobs, hardware, mantels,
stained glass, light fixtures, columns.

Cherub Antiques Gallery
2918 M St., NW
202-337-2224
Early-20th-c. American, European,
incl. Art Deco, & Art Nouveau,
furnishings & objects, art.

Darrell Dean Antiques & Decorative
Arts
1524 Wisconsin Ave., NW
202-333-6330
www.darrelldeanantiques.com
Furnishings & decorative objects
sourced internationally, folk art,
architecturals, garden items.

Frank Milwee Antiques
2912 M St., NW
202-333-4811
Wine-related items, tableware, silver,
English watercolors.

Good Wood
1428 U St., NW
202-986-3640
19th- & 20th-c. furniture, stained
glass, other decorative items.

Guarisco Gallery
2828 Pennsylvania Ave., NW
202-333-8533
19th- to early-20th-c. American, English,
& European paintings, sculpture.

Hemphill Fine Arts
1027 33rd St., NW
202-342-5610
20th-c. fine art, sculpture, photography.

Marston Luce
1651 Wisconsin Ave., NW
202-333-6800
French country furniture, accessories,
garden items.

Metternich Canal Square
1054 31st St.
202-944-9600
19th-c. Austrian Biedermeier furniture.

Michael Getz Antiques
2918 M St., NW
202-338-3811
18th- to 20th-c. silver, fireplace items,
decorative accessories.

Miller & Arney Antiques
1737 Wisconsin Ave., NW
202-338-2369
www.millerarney.com
18th- & early-19th-c. furnishings,
Chinese export porcelain, prints.

Miss Pixie's
1810 Adams Mill Rd., NW
202-232-8171
www.misspixies.com
19th- & 20th-c. furnishings, parasols,
glass, silver, clothing.

Old Print Gallery
1220 31st St., NW
202-965-1818
Antiquarian prints & maps, political
cartoons, Civil War scenes, botanicals.

Opportunity Shop of the
Christ Child Society
1427 Wisconsin Ave., NW
202-333-6635
Consigned furniture & decorative
items, crystal, silver, home goods.

Osuna Gallery
1914 16th St., NW
202-296-1963
Furniture, Old Master & 19th-c.
paintings.

St. Luke's Gallery
1715 Q St., NW
202-328-2424
Paintings, sculpture, drawings, prints.

Susquehanna Antiques
3216 O St., NW
202-333-1511
18th- & 19th-c. American & English
furnishings, paintings.

The Tartt Gallery
2017 Q St. NW
202-332-5652
19th- & 20th-c. photography
& American outsider art.

PART THREE: SOUTH

Loudoun County, Northern Virginia's Hunt Country

Leesburg

Black Shutter Antique Center
1 Loudoun St., SE
703-443-9579
www.blackshutterantiques.com
45 dealers: furniture, decorative items, collectibles.

Four Shabby Chicks
106 Harrison St., SE
703-669-0380
www.fourshabbychicks.com
Shabby chic & vintage furnishings.

Leesburg Court of Shoppes Mall
19487 James Monroe Hwy.
703-777-7799
40 dealers: Victorian to1950s furnishings, collectibles.

Molly Sproket Antiques
120-C E. Market St.
703-669-9688
1700-1940 American, English, & Asian furniture.

Otter Creek Collections
10 S. King St.
703-669-0140
www.ottercreekinc.com
Furniture, art, accessories.

Middleburg

Greystoke & Verner Antiques
1 W. Washington St.
540-687-6875
www.greystokeandverner.com
18th- to 20th-c. furnishings & art.

JML French Antiques
17 E. Washington St.
540-687-6323
www.jml-french-antiques.com
17th- to 19th-c. furniture, tea sets, art.

Middleburg Antique Emporium
107 W. Washington St.
540-687-8680
www.middleburgantiqueemporium.com
45 dealers: 18th- to mid-20th-c. English & American furniture, decorative arts.

Red Fox Fine Art
1 N. Madison St.
540-687-5780
1750-1950 American paintings (some sporting), bronzes.

Thrill of the Hunt Antiques
100 E. Washington St.
540-687-6988
Multi-dealer shop.

Purcellville

Mary Ellen Stover Antiques
120 N. 21st St.
540-338-2632
18th- & early-19th-c. American furniture & decorative accessories.

Really Great Finds
42410 Stumptown Rd.
& 600 E. Main St.
703-779-7709; 540-338-7799
www.reallygreatfinds.com
Shabby chic decor & garden iron.

Other

An American in Paris
694 Federal St.
Paris
540-592-9008
Pre-1850 formal & high country furniture, primitives, folk art, textiles.

Bee Keepers Cottage
43738 Hay Rd.
Ashburn
703-726-9411
Shabby chic decor.

Delaplane Store and Antique Center
3054 Delaplane Grade Rd.
Delaplane
540-364-2754
18th- to 19th-c. American high country painted & formal furniture, decorative accessories, folk art.

Malcolm Magruder
Millwood
540-837-2438 (by appt.)
18th- & early-19th-c. American furniture & decorative arts: English pottery, paintings, period jewelry.

Norma Tolmach Antiques
112 Oakgrove Rd., #108
Sterling
703-437-8800
www.normatolmachantiques.com
Irish, English, & French country pine furniture & accessories.

The Old Lucketts Store Antiques
42350 Lucketts Rd.
Lucketts
703-779-0268
www.luckettstore.com
Vintage & shabby chic furnishings, decorative & garden items.

Asheville, North Carolina

Aberdeen & Co.
828-236-3636 (by appt.)
British & American country furniture & accessories.

Antique Market Gallery
52 Broadway St.
828-259-9977
28 dealers: furniture, glassware, collectibles.

Antique Tobacco Barn
75 Swannanoa River Rd.
828-252-7291
80 dealers: wide variety.

Biltmore Station Antiques & Collectibles
130 Swannanoa River Rd., #A
828-250-0229
45 dealers: variety of items.

Brunk Auctions
117 Tunnel Road
828-254-6846
www.brunkauctions.com

Charlton Bradsher American Antiques
828-251-1904 (by appt.)
www.charltonbradsher.com
Early American & Southern back country folk art, furniture in original surface, pottery, textiles.

Chatsworth Art & Antiques
54 N. Lexington Ave.
828-252-6004
English furniture, silver, paintings, small accessories.

Cottage Walk
6 All Souls Crescent
828-277-9066
European furniture.

Deluxe Retro-Modern
602 Haywood Rd.
828-251-9074
Furnishings, 1920-1960.

Fireside Antiques & Interiors
30 All Souls Crescent
828-274-5977
English Victorian furniture, porcelains.

King-Thomasson Antiques
65 Biltmore Ave.
828-252-1565
18th-c. English country furniture.

Lexington Park Antiques
65 W. Walnut St.
828-253-3070
90 dealers: wide variety.

Oddfellows Antique Warehouse
23 Rankin Ave.
828-350-7800
Victorian & 20th-c. European
& British furniture.

Stuf Antiques
52 Broadway St.
828-254-4054
Variety from toasters to Tiffany.

Tommy Tuten & Johnny Penland Auctions
155 Craven St.
828-253-7712

Village Antiques at Biltmore
755 Biltmore Ave.
828-252-5090
18th- & 19th-c. French, English,
& American furniture.

Other

Balsam Antique Mall
25 Muse Business Pike
Waynesville
828-452-7070
60 dealers.

Charleston, South Carolina

Alkyon Arts & Antiques
120 Meeting St.
843-276-5899
Decorative arts: paintings, bronzes,
marbles, vases, mirrors, clocks.

Architectural Antique Warehouse
1011 St. Andrews Blvd.
843-571-3389
Architectural salvage.

A'Riga IV Antiques
204 King St.
843-577-3075
18th- & 19th-c. decorative arts,
ceramics, medical & apothecary.

Audubon Gallery
190 King St.
843-853-1100
www.audubongallery.com
17th- to 19th-c. natural history art.

Carolina Antique Maps & Prints
91 Church St.
843-722-4773 (by appt.)
16th- to19th-c. maps, charts, natural
history art, Civil War & historical
prints, Charleston items.

Charleston Antique Mall
4 Avondale Ave.
843-769-6119
25 dealers: furniture, glassware,
paintings, tea sets.

Chicora Antiques
102 Church St.
843-723-1711
www.chicoraantiques.com
18th- &19th-c. English & American
furnishings, decorative arts.

Church St. Galleries
100 Church St.
843-937-0808
18th- & 19th-c. English furniture,
paintings, porcelain.

Dailey-Grommé 20th Century
208 King St.
843-853-2299
Art Deco & 20th-c. Moderne furniture
& design.

George C. Birlant and Co.
191 King St.
843-722-3842
18th- & 19th-c. fine English furniture,
silver, china, crystal.

George C. Williams
155 King St.
843-377-0290
www.georgecwilliams.com
Early American furniture, accessories,
Charleston decorative arts.

Golden & Associates Antiques
206/197 King St.
843-723-8886; 843-853-4706
18th- & 19th-c. English, American,
& Continental furniture, decorative
accessories, garden items.

Helen Martin Antiques
169 King St.
843-577-6533
Furniture, glassware, collectibles.

Iva's Attic Antiques & Collectibles
825 Savannah Hwy.
843-766-2267
Porcelain, furniture, glassware,
collectibles, art.

John Gibson Antiques
183 King St.
843-722-0909
Estate jewelry, Art Deco items.

Julia Santen Gallery
216-B King St.
843-534-0758
Vintage poster art.

King St. Antique Mall
495 King St.
843-723-2211
35 dealers: French, Italian,
& Dutch furniture.

L & W New and Used Thrift Store
4226-A Rivers Ave.
843-225-5968
Furniture, glassware, collectibles.

Livingston Antiques
163 King St.
843-723-9697
www.livingstonantiques.com
18th- and 19th-c. furniture, decorative
items, fine art, incl. English pieces.

Moore House Antiques
150 King St.
843-722-8065
www.moorehouseantiques.com
18th- & early-19th-c. decorative arts,
American furniture, Charleston-made
pieces.

Queen Charlotte Antiques
173 King St.
843-722-9121
18th- & 19th-c. English & French
furniture, mirrors, paintings, lighting,
garden items.

Roumillat's
2241 Savannah Hwy.
843-766-8899
American, English, & French furniture.

Terrace Oaks Antique Mall
2037 Maybank Hwy.
843-795-9689
20 dealers: wide variety.

Zinn Rug Gallery
76 Wentworth St.
843-577-0300
www.zinnruggallery.com
Oriental & tribal rugs.

Atlanta, Georgia

Antonio Raimo Galleries
700 Miami Circle
404-841-9880
Books, paintings, prints.

Architectural Accents
2711 Piedmont Rd.
404-266-8700
European & American architecturals,
lighting, hardware.

Arthur Oriental Rugs
25 Bennett St.
404-350-9560
Oriental, Persian, Chinese, Turkish, Art
Deco, tribal rugs, tapestries.

Beaman Antiques
22-J Bennett St.
404-352-9388
18th- & 19th-c. furniture.

Bobby Dodd Antiques
695 Miami Circle
404-231-0580
18th- & 19th-c. furnishings.

Dearing Antiques
709 Miami Circle
404-233-6333
Country English & French furniture, decorative items.

English Accent Acquisitions
22-H Bennett St.
404-351-9433
English furnishings, Staffordshire.

Franya Wade Antiques and Interiors
668 Miami Circle
404-352-2300
18th- & 19th-c. furniture & accessories.

Gables Antiques
711 Miami Circle
800-753-3342
Country French furnishings & accessories, porcelain, ironstone.

Gryphon Antiques
802 Miami Circle
404-262-9516
1920s, '30s, '40s furniture.

Interiors Market
55-A Bennett St.
404-352-0055
Multi-dealer shop.

J. Tribble Antiques
764 Miami Circle, Ste. 122
404-846-1156
19th- & 20th-c. fine & decorative arts.

Kilim Collection
22-A Bennett St.
404-351-1110
Tribal carpets.

Orientiques
700 Miami Circle
404-467-8100
Asian furniture & porcelains.

The Stalls
116 Bennett St.
404-352-4430
Multi-dealer shop.

Thomas Deans and Co.
Tula Art Center
75 Bennett St.
404-352-3778
British watercolors, drawings, paintings, 1750 to present.

William Word Antiques
707 Miami Circle
404-233-6890
18th- & 19th-c. English & Continental furnishings, accessories, porcelain.

Williams Antiques
699 Miami Circle
404-231-9818
18th- & 19th-c. English, French, & Continental furnishings.

Chamblee

Antique Factory
5505 Peachtree Rd.
770-455-7570
Art Deco, '50s Moderne, Mission oak & vintage steel furniture, primitives, folk art, retro, advertising.

Atlanta Antique Gallery
3550 Broad St., Ste. A
770-457-7444
www.atlantaantiquegallery.com
Decorative items (incl. Art Deco), toys, art pottery & glass, silver, jewelry, linens, porcelain.

Biggar Antiques
5576 Peachtree Rd.
770-451-2541
Furniture, signs, sports & fishing ephemera, pin-ups, postcards.

Blanton House
5449 Peachtree Rd.
770-458-1453
American formal & country furniture, accessories, collectibles.

Broad Street Antique Mall
3550 Broad St.
770-458-6316; 877-645-4728
American & English furniture & art. Black Americana, decorative, scientific, & sporting items.

Chamblee Antiques & Collectibles
3509 Broad St.
770-458-8336
www.chambleeantiques.com
Art, mirrors, glass, lace linens, christening gowns, silver, china, jewelry.

Eugenia's Antique Hardware
5370 Peachtree Rd.
770-458-1677; 800-337-1677
www.eugeniaantiquehardware.com
Door, window, & furniture hardware, bathroom accessories, lighting.

Great Gatsby's Antiques and Auctions
5070 Peachtree Industrial Blvd.
770-457-1903
www.greatgatsbys.com
18th- to 19th-c. American & European furniture & decorative accents.

Kishi's Rugs & Antiques
5496 Peachtree Rd.
770-331-1787
Decorative rugs, Aubussons, tapestries.

Moose Breath Trading Co.
5461 Peachtree Rd.
770-458-7210; 770-458-1572
www.moosebreathtrading.com
Funky decorative pieces.

My Sister's Closet
5350 Peachtree Rd.
770-458-8362
www.mysisterscloset online.com
Resale & consignment shop.

Rust 'n' Dust Antiques
5486-5492 Peachtree Rd.
770-458-1614
Furniture, radios, collectibles, architecturals, tin toys.

Townsend Fine Antique Clocks
3524 Broad St.
770-986-8981
www.townsendclocks.com
American & European mantel, wall & grandfather clocks.

The Treasure Mart
3641 Pierce Dr.
770-458-1200
www.thetmart.com
Consignment shop.

The Way We Were
5493 Peachtree Rd.
770-451-3372
European furniture & decorative accessories, blue & white porcelains.

Savannah, Georgia

Abercorn Antique Village
201 E. 37th St.
912-233-0064
www.abercornantiques.com
50 dealers: iron beds to French armoires, decorative accessories.

Alex Raskin Antiques
441 Bull St.
912-232-8205
Furniture, accessories, paintings, Oriental rugs.

Anna's Antiques
20 Bull St.
912-236-7112
www.federalantiques.com
18th- & 19th-c. English & American furniture, accessories.

Antiques Emporium of 38th Street
122 E. 38th St.
912-236-8444
Multi-dealer shop.

Clipper Trading
201 W. Broughton St.
912-238-3660
www.clippertrading.com
Asian furniture, accessories, artifacts.

Habersham Antiques & Collectibles Market
2502 Habersham St.
912-238-5908
60+ dealers: shabby chic, primitives, Art Deco, mid-20th-c. Moderne.

J. D. Weed & Co. Antiques
102 W. Victory Dr.
912-234-8540
www.jdweedco.com
18th- & 19th-c. American furniture & decorative accessories.

James Morton Antiques
222 E. Jones St.
912-233-0360
English & Continental furniture,
porcelain, decorative arts.

Jere's Antiques
9 N. Jefferson St.
912-236-2815
English & European furniture,
decorative items.

Maggies Antique Mall
2819 Bull St.
912-234-8833
Multi-dealer shop.

Pinch of the Past
109 W. Broughton St.
912-232-5563
Architectural salvage.

Savannah Galleries
30 E. Bryan St.
912-232-1234
American & English furniture,
porcelain, silver, decorative arts.

Southern Antiques and Interiors
28 Abercorn St.
912-236-5080
www.southernantiques.com
English, Continental, & American
furniture, Oriental rugs, accessories.

Southern Gents Antiques
208 Bay St.
912-232-9122
Glassware, pressed & cut glass,
Staffordshire, flow blue, estate jewelry,
decorative arts.

V & J Duncan
12 E. Taylor St.
912-232-0338
Maps, photographs, books, prints.

Northern Florida: The Treasure Coast

Jacksonville

Avondale Antique Mall
3651 Park St.
904-384-8787
Multi-dealer mall: furniture, art,
jewelry, glassware.

Classic Antiques
5262 Beach Blvd.
904-396-4611
Furniture, incl. Mission & Art Deco,
lamps, stained glass, art, mirrors,
whimsy, memorabilia.

Mussallem Oriental Rugs & Fine Arts
5801 Philips Hwy.
904-739-1551
Formal Continental furnishings
& decorative arts, fine art, sculpture,
art glass, Oriental rugs.

PrimRose Antique Mall
2730 Park St.
904-388-7673
American & English furnishings,
collectibles, glassware.

Tin City Antique Mall
11740 San Jose Blvd.
904-425-0000
Furniture, linens, glass, art pottery,
primitives, kitchen & garden items.

St. Augustine

A Step Back in Time
60 San Marco Ave.
904-810-5829
Victorian & early-20th-c. furniture,
decorative items, art pottery, majolica,
flow blue, glassware, jewelry, toys.

Barclay-Scott Antiques
4 Rohde Ave.
904-824-7044
www.barclayscott.com
18th- & 19th-c. American & European
furniture, linens, jewelry, ceramics.

Bouvier Antique Maps and Prints
11D & E Aviles St.
904-825-0920
www.bouviermaps.com
Floridiana, botanicals & prints,
Medieval manuscripts, 16th-c. maps.

Jena's Antiques & Art
56 San Marco Ave.
904-823-3456
Furniture, decorative items, art,
paintings of St. Augustine.

Old City Stained Glass & Antiques
130 King St.
904-819-0709
www.oldcity-stained-glass.com
Architecturals, incl. stained-glass.

Out There Antiques and More
6410 US-1 North Hwy.
904-826-4467
40+ dealers: furnishings, art,
collectibles, glassware, jewelry.

St. Augustine Antique Emporium
62 San Marco Ave.
904-829-0544
33+ dealers: stained glass, jewelry,
cameras, art pottery, kitchen items.

The Antique Market
325 State Rd. 16 (west of Rt. 1)
904-824-9394
English, European, & Indian
furniture, china, linen, architecturals,
decorative items.

The Antique Warehouse
6370 US-1 North Hwy.
904-826-1524
www.antqware.com
1850s to 1950s furniture, decorative
& architectural items, incl. Art Deco.

The Linen Room
Lightner Museum Antique Mall
25 Granada St.
904-824-9948
www.antique-mkt.com/linenroom
Victorian & Edwardian linens, lace,
English china, glassware, Persian
rugs, & nurseryware.

Uptown Antiques of St. Augustine
63 & 67 San Marco Ave.
904-824-9159
50 dealers: furniture, home decor,
collectibles, jewelry, glass, pottery,
kitchen items, toys.

West Palm Beach, Florida

Antiques, Antiques
3700 South Dixie Hwy., #7
561-655-9302
Shabby chic, incl. mirrored
furniture, screens.

Blackamoor Antiques
3611 South Dixie Hwy., Ste. A
561-721-1340
www.blackamoor.com
European & Asian furniture, porcelain,
accessories, art.

Brass Scale Antiques
3719-3723 South Dixie Hwy.
561-832-8410
18th- & 19th-c. decorative furnishings,
garden statuary, architecturals.

Cashmere Buffalo
3709 South Dixie Hwy.
561-659-5441
Mid-20th-c., Moderne, & Art Deco
home furnishings, linens, sterling,
hollowware, jewelry.

Chris Ellis Consignment Collection
3636 South Dixie Hwy.
561-659-1919
Chandeliers, furniture, lamps,
mirrors, accessories.

Christa's
3737 South Dixie Hwy.
561-655-4650
www.cssseashell.com
Furniture, incl. dining room pieces,
seashell designs.

D & G Antiques
3234 South Dixie Hwy.
561-835-0461
www.dandgantiques.com
Furniture, decorative & garden items.

Decorations of Palm Beach
3632 South Dixie Hwy.
561-655-9727
Decorative arts & furniture.

Dolce Antiques
3700 South Dixie Hwy., #8
561-832-4550
Mid-20th-c. design & lighting.

Emilie-Marie
3720 South Dixie Hwy.
561-832-6505
17th- to 19th-c. English & Continental
furniture & decorations, garden items.

Eric Dumont
3705 South Dixie Hwy.
561-820-9778
www.ericdumontinc.com
18th- to early-20th-c. French furniture,
decorative accessories.

Galere
3733 South Dixie Hwy.
561-832-3611
www.galere.net
20th-c. Moderne furniture, lighting,
glass, incl. name designers.

Greta S. Decorative Antiques
3803½ South Dixie Hwy.
561-655-1533
French & English decorative
furnishings: Victorian bamboo,
majolica, mirrors, sconces, toile.

Heath & Co.
3707 South Dixie Hwy.
561-833-0880
Lamps, sconces, chandeliers,
furniture, jewelry, bric-a-brac.

Incurable Collector
3717 South Dixie Hwy.
& 407 Roseland Dr.
561-820-0023
17th- to 19th-c. Continental furniture,
lighting, decorative & unique pieces.

J & M Antiques
3714 South Dixie Hwy.
561-655-0899
18th- & 19th-c. Continental furniture,
paintings, lamps, mirrors, accessories.

James & Jeffrey Antiques
3703-A South Dixie Hwy. (furnishings)
3619 South Dixie Hwy. (garden)
561-832-1760; 800-991-3499
www.jamesandjeffrey.com
18th- & 19th-c. French, Italian,
& English furniture, accessories.
Architectural & garden elements.

John Prinster Art Deco Moderne
3735 South Dixie Hwy.
561-835-1512
www.john-prinster.com
Lighting, furniture, sculpture,
ceramics, glass, 1920s to 1940s.

Michael Maclean Antiques
3803 South Dixie Hwy.
561-659-0971
17th- to 19th-c. European furniture,
lighting, art, screens, accessories.

N. P. Trent Antiques
3729 South Dixie Hwy.
561-832-0919
www.nptrentantiques.com
17th- to 19th-c. Continental & English
furniture, accessories.

Objects in the Loft
3611 South Dixie Hwy., Ste. C
561-659-0403
20th-c. furnishings & decorative
accessories, vintage rattan.

Pierre Anthony Antiques and Interiors
3638 & 3300 South Dixie Hwy.
561-832-0556; 561-832-1990
www.pierreanthony.com
17th- to 20th-c. furniture, lighting,
art, accessories.

Renata Metelska's Fine Arts
3300 South Dixie Hwy., #2
561-805-7792
19th- to 20th-c. American & European
fine & decorative arts.

Rococo Joe Designs
3700 Georgia Ave.
561-659-9350
Spanish, Portuguese, Moroccan,
American tiles, furniture.

The Elephant's Foot Antiques
3800 South Dixie Hwy.
561-832-0170
American, English, European,
& Asian furniture, lighting,
accessories, antiquities.

Wardall Antiques and Decorations
3709 South Dixie Hwy.
561-832-0428
American & European furniture
& decorative arts, lighting, mirrors.

Wilson Antiques
3716 South Dixie Hwy.
561-802-3881
Furnishings from Italy, France,
& Sweden, cast iron, faux bois.

William Snow Antiques
3617 South Dixie Hwy.
561-628-5223
www.williamsnowantiques.com
English & Continental furnishings,
books, decorative accessories.

New Orleans, Louisiana

Ann Koerner Antiques
4021 Magazine St.
504-899-2664
American & international antiques,
incl. Southern pieces.

Bush Antiques
2109 Magazine St.
504-581-3518
Decorative items & furnishings, incl.
French furniture. Religious artifacts,
lighting, ironwork.

Didier
3439 Magazine St.
504-899-7749
19th-c. American furniture
& decorative arts.

French Antique Shop
225 Royal St.
504-524-9861
18th- & 19th-c. French furnishings
& chandeliers.

Ida Manheim Antiques
409 Royal St.
888-627-5969
Continental furniture,
fine art, accessories.

Keil's Antiques
325 Royal St.
504-522-4552
Furniture, art, jewelry.

M. S. Rau Antiques
630 Royal St.
504-523-5660
American & European furniture,
objets d'art.

Macon Riddle, *Let's Go Antiquing*
504-899-3027
www.neworleansantiquing.com
Shopping service & guide.

Maison de Provence
3434 Magazine St.
504-895-2301
18th- & 19th-c. Continental & Swedish
furniture, decorative arts.

Mire Antiques
2050 Magazine St.
504-568-9944
European & Art Deco furniture,
mirrors, clocks, accessories.

Neal Auction Co.
4038 Magazine St.
504-899-5329

New Orleans Auction Galleries
801 Magazine St.
504-566-1849

Passages Antiques
3939 Magazine St.
504-899-3883
18th- & 19th-c. European furnishings,
objets d'art, paintings, porcelains,
mirrors, statuary.

Peter Patout Fine Art & Antiques
504-481-4790 (by appt.)
Classical American & Louisiana Creole
furniture & paintings.

Royal Antiques
307 Royal St.
504-524-7033
www.royalantiques.com
18th- & 19th-c. French & English
furniture, decorative arts.

Whisnant Galleries
222 Chartres St.
504-524-9766
17th-c. art, jewelry, arms, armor.

Williamson Designs
617 Chartres St.
504-568-9615
French & Continental furniture,
accessories, chandeliers, art.

Wirthmore Antiques
3727 Magazine St.
504-269-0660
French & Italian furniture, linens,
faience, mirrors, chandeliers, tile
flooring, art.

Louisiana's Cajun Country

Breaux Bridge

Au Vieux Paris
1040 rue Henri Penne
337-332-2852
www.auvieuxparisantiques.com
17th- to 19th-c. French furniture &
decorative accessories.

Breaux Bridge Antique Mall
130 E. Bridge St.
337-507-3608
12 dealers: Victorian to primitive to Art
Deco, furnishings, glassware, pottery,
kitchen items, jewelry, toys.

Janelle's Antiques
200 E. Bridge St.
337-332-5409
Buffets, secretaries, tables.

Le Napoleon Antiques & Collectibles
101 E. Bridge St.
337-332-5558
10 dealers: primitive to French
furniture, pottery, linens, kitchenware.

Louisiana Purchase Antique Market
507 S. Main St.
337-332-4348
Multi-dealer mall: varied furnishings.

Lucullus à Pont Breaux Antiques
107 N. Main St. (rue Principal)
337-332-2625
www.lucullusantiques.com
Culinary items: glassware, china,
silver, crystal, dining furniture.
Chandeliers, art.

Precious Past Antiques
125 S. Main St.
337-332-1414
Furniture, accessories, architecturals.

Lafayette

Jefferson Street Market
538 Jefferson St.
337-233-2589
65 dealers: primitive, rustic, Art Deco,
French, & Italian furnishings.

Melange Antiques
113 Heymann Blvd.
337-291-1139
Furniture, ironwork, olive jars.

The Renaissance Market
321 Oil Center Dr.
337-234-1116
Furniture & collectibles.

Washington

A French Farmhouse
104 N. Gardner St.
337-826-0506
French furnishings, French
& Belgian linens.

Maison de Vieux Temp
110 N. Main St.
337-826-3002
1845-1930s furniture, mostly
American, collectibles, decorative
items, incl. Depression glass.

Nanny Belle's Antiques
402 S. Main St.
337-826-8793
Multi dealer shop: 20th-c. & earlier
furnishings, china, glassware, linens.

Old School House Antique Mall
210 Church St.
337-826-3580
100+ dealers: furnishings & decorative
items, 18th c. on.

Plantation Antique Mall & Auction House
203 N. Main St.
337-826-3967
Furnishings & collectibles.

Nashville, Tennessee, & the Heart of Country Antiques Show

American Classical Antiques
2116 8th Ave., S.
615-297-5514
www.antiquesbygail.com
Early-19th-c. Neoclassical art,
furniture, decorative accessories.

Antique Mall of Green Hills
4108 Hillsboro Pike
615-383-9851
25 dealers: wide selection.

Artifacts
105 Heady Dr.
615-354-1267
Iron work, chandeliers.

Bellevue Antique Mall
160 Belle Forest Circle
615-646-5828
22 dealers: wide variety.

Berenice Denton's Cottage and Estate Sales
2209 Bandywood Dr., Ste. C
615-292-5765
www.berenicedenton.com
Furniture, collectibles, paintings,
prints, decorative accessories.

Carissa's Armoires & Antiques
1801 21st Ave., S.
615-292-6994
www.carissaarmoires.com
Armoires, tables, accessories.

Chancery Lane Antiques
5133 Harding Rd., C-1
615-354-0400
www.chancerylane.com
British ivory, tortoiseshell,
& horn objects, jewelry, silver by
Hester Bateman, Matthew Boulton.

Davishire Interiors
2106 21st Ave., S.
615-298-2670
www.davishire.com
Continental furnishings,
art, accessories.

Dealer's Choice Antiques & Auctions
2109 8th Ave., S.
615-383-7030
Furniture, glassware, collectibles.

Downtown Antique Mall
612 8th Ave., S.
615-256-6616
63 dealers: wide variety.

Eighth Avenue Antique Mall
2015 8th Ave., S.
615-279-9922
40 dealers.

Garden Park Antiques
7121 Cockrill Bend Blvd.
615-350-6655
www.gardenpark.com
Decorative architectural & garden
pieces, lighting, fire screens, mirrors.

Gilchrist and Gilchrist Antiques
2823 Bransford Ave.
615-385-2122
Furniture, collectibles.

Glenn's Antique & Auction Gallery
2919 Nolensville Pike
615-832-5277

Hermitage Home Antique
4805 Old Hickory Blvd.
615-627-7972
American & Chinese furniture,
accent pieces.

Jalan-Jalan
2503 Winford Ave.
615-780-2600
www.jalanjalanantiques.com
Late-19th to early-20th-c. teak
furniture, architecturals.

Jelly Cupboard Antiques
478 Allied Dr., Ste. 105
615-305-0853
Country furniture, folk art.

Karmal-Skillington
2019 8th Ave., S.
615-460-7197
www.karmal-skillington.com
Armoires, smoking & dining chairs, chandeliers, harvest tables.

Pembroke Antiques
6610 Hwy. 100
615-353-0889
English & informal furnishings.

Pia's Antique Gallery
1800 8th Ave., S.
615-256-3890
18th- & 19th-c. European furniture, decorative items, silver, lamps.

Polk Place Antiques
6614 Hwy. 100
615-353-1324
American Federal period furniture.

Pre to Post Modern
2110 8th Ave., S.
615-292-1958
Vintage furnishings.

Preservation Station Architecturals
2309 Franklin Pike
615-292-3595
Mantels, doors, stained glass, lighting.

Quarter Horse Antiques
3110 Belmont Blvd.
615-383-5994
Porcelain, glass, silver.

Richters
4003 Hillsboro Rd.
615-385-0140
Furniture, decorative arts, jewelry, incl. signed Edwardian period jewelry.

Tennessee Antique Mall
654 Wedgewood Ave.
615-259-4077
Variety of furnishings, collectibles.

Williams American Art Galleries
4119 Hillsboro Rd.
615-297-2547
www.williamsamericanart.com
American paintings, 1840-1950; '30s-'50s Mexican Taxco sterling; jewelry; American folk art; Navajo textiles.

The World's Longest Yard Sale: from Kentucky to Alabama

ALABAMA

Birmingham

Architectural Heritage
2807 2nd Ave., S.
205-322-3538
www.architecturalheritage.com
Stone, mantels, doors, statuary, lighting.

Christopher House
2330 7th Ave., S.
205-870-7106
www.christopherhouseantiques.com
European & American furnishings.

Europa Antiques
2805 2nd Ave., S.
205-254-0122
European furnishings.

Hanna Antiques
2424 7th Ave., S.
205-323-6036
120 dealers: variety of items.

Jackson Galleries
2227 1st Ave., S.
205-714-9933
www.jacksonantiquegalleries.com
English & Continental furniture, decorative arts.

Mary Helen McCoy Fine Antiques
2732 Cahaba Rd.
205-870-4777
17th- to 19th-c. French furniture & decorative arts.

Très Provence
2616 3rd Ave., S.
205-251-8989
18th- to 20th-c. European furniture, accessories, garden items.

KENTUCKY

Lexington

Ann Greely Interiors and Antiques
497 E. Main St.
859-367-0200
Furniture, decorative items, paintings.

Antique Lamplight Gallery at Antiquities II
636 W. Main St.
859-231-1871
www.antiquelamplight.com
Fine furniture, lighting, accessories.

Belle Maison
523 W. Short St.
859-252-9030
French furniture, accessories, garden planters, urns, arbors, statuary.

Bluegrass Antique Market
801 Winchester Rd.
859-258-2105
Late-19th-c. to 1950s furniture & accessories.

Cow Girl Attic
135 Delaware Ave.
859-225-3876
Architectural artifacts, furniture, garden items.

Greentree Antiques
521 W. Short St.
859-455-9660
www.greentreeantiques.com
18th- & early-19th-c. fine furniture, decorative items.

Heritage Antiques
380 E. Main St.
859-253-1035
18th-, 19th-, & 20th-c. furnishings.

Lafayette Galleries
Lexington Center
859-253-1633
17th- to 19th-c. American & English silver, plates, crystal, prints.

Lexington Antique Gallery
637 E. Main
859-231-8197
22 dealers: 18th- to 19th-c. furniture, silver, linens, other items.

Louisville

Bittners
731 E. Main St.
502-584-6349
Furniture, rugs, paintings.

Derby City Antique Mall
3819 Bardstown Rd.
502-459-5151
140 dealers.

Elaine Claire
712 E. Market St.
& 211 Clover Lane
502-584-0843
French furniture, paintings, lighting, decorative accessories.

European Antique Market
414 Baxter Ave.
502-585-3111
www.euroantiquemarket.com
17th- to 20th-c. formal & country French & European furniture, architecturals, lighting, art.

Isaacs & Isaacs Antiques
3937 Chenoweth Sq.
502-897-2232
www.isaacsantiques.com
18th-c. English furniture.

Joe Ley Antiques
615 E. Market St.
502-583-4014
www.joeley.com
Furnishings, carousel horses, garden items.

Louisville Antique Mall
900 Goss Ave.
502-635-2852
www.louisvilleantiquemall.com
300 dealers: 18th- to 20th-c. furniture,
decorative items, collectibles.

Oakridge Antiques
11707 Main St.
502-245-0004
English china, clocks, furniture.

Red Barn Mall
12125 Old Shelbyville Rd.
502-245-8330
60 dealers.

Scott F. Nussbaum Antiques
2036 Frankfort Ave.
502-894-9292
Period furniture, porcelain, paintings,
silver, jewelry, glassware, crystal.

Tin Horse Antiques
1040 Bardstown Rd.
502-584-1925
Furniture, glassware,
paintings, collectibles.

Trace Mayer Antiques
3700 Lexington Rd.
& 3937 Chenoweth Sq.
502-899-5335; 502-893-8444
English, Continental, & American
furniture, decorative items.

TENNESSEE

Chattanooga

Architectural Exchange
1300 McCallie Ave.
423-697-1243
Doors, windows, statues, columns,
stained glass.

Church's Antiques & Estate Pieces
1819 Taft Hwy.
423-886-9636
Furniture, glass, china, silver.

Dacus Antiques and Estate Sales
2506 E. 29th St.
423-622-1715
1930s mahogany furniture.

East Town Antique Mall
6503 Slater Rd.
423-899-5498
70 dealers: furnishings, silver, pottery,
collectibles, etc.

L. P. Cline Antiques
508 Broad St.
423-265-4786
English & French furniture.

The Antique Market
1101 Hixson Pike, Ste. E
423-267-0505
French furniture.

The Chattanooga Auction House
1206 Market St.
423-266-6603

The Galleries at Southside
1404 Cowart St.
423-267-8101
50 dealers.

PART FOUR: MIDWEST

Cincinnati, Ohio

Brass Armadillo Antique Mall
10132 Business Center Dr.
513-874-7855
www.brassarmadillo.com
500 dealers: from silver, furniture,
ceramics, to toys.

Brass Eagle Antiques
6079 Montgomery Rd.
513-631-6135
Furniture, jewelry, pottery, glassware,
Oriental rugs, china.

Chester Dowers Auctions
8655 Livingston Rd.
513-245-9111

Cheviot Trading Co.
3621 Harrison Ave.
513-661-3633
Jewelry, watches, collectibles,
1870-1940s.

Covered Bridge Antique Mall
7508 Hamilton Ave.
513-521-5739
30 dealers: variety of items from
around the world.

English Traditions
2716 Erie Ave.
513-321-4760
www.englishtraditions.com
English, Irish, & French furniture,
1800-1900.

Federation Antiques
2124 Madison Rd.
513-321-2671
www.federationantiques.com
American, English, & Continental
furniture, porcelain, lighting, fine art.

French Country Road
1995 Madison Rd.
513-561-2750 (by appt.)
19th-c. French country furnishings.

French Rendez-Vous
9410 Montgomery Rd.
513-792-0252
www.frenchrendezvous.com
French country items, from lamps
to linens.

Grand Antique Mall
9701 Reading Rd.
513-554-1919
160 dealers: general selection,
cast iron, architecturals.

Greg's Antiques
1404 Main St.
513-241-5487
www.gregsantiques.com
Victorian furniture, architecturals,
landscape accoutrements.

Grosvenor Brant Antiques
3407 Monteith Ave.
513-871-1333
English & Continental furniture,
porcelains, Chinese export, prints,
early brass, copper, silver.

Main Auction Galleries
137 W. 4th St.
513-621-1280
www.mainauctiongalleries.com

Patricia Weiner Gallery
9393 Montgomery Rd.
513-791-7717
19th- & early-20th-c. American
& European paintings, incl. artists of
Cincinnati's Golden Age.

Reyne Gallery
17 E. 8th St., 3rd fl.
513-651-4198
www.reyne.co
20th-c. decorative arts: Art Nouveau
lamps, glass, pottery, bronze,
furniture, paintings.

Wooden Nickel Antiques
1400 Central Pkwy.
513-241-2985
www.woodennickelantiques.net
Victorian & Continental furniture,
architectural & garden items.

Other

Duck Creek Antique Mall
3715 Madison Rd.
Oakley
513-321-0900
www.duckcreekantiquemall.com
170 dealers: furniture, collectibles, stoneware, etc.

Alton, Illinois, & St. Charles, Missouri

ILLINOIS

Alton

Alton Antique Center
401 E. Broadway
618-463-0888
6 dealers: 19th-c. French provincial furniture, glassware, collectibles.

Alton Landing Antiques
110 Alton St.
618-462-0443
19th-c. American furniture.

Christian Hill Antiques
219 William St.
618-463-0517
1880s-1940s cottage items.

Country Meadows
401 E. Broadway
618-465-1965
Country primitives, incl. bowls, crocks.

George St. Antique Mall
108 George St.
618-463-1693
35 dealers: from glassware to toys & collectibles.

MJ's Antiques
356 E. Broadway
618-463-4724
American & European furniture, pottery, collectibles.

Prairie Peddler Antiques
200 State St.
618-465-6114
18th- & early-19th-c. American formal & country furniture, accessories: rugs, ceramics, folk art, lighting, paintings.

Red Barn Antiques
3616 Edwardsville Rd. (Rt. 143)
618-659-0145
1860-1920 rustic country furniture, collectibles.

Riverbend Treasures
205 E. Broadway
618-465-5400
18th- & 19th-c. furniture, glassware, collectibles.

Rubenstein's Antiques
728 E. Broadway
618-462-5243
Bathtubs, copper & brassware, collectibles.

Shelton & Company Antiques
319 E. Broadway
618-462-7010
Furniture, primitives, pottery, farm collectibles, trunks & luggage, decorative items, jewelry, textiles.

Upstairs Antiques Mall
323 E. Broadway
618-465-1200
12 dealers: furniture, clocks, unusual items, incl. dinosaur teeth, arrowheads.

Weathered Treasures Mall
5707 Godfrey Rd.
618-466-5170
12 dealers: furniture, glassware, rugs, paintings, silver, toys.

Wilson's Antiques
217 E. Broadway
618-465-3798
Mostly American furniture, 1800-1950.

Grafton

Fleaflicker's Collectibles
128 E. Main St.
618-786-2415
Pottery, glass, collectibles, 1900 on.

Harrison's
224 E. Main St.
618-786-3370
Glassware, pottery, art, collectibles, furniture.

MISSOURI

St. Charles

Airedale Antiques
917 S. Main St.
636-940-9553
Architecturals, prints, glass, furniture, collectibles.

Blossom
806 N. 2nd St.
636-949-3956
Shabby chic & cottage-style furnishings, iron beds, cupboards, pottery, textiles.

French Connection Antiques & Interiors
826 N. 2nd St.
636-947-7044
American furniture (1850-1930), incl. dining room sets, lighting.

Hobbit's Hole Antiques
341 N. Main St.
636-947-6227
Glassware, collectibles, American furniture, 1850-1900.

Maison Rive
603 S. Main St.
636-940-0266
Lighting, pottery, furniture from the U.S. & France.

Mattie's Heritage Antiques
1417 N. 2nd St.
636-723-1665
1890s to 1930s American & European furniture, incl. walnut & painted pieces, silver, china, glass.

Old Mill House Antiques & More
8910 N. 2nd St.
636-723-8333
Furniture, glassware, collectibles, paintings, from 1800 on.

Winnebago County, Illinois, & Rock County, Wisconsin

ILLINOIS

Love's Park

Chris' Antiques & Collectables
5152 Harlem Rd.
815-654-1610
Furniture, rustic, primitives, smalls.

Pleasant Valley Antiques
930 Windsor Rd.
815-877-7899
Furniture & accessories, incl. primitives & smalls.

Trinkets & Treasures
8105 Forest Hills Rd.
815-877-6608
Furniture, decorative items, glassware, dishes.

Rockford

Action Auctioneering
1339 S. Meridian Rd.
815-965-0669
Monthly outdoor auctions, usually on 3rd Sat.

Book Stall of Rockford
1032 Crosby St.
815-963-1671
First editions, hard-to-find, & antiquarian books.

Eagle's Nest Antiques
7080 Old River Rd.
815-633-8410
Country furniture, stoneware, folk art, Americana.

East State St. Antique Malls I & II
5411 & 5301 E. State St.
815-229-4004; 815-226-1566
320 dealers: furnishings, architecturals, children's prints, maps, art & antique reference books.

Oddly Enough Curio Shoppe
1030 Auburn St.
815-963-1172
Glassware, dishes, furniture, etc.

Sandy Hollow Flea Market
3913 Sandy Hollow Rd.
815-397-6683
60 vendors.

Three Angels Emporium
2409 Charles St.
815-484-9791
Consignment & estate sale shop.

West End Auction House
4907 W. State St. (Rt. 20)
815-962-3581
Weekly auctions.

Rockton

Country Cottage
122 S. Prairie St.
815-624-8393
www.cyndyscountrycottage.com
Rustic & country furniture,
accessories, shabby chic, vintage,
retro, seasonal items.

Main Street Antique Mall
203 W. Main St.
815-624-7514
30 dealers: furniture, decorative
items, collectibles.

South Beloit

Anamosa Arts & Antiques
1020 Gardner St. (Hwy. 75)
815-389-1679
Large mall with furniture, decorative
items, lamps, architecturals, sinks.

Fire Station Antique Mall
440 Gardner St. (Hwy. 75)
815-389-8111
Furniture, lamps, china, etc.

Fire Station Antique Mall #2
417 Eastern Ave.
815-389-8111
Old & new resale; stuff in the rough.

Roscoe Antique Mall of South Beloit
1019 Gardner St.
815-389-8800
Furniture & decorative items.

Other

Antiques at Hillwood Farms
Pecatonica
815-239-2421 (by appt.)
Early American & English furniture
& decorative arts.

Bargain Barn
11951 Main St. (Hwy. 251)
Roscoe
815-623-3364
Furniture, home decor items,
collectibles. Weekend flea market.

WISCONSIN

Janesville

A Square Peg
1159 Summerhill Dr.
608-755-1930
Furnishings, glassware, collectibles.

General Antiques Store
8301 East US Hwy. 14
608-756-1812
Early-19th-c. furniture, art glass,
accessories.

Indian Arts and Artifacts
20 N. Main St.
608-757-2255
Native American art, from 1200 AD
to the present.

Spaulding House
3941 Milton Ave.
608-756-5422
18th- & 19th-c. collectibles,
fine art, furnishings.

Treasure Seekers
644 College St.
608-868-4939
Furniture & collectibles, 1800-1900.

Other

Gaslight Antiques
626 Millar Rd.
Beloit
608-362-1110
Furniture, lamps, dishes, glassware,
collectibles, early 1900s.

Powell's Antique Shop
14 W. Geneva
Elkorn
262-723-2952
Early-19th-c. lighting & glassware.

Springfield, Waynesville, & Lebanon, Ohio

Lebanon

Ambassador Antiques
40 E. Mulberry St.
Lebanon
513-934-5677
American & European furniture,
decorative arts.

Hardy's Interiors and Antiques
208½ Wright Ave.
513-932-2951
American & English furnishings,
Victorian, Arts & Crafts, art,
lamps, architecturals.

Shoe Factory Antique Mall
120 E. South St.
513-932-8300
40 dealers: knickknacks to furniture.

William & Mary Antiques
23 S. Broadway
513-932-4030
Pre-1850 American cherry
& walnut cupboards.

Springfield

AAA I-70 Antique Mall
4700 S. Charleston Pike
937-324-8448
www.aaa-i-70-antique-mall.com
200+ dealers: furnishings &
collectibles.

American Antiquities Gallery
126 E. High St.
937-322-6281
Furnishings, architecturals, etc.

Berner's Auction Gallery
4785 E. National Rd.
937-325-9925

Heart of Ohio Antique Center
4785 E. National Rd.
937-324-2188
www.heartofohioantiques.com
650+ dealers: furnishings
& collectibles.

Springfield Antique Centre
1735 Titus Rd.
937-322-8868
Furnishings from all over the U.S.

Waynesville

American Pie Antiques
43 S. Main St.
513-897-5195
American country furniture
(with original paint), 1850-1920.

Brass Lantern Antiques
100 S. Main St.
513-897-9686
English Victorian furniture
(mostly Eastlake).

Lilly's Corner Shoppes
105 S. Main St.
513-897-0388
Early American furniture.

Little Red Shed Antiques
85 S. Main St.
513-897-6326
www.littleredshedantiques.biz
Furniture, glass, china, books,
primitives, silver, 1800s-1960.

My Wife's Antiques
77 S. Main St.
513-897-7455
English & American furniture,
1750-1890.

Olde Glory Antiques
185 High St.
513-897-4718
American furniture, 1700-1870.

Spencer's Antiques & Imports
274 S. Main St.
513-897-7775
www.spencersantiques.com
American oak furniture, 1890-1920.

Waynesville Antique Mall
69 S. Main St.
513-897-6937
60 dealers: wide variety.

Other

Honeycreek Galleries
131 S. Main St.
New Carlisle
937-845-3443
Costume jewelry, flow blue china,
kitchenware, furniture, art glass.

Johnson's Lamp Shop & Antiques
8518 E. National Rd.
South Vienna
937-568-4551
Old & traditional lamps, chandeliers.

South Charleston Antique Mall
134 S. Chillicothe
South Charleston
937-462-8084
15 dealers: china, coins, stamps,
glassware, furniture.

Weber's Antiques Americana
Rt. 343 & Clay St.
Clifton
937-767-8581
10 dealers: Victorian to early-20th-c.
furniture, household & decorative
items, collectibles.

Indiana's Antique Alley

Cambridge City

Cows in the Creek Antiques
119 W. Main St.
765-478-6666
Country primitives & cottage elegance.

Hole in the Wall Antiques
115 W. Main St.
765-478-6363
English, European, American furniture,
glassware, collectibles.

Vinton House Antiques
20 W. Main St.
765-478-9371
Furniture, primitives, accessories.

Centerville

Sunstar Antiques
134 W. Main St.
765-977-2487
Glass, porcelain, 1950s kitchenware.

Webb's Antique Mall
200 W. Union St.
765-855-5551
500+ dealers: from marbles to dining
room sets.

Wheeler's Antiques
106 W. Main St.
765-855-3400
Furniture & Americana, 1830-1950.

Dublin

Old Storefront Antiques
1827 Main St.
765-478-4809
Drugstore collectibles. Country
& primitive furniture, other items,
1880–1950.

The Old Trunk
58 Johnson St.
765-478-4168
Primitives, glassware, garden items.

Indianapolis

Colby Antiques
1111 E. 61st St.
317-253-2148
18th- & 19th-c. English
& Continental furniture.

Red Barn Antique and Flea Market
325 E. 106th St.
317-846-8928
Small furniture, primitives, country
items, tools, books, collectibles.

Southport Antique Mall
2028 E. Southport Rd.
317-786-8246
Furniture, decorative accessories,
china, silver, glassware, textiles.

Surroundings
1111 E. 61st St.
317-254-8883
18th-, 19th-, & 20th-c. American
& European furnishings, interior
& garden accessories.

Knightstown

**Antiques on Carey Knightstown
Antique Mall**
136 W. Carey St.
765-345-5665
80 dealers: furniture, yellowware,
stoneware, toys.

Bittersweet Antiques
121 E. Main St.
765-345-7480
20 dealers: wide selection.

Glass Cupboard Antique Mall
115 E. Main St.
765-345-7572
25 dealers: furnishings, glassware,
primitives, collectibles.

Portland

Farmstead Antiques
4327 South US 27
260-726-4930
Wide variety of furnishings,
collectibles, etc.

Jay Garment Antique Mall
500 S. Meridian St.
260-726-8891
100 dealers: wide range of items.

Other

Glass House Antiques
135 E. 5th St.
Connorsville
765-825-3571
4 dealers: furniture, glass, pottery,
ceramics.

Old National Trail Dealer Warehouse
113 W. Washington St.
Dunreith
765-345-7247
Specializing in early American
furniture & collectibles.

West Des Moines,
Valley Junction,
& Walnut, Iowa

Des Moines

Bartlett's Antiques & Collectibles
820 35th St., Ste. A
515-255-1362
Primitive American furniture,
collectibles, 1850-1900.

Brass Armadillo
701 NE 50th Ave.
515-282-0082; 800-775-2140
www.brassarmadillo.com
450 dealers: 19th- & 20th-c. furniture,
decorative accessories.

Majestic Lion
5048 2nd Ave.
515-282-5466
www.majesticlion.com
150 dealers: Victorian furniture.

Que Sera
5907 Grand Ave.
515-279-2750
French & American furniture,
housewares, collectibles, 1800-1930.

**West Des Moines/
Valley Junction**

A Okay Antiques
124 5th St.
515-255-2525; 800-968-4993
From Victorian to mid-c. Moderne.

Century Shop
333 5th St.
515-274-1419
Vintage & collectible items, folk art,
furniture, 1850-1950.

Elinor's Woods 'n Wares
102 5th St.
515-274-1234
Early country antiques (original paint),
toys, textiles, stoneware.

Fifth Street Finds
115 5th St.
515-279-3716
10 dealers: lighting, home & garden
decor, shabby chic & French country,
architecturals, primitives.

Porch Light Antiques
317 5th St.
515-255-5900
www.porch-light-too.net
Vintage farm & cottage
furniture, accessories.

Walnut

Antique Furniture Emporium
226 Antique City Dr.
712-784-3839
Late-19th- to early-20th-c. furniture.

Barn Mall
615 Highland
712-784-3814
34 dealers: wide selection.

Bear Trap Antiques
608 Highland
712-784-3779
19th-c. American furniture, glassware,
plates, collectibles, coins.

CJ's Antiques
218 Antique City Dr.
712-784-3799
Furniture, glassware, collectibles,
1850-1950.

Corn Country Antiques
212 Pearl St.
712-784-3992
19th-c. silverware, clocks,
glassware, furniture.

Farm Fresh Antiques
200 Pearl St.
712-784-2275
Furniture & accessories.

Granary Mall
603 Pearl St.
712-784-3331
100 dealers: American furniture,
art, glass, stoneware, architecturals,
Civil War artifacts.

Madison &
the Wisconsin Dells

Lake Delton

Antique Mall of Wisconsin Dells II
(⅛ mi. off Hwy. I 90/94, next to
Wisconsin Opry)
608-356-7600
200 dealers: varied international items.

Wisconsin Opry Flea Market
Hwy. 12 (¼ mi. south of Hwy. I 90/94,
Exit 92)
608-254-7951
May to Aug.: variety of items.

Madison

Antiques Mall of Madison
4748 Cottage Grove Rd.
608-222-2049
130 dealers: variety of furnishings &
collectibles.

Atomic Interiors
1021 S. Park St.
608-251-5255
1950s & vintage goods.

Janet's Antiques & Art
3800 University Ave.
608-238-3300
18th- & 19th-c. furniture & decorative
items, Mission pieces, art glass, china.

Monroe St. Antiques
2606 Monroe St.
608-231-0998
Furniture, lamps, books, sterling,
1800-1950.

Northgate Antique Mall
1293 N. Sherman Ave.
608-246-8402
40 dealers: wide variety, incl. shabby
chic & glassware.

Randall Hopkins Art & Antiques
807 E. Johnson St.
608-255-6222
18th- & early-19th-c. English &
American furniture & decorative arts,
19th-c. British paintings.

Westside Antiques Mall
6714 Odana
608-836-8881
30 dealers: wide range of items.

Mt. Horeb

First St. Antiques
111 S. First St.
608-437-6767
15 dealers: butternut cupboards to
1950s kitchenware.

Hoff Mall Antique Center
101 E. Main St.
608-437-4580
25 dealers: furniture, glass, pottery,
lamps, silver, collectibles, toys.

Isaac's Antiques
132 E. Main St.
608-437-6151
50 dealers: wide variety.

Reedsburg

Antique Mall of Reedsburg
121 S. Webb
608-524-0000
60 dealers: wide range of items.

Main St. Antiques
190 E. Main St.
608-768-3300
American furniture, collectibles,
pottery, books, Asian artifacts.

The Antique Shop
195 Main (Hwy. 23/33, lower level)
608-524-4141
Early-20th-c. furniture & collectibles.

Wisconsin Dells

Antique Mall of Wisconsin Dells I
720-730 Oak St.
608-254-2422; 608-254-7465
40 dealers: wide variety.

Days Gone By® Antique Mall
729-731 Oak St.
608-254-6788
65+ dealers: glassware & collectibles,
incl. toys & Red Wing pottery.

Oak St. Antique Mall
725 Oak St.
608-254-4200
50 dealers: collectibles, glassware,
furniture.

Marshall & Michigan's
Antique Alley

Adrian

Birdsall Depot
4106 North Adrian Hwy.
517-265-7107
Primitives & collectibles.

Marsh's Antique Mall
138 S. Winter St.
517-263-8826
30+ dealers: oak & Victorian furniture,
decorative items, collectibles.

Allen

A Horse of Course
106 Prentiss St. (Corner, Hwy. US-12)
517-869-2527; 517-524-6402
Primitives, trunks.

Allen Antique Mall
9011 W. Chicago Rd. (Hwy. US-12)
517-869-2788
242 dealers: furniture, Native American
artifacts, sports memorabilia, etc.

Ann Arbor

Ann Arbor Antiques Market
5055 Ann Arbor-Saline Rd.
www.annarborantiquesmarket.com
Monthly shows: early Americana
to Art Deco. 3rd Sun., May-Aug.
& Oct.; 3rd weekend, Apr. & Sept.;
1st Sun., Nov.

Hitching Post Antique Mall
1322 E. Monroe Rd. (Hwy. M-50)
517-423-8277
Furniture, decorative items, books on
antiques. Flea markets: Memorial Day,
July 4th, Labor Day.

Blissfield

Blissfield Antique Mall
at Hwys. 101 & 103, US-223
517-486-2236
55+ dealers: home furnishings,
collectibles.

Green's Gallery of Antiques
115 S. Lane St.
517-486-3080
Furniture & decorative items (incl.
Mission & Victorian), primitives,
architecturals.

Clinton

Oak City Antiques
1101 Hwy. US-12
517-456-4444
Furnishings,collectibles, etc.

The Turn-of-the-Century Lighting Co.
116 W. Michigan Ave.
517-456-6019
Victorian gas & electric lighting.

Irish Hills

Irish Hills Antiques
10600 Hwy. US-12 (1 mi. east of M-50)
517-467-4646
Furniture, decorative items, wood- &
coal-burning parlor & kitchen stoves.

Muggsies Antiques and Collectibles
13982 W. Hwy. US-12
517-592-2659; 517-467-4725
Furniture & decorative items, incl.
children's items.

The Enchanted Schoolhouse
14012 Hwy. US-12 (2 mi. west of M-50;
5 mi. east of US-127)
517-592-4365
Furniture, decorative items, folk art,
primitives, artist originals.

Marshall

Amazing Grace Antiques
106 W. Michigan Ave.
269-781-3595
19th-c. American furniture, glassware,
collectibles.

Cronin Antique Center
101 W. Michigan Ave.
269-789-0077
22 dealers: advertising items,
furniture, glassware.

**Keystone Architectural and General
Antiques**
110 E. Michigan Ave.
269-789-1355
Statues, stained glass,
fixtures, gargoyles.

Marshall Town and Country Antiques
151 W. Michigan Ave.
269-781-4642
30 dealers: wide variety.

Shops at the Marshall House
100 Exchange St.
269-781-9450
Quilts & some antiques.

Tecumseh

Hitching Post Antique Mall
1322 E. Monroe Rd. (Hwy. M-50)
517-423-8277
20 dealers: furniture, accessories,
books on antiques.

Tecumseh Antique Mall 2
112 E. Chicago Blvd. (Hwy. M-50)
& 1111 W. Chicago Blvd.
517-432-6441; 517-423-6082
130+ dealers in two locations.

Other

Antique Stove Shop
415 Fleming Rd.
Tekonsha
517-278-2214
Kitchen ranges, parlor stoves.

Manchester Antique Mall
116 E. Main St.
Manchester
734-428-9357
25 dealers: furniture, primitives, rugs,
silver, porcelain, glass, collectibles.

Pinetree Centre Antique Mall
129 N. Main (Hwy. M-50)
Brooklyn
517-592-3808
60 dealers: furniture, accessories.

PART FIVE: WEST

Texas Hill Country

Boerne

Boerne Downtown Emporium
179 S. Main St.
830-249-3390
16th- to 18th-c. English furniture
& china.

Burlap Horse Antiques
210 S. Main St.
830-249-0204
Continental European (esp. Spanish
& French) furniture.

Good & Co.
248 S. Main St.
830-249-6101
French & American farm
chairs, tables.

Henfeathers
212 E. Main St.
830-990-8998
Primitive furnishings, china.

Hill Country Antiques
112 S. Main St.
830-816-2761
6 dealers: Victorian & rustic furniture,
pottery, paintings, old photographs.

Comfort

Antiques on High
641 High St.
830-995-3662
18th- to 19th-c. American furniture,
stained glass, church pews, art, rugs.

Antiquities Etc.
702 High St.
830-995-4190
Primitives & folk art, furniture, gifts.

Comfort Antique Mall
734 High St.
830-995-4678
30+ dealers: 18th- to 20th-c. furniture,
lamps, decorative objects, fine art.

Comfort Common
717 High St.
830-995-3030
Primitive furniture, stoneware.

Cypress Creek Antiques
702 High St., Ste. A
830-995-3570
American country furniture, 1860-1950.

Highbrow & Hicks
22 Hwy. 87
830-995-4192
5 dealers: early American & Victorian
furniture, decorative objects.

Wilson Clements Antiques & Gifts
405 7th St.
830-995-5039
Early 1900s Mexican furnishings & art.

Fredericksburg

Adze Country Mill
208 N. Washington St.
830-997-4278
French & English furniture, 1850-1950.

Antique Mall of Fredericksburg
1102 E. Main St.
830-997-6329
25 dealers: furniture & collectibles
from around the world.

Der Alte Fritz Antiques
409 E. Main St.
830-997-8249
3 dealers: 17th- to 18th-c. German
furniture & rugs.

Jackson's Uptown Market
330 W. Main St.
830-997-0073
18th- to 20th-c. American
& European furniture.

Lone Star Antique Mall
905 E. Main St.
830-997-6767
30+ dealers: 17th- to 20th-c.
furnishings, collectibles.

Showcase Antiques
119 E. Main St.
830-997-5505
American brilliant cut glass, Victorian
art, silver, 1850-1950.

New Braunfels

Cactus Jack's Antiques Etc.
1706 Hunter Rd.
830-620-9602
18th- & 19th-c. American furniture
& decorative items.

Furniture & Antique Consignment
236 W. San Antonio St.
830-609-0004
18th- to 20th-c. American & Victorian
furniture, paintings, decorative objects.

Hampe House
1640 Hunter Rd.
830-620-1325
1840-1920s American furniture,
decorative accessories.

Hillcrest Antique Gallery
7570 Hwy. 35 North, #70
830-620-5056
30 dealers: glass, jewelry, lamps,
mirrors, furniture.

Palace Heights Antiques Mall
1175 Hwy. 81 East
830-625-0612
10 dealers: collectibles & furniture.

Other

Fredericksburg Trade Days
Hwy. 290 (east of Fredericksburg)
Stonewall
830-990-4900
www.fredericksburgtradedays.com
Weekends, mid-month, June through
Dec. Primitives, shabby chic,
farm tools, ranch furnishings.

East Texas

Forney

Antiques East I & II
10486 & 10470 West Hwy. 80
972-564-1303; 972-564-1331
75 dealers: furniture, glassware,
collectibles, 18th-c. to present.

De Ridder Antiques
10462 West Hwy. 80
972-564-4468; 972-552-3130
www.deridderantiques.com
European country pine furniture,
statues, collectibles, decorative objects.

Little Red's Antiques
10274 West Hwy. 80
972-564-2200
English, Austrian, & French furniture,
19th-c. glassware.

Philbeck's Antiques
119 East Hwy. 80
972-564-9842
European pine furnishings, Texas
pine reproductions.

Gladewater

Antiques II
112 S. Main St.
903-845-6493
30 dealers: wide range of furnishings.

Bygone Tymes Mall
300 Phillips Dr.
903-845-2655
Mid-19th- to mid-20th-c.
American furniture.

Coach House Antiques
121 S. Main St.
903-845-5503
15 dealers: wide range of furnishings
& collectibles.

Gladewater Antique Mall
100 E. Commerce Ave.
903-845-4440
15 dealers: wide variety of items.

Now & Then Antique Mall
109 W. Commerce Ave.
903-845-5765
25 dealers: furnishings & collectibles.

Red Rooster Antiques
211 N. Main St.
903-844-9240
American furniture, 1800-1900.

St. Clair Antique Emporium
104 W. Pacific Ave.
903-845-4079
25 dealers: range of furnishings,
incl. glassware & collectibles.

Tyler

Antiques and Uniques
433 S. Vine Ave.
903-593-2779
Custom lamps & shades made
from antiques.

Antiques on Broadway
320 S. Broadway Ave.
903-531-2399
58 dealers: 18th- to 19th-c.
shabby chic, country, English &
French furnishings.

ETEX Auctioneers
314 W. Rusk St.
903-592-7022

French Peas
4525 Old Bullard Rd.
903-939-3907
American pottery & dishes, early
1900s to present.

John Sauls Antiques
310 W. Rusk St.
903-593-4668
Early Texas furnishings, collectibles,
lamps, quilts. Asian ceramics.

Old City Antique Mall
302 E. Locust St.
903-592-7123
20 dealers: variety, furniture to furs.

The London Shop
100 W. 8th St.
903-592-4541
17th- to 18th-c. English furniture.

Other

Canton First Monday Trade Days
Hwy. 64 East
Canton
903-567-6556

Denver & Colorado Springs, Colorado

Colorado Springs

Adobe Walls Antique Mall
2808 W. Colorado Ave.
719-635-3394
Vintage Old West items. Native American baskets, pottery, beadwork, textiles, art.

Carrs Antique Gallery
21 N. Nevada
719-633-6070
www.carrsantiquegallery.com
50 dealers: furnishings & accessories.

Legend Antiques Warehouse
2165 Broadway
719-448-9414
www.legendantiques.com
European & American country furnishings, clocks, chandeliers, mirrors, pottery, rugs, tapestries, art.

Rich Designs Gallery
1731 Mt. Washington Ave.
719-475-1200
www.richdesignsgallery.com
Decorative furniture & accessories, incl. Chinese lacquer cupboards, rugs, benches.

Van Briggle Art Pottery
600 S. 21st St.
719-633-7729
www.vanbriggle.com
Early-20th-c. art pottery (& new based on originals).

Denver

Antique Center on Broadway
1235 S. Broadway
303-744-1857
www.antiquecenteronbroadway.com
19th- to early-20th-c. American & French furnishings. Czech & English enamelware, antique maps.

Black Tulip Antiques
1370 S. Broadway
303-777-1370
www.blacktulipantiques.com
European & American tables, armoires, chairs.

Borgman's Antiques
1700 E. 6th Ave.
303-399-4588
www.borgmansantiques.com
17th- to 20th-c. English, Continental, Asian, & American furnishings, rugs, china, crystal, art, architecturals.

Bruhn's Auction
50 W. Arizona Ave.
303-744-6505
www.bruhnsauction.com

Camera Obscura Gallery
1309 Bannock St.
303-623-4059
www.cameraobscuragallery.com
19th- & 20th-c. photographs, incl. Edward S. Curtis & William H. Jackson.

Cashi Gallery
3548 Walnut St.
303-297-2947
& 200 S. Broadway
303-722-2545
www.cashigallery.com
18th- & 19th-c. Chinese & Philippine furniture.

Collection Antique and Design Market
899 Broadway
303-623-4200
www.theinternationalcollection.com
100 dealers: furnishings sourced worldwide, incl. mountain style, architecturals, garden items.

David Cook Fine American Art
1637 Wazee St.
303-623-8181
www.davidcookfineart.com
American & Native American art.

Eron Johnson Antiques
451 Broadway
303-777-8700
www.eronjohnsonantiques.com
17th- to 19th-c. furniture, lighting, accessories, architecturals, from around the world.

John Boulware Antiques
1416 S. Broadway
303-733-7369
Pre-1830 Pennsylvania & New England furnishings (incl. early finishes), folk art, samplers, signs.

Lewis Bobrick Antiques
1213 E. 4th Ave.
303-744-9203
www.lewisbobrickantiques.com
Mexican, American, & Native American furniture, decorative arts, jewelry, fine & folk art, rugs.

Native American Trading Co.
1301 Bannock St.
303-534-0771
www.nativeamericantradingco.com
Native American weavings, pottery, baskets, jewelry, artifacts.

Priddy's Auction Galleries
5411 Leetsdale Dr.
303-377-4411
18th- to19th-c. European & American furnishings: Mission furniture, rugs, silver, art, architecturals.

Sheptons Antiques
389 S. Broadway
303-777-5115
www.sheptonsantiques.com
Furnishings, lighting, textiles, accessories from around the world. Architecturals & ethnic art.

Starr Antiques
2940 E. 6th Ave.
303-399-4537
www.starrantiques.com
18th- & early-19th-c. American furniture, folk art, glass, silver, boxes, paintings, ceramics, decoys, baskets.

The Estate Brokers
2440 Clay St.
303-475-5305
www.theestatebrokers.com

Other

Brass Armadillo Mall
11301-West Hwy. 70
Wheat Ridge
303-403-1677
600 dealers: wide variety.

Colorado Antique Gallery
5501 S. Broadway
Littleton
303-794-8100
250 dealers: European, American, & Asian furniture, art, glass, jewelry, silver, china, linens, architecturals.

Ruxton's Trading Post
22 Ruxton Ave.
Manitou Springs
719-685-9024
www.ruxtons.com
Cowboy & Native American art & artifacts, incl. Navajo rugs, weavings.

Santa Fe, Albuquerque, Taos, & New Mexico's Tribal Arts Shows

Albuquerque

Antique Connection Mall
12815 Central Ave., NE
505-296-2300
www.antiqueconnectionmall.com
70+ dealers: Victorian to mid-20th-c. Moderne furniture, decorative items, jewelry. Western furnishings.

Cowboys and Indians Antiques
4000 Central Ave., SE
505-255-4054
www.cowboysandindiansnm.com
Native American art & artifacts, Mexican pottery & art. Spanish colonial art, santos, decorative items.

Gertrude Zachary's Secret Antiques
416 2nd St., SW
505-244-1320; 800-682-5768
www.gertrudezachary.com
American & European furniture, decorative objects, architectural elements, fountains.

Morningside Antiques
4001 Central Ave., NE
505-268-0188
Furniture & decorative arts, incl. silver,
glass, ceramics, metalwork.

Santa Fe
Christopher Selser Antiques
830 Canyon Rd.
505-984-1481
Native American & New Mexican
furnishings, art, artifacts.

Gerald Peters Gallery
1011 Paseo de Peralta
505-954-5700
19th- & 20th-c. American art, incl.
Western, Taos Society, Santa Fe
Art Colony, Georgia O'Keeffe.

H. Malcolm Grimmer
6 Shorthorn Lane
505-982-8669
Native American art, incl. Plains,
Southwest, Northwest Coast, Eskimo,
& Eastern tribes.

Joshua Baer & Co.
142 Lincoln Ave., #5
505-988-8944
Navajo blankets & rugs.

Mary Corley Antiques
215 N. Guadalupe St.
505-984-0863
www.mcorleyantiques.com
European country furnishings.

Matthew Chase
440 Galisteo St.
505-986-1095
Native American art, beadwork,
pottery, blankets, incl. Taos Society of
Artists & Santa Fe Art Colony.

Morning Star Gallery
513 Canyon Rd.
505-982-8187
www.morningstargallery.com
Native American art.

Nomads of Santa Fe
207 Shelby St.
505-986-0855
Moroccan furnishings & textiles.

Northstar Trading Co.
1812 2nd St.
505-988-1388
Oriental carpets, architecturals, art &
decorative items from Thailand, India,
Burma, & Vietnam.

Rio Bravo Trading Co.
411 S. Guadalupe St.
505-982-0230
Old West accessories: spurs, boots,
rawhide chaps, hats. Native American
jewelry, Navajo rugs.

William Siegal Galleries
135 W. Palace Ave.
505-820-7744
African, Chinese, Indonesian,
& pre-Columbian art, textiles, pottery,
baskets, masks.

Taos
Bosshard Fine Art Furnishings
112 Camino de La Placita
505-989-9150
www.johnbosshard.com
Asian furnishings, incl. lighting,
baskets, textiles, lacquerware,
architecturals, tribal & Buddhist art.

Patrick Dunbar Antiques
222 Paseo del Pueblo Norte
505-758-2511
www.patrickdunbarantiques.com
Colonial decorative furnishings,
architecture, sculpture. Architectural
elements from India.

Glendale, Arizona
Glendale
A Mad Hatter's Antiques & Collectibles
5734 W. Glendale Ave.
623-931-1991
www.amadhatter.com
1870s to 1960s furnishings, incl.
Victorian, Western, country, cottage,
lodge, primitives, garden items.

ABD Antique Appraisers
5809 W. Glendale Ave.
623-931-0235
18th- to 20th-c. furniture, glass,
jewelry, art, china.

Antique Haven
5805 W. Glendale Ave.
623-939-3420
Early-20th-c. vintage jewelry, glassware.

Empire Antiques
5609 W. Glendale Ave.
623-931-0558
19th- & 20th-c. European (mostly
French) furniture & accents.

Gatehouse Antiques
7023 N. 57th Dr.
623-435-1919
Mid-19th- to mid-20th-c. china, glass,
jewelry, paper, sterling. Native
American & Western memorabilia.

Granny G's Shady Nook
5303 W. Glendale Ave.
623-939-1462
Mid-19th- to mid-20th-c. books
& Victoriana.

Lois' Loveables
5807 W. Glendale Ave.
623-934-8846
Figurines, jewelry, lace, perfume
bottles, prints, art glass & pottery,
1950s to present.

Matilda's Vintage Closet
7013 N. 58th Ave.
623-847-1847
www.vintagefinery.com
1930s to 1950s after-five & cocktail
attire, accessories, incl. jewelry.

Maudie Mae's
5817 W. Glendale Ave.
623-463-3363
19th- to mid-20th-c. furniture, incl.
Victorian & country. Paper documents,
jewelry, 1950s clothing.

Pal's Forever
7003 N. 58th Ave.
623-930-1495
20th-c. furnishings, incl. kitchen tables
& hutches, jewelry.

Picket Fence Antiques
5825 W. Glendale Ave.
623-930-7121
1900 to 1960s furniture, cookie jars,
advertising signs, toy cars.

Sandy's Dream Dolls
7154 N. 58th Dr.
623-931-1579
www.sandysdreamdolls.com
Victorian dolls, dollhouse furniture,
children's dishes.

Smilin' Jack's Pedal Cars
5625 W. Glendale Ave.
623-435-0783
1950s vintage & new toys, incl. cars
& dollhouses.

Strunk's Hollow
6960 N. 57th Dr.
623-842-2842
19th-c. to present beer memorabilia,
1950s chrome sets, glassware, Fiesta
ware, pottery, sleds.

The Apple Tree
5811 W. Glendale Ave.
623-435-8486
www.appletreecountryshop.com
19th-c. East Coast colonial-style &
country furniture, decorative items.

Other
R. G. Munn Auction
Cloudcroft
505-687-3676

PART SIX: PACIFIC COAST

The Los Angeles Area: Santa Monica, Pasadena, & Orange

Los Angeles

A. N. Abell Auctions
2613 Yates Ave.
323-724-8102; 800-404-2235
www.abell.com

Big Daddy's Antiques
333 W. 131st St.
310-769-6600
www.bdantiques.com
Furniture & decorative items: painted country to Chinese, architecturals, garden items.

Jaipur
500 N. La Brea Ave.
323-939-7500
www.indianfurnishings.com
Indian furniture & accessories.

LA Moderne Antiques
947 N. La Cienega Blvd., Ste. A
310-360-1656
www.lamoderne.com
20th-c. furniture, accessories, collectibles, fine art.

Neil Lane
8840 Beverly Blvd.
310-275-5015
Estate jewelry & other items.

Richard Gould Antiques
808 N. La Cienega Blvd.
310-657-9416
www.richardgouldantiques.com
17th-, 18th-, & early-19th-c. English & American decorative arts, China trade & English ceramics.

Sam Kaufman
7965 Beverly Blvd.
323-857-1965
www.samkaufman.com
Mid-20th-c. furniture, lighting, decorative objects by leading designers.

West Hollywood

Blue House Antique Furniture
8440 Melrose Ave.
323-852-0747
www.bluehouseantiques.com
Furniture & accessories from France, U.K., & Sweden.

Evans and Gerst Antiques
520 N. San Vicente Blvd.
310-657-0112
18th- & early-19th-c. Continental & English furniture & accessories.

Hideaway House Antiques
143 N. Robertson Blvd.
310-276-4319
Furnishings from the U.K., Europe, Asia, India, & Scandinavia.

R. M. Barokh Antiques
8479 Melrose Ave.
323-655-2771
www.rmbarokhantiques.com
Period English & Continental, especially Italian, furniture, art.

Ralf's Antiques
807 N. La Cienega Blvd.
310-659-1966
www.antiques&finearts.com
15th- to 19th-c. English & Continental country & formal furniture, paintings, accessories.

Other

Antiquarian Traders
9031 W. Olympic Blvd.
Beverly Hills
310-247-3900
www.antiquariantraders.com
Furniture, pianos, rugs, paintings, mirrors, clocks, chandeliers, vases, urns, bronzes, architecturals.

Wertz Brothers
11879 Santa Monica Blvd.
West Los Angeles
310-477-4251
Furniture & accessories from all periods & around the world.

Orange

Architectural Salvage by Tony
123 N. Olive St.
714-538-1900
Architectural objects.

Country Roads Antiques
204 W. Chapman Ave.
714-532-3041
Country, primitive, shabby chic, folk art, garden items.

Sloane's Antiques
2055 N. Glassell St.
714-637-0444
19th- & 20th-c. European furniture.

Summerhill Antiques
110 S. Glassell St.
714-771-7782
Furnishings, specialty lighting.

Woody's Antiques
173 N. Glassell St.
714-744-8199
www.woodysantiques.com
Vintage Heywood Wakefield, streamline, & Moderne furniture.

Pasadena

Pasadena Antique Center
480 S. Fair Oaks Ave.
626-449-7706
70 dealers: variety 19th- & 20th-c. furnishings: European items, rugs, linens, art, lighting, collectibles.

Pasadena Antique Mall
35 S. Raymond Ave., Ste. 130
626-304-9886
www.pasadenacitysearch.com
60 dealers: 18th- to mid-20th-c. furnishings, pottery, art, glass, crystal, decorative items, etc.

Thomas R. Field Antiques
1127 Mission St.
(South Pasadena)
626-799-8546
www.thomasrfieldantiques.com
Early American furniture & folk art.

West World Imports
171 E. California Blvd.
626-449-8565
www.westworldimports.com
French & English country furniture accessories.

Santa Monica

Historia Antiques
1322 2nd St., Ste. 2
310-394-3384
Spanish Colonial art & furnishings.

Paris 1900
2703 Main St.
310-396-0405
www.paris1900.com
Vintage clothing, incl. bridal, accessories, jewelry, linens.

Rosemarie McCaffrey Antiques
1203 Montana Ave.
310-395-7711
17th- to 19th-c. European furnishings, French country, art, tapestries, Apt pottery, mirrors.

Vintage Animation Gallery
1404 3rd St. Promenade
310-393-8666
Original animation artwork: Disney,
Warner Bros., Hanna Barbera,
M-G-M, Walter Lantz.

Wertz Brothers Antique Mart
1607 Lincoln Blvd.
Santa Monica
310- 452-1800
190+ dealers: antique & vintage
furniture, decorative accessories,
lighting, statuary, jewelry.

California's Monterey Peninsula

Carmel

Anderle Gallery
Lincoln (betw. Ocean & 7th)
831-624-9450
Tribal arts, Japanese & Korean
furnishings, doors.

Artist Forum
223 Forest Ave.
831-375-4278
Arts & Crafts furnishings, fine &
decorative art, pottery, lighting.

Conway of Asia
7th & Dolores W/S
831-624-3643
Furnishings & rugs from Persia, India,
Tibet, Burma, & Thailand.

End of an Era Antiques
Lincoln (betw. Ocean & 7th)
831-620-1372
18th- & 19th-c. Americana, furniture,
European porcelain, Asian furnishings,
decorative arts.

Great Things Antiques
Ocean Ave. (betw. Dolores & Lincoln)
831-624-7178; 877-249-6260
French furniture & accessories.

Maxine Klaput Antiques
Mission & 7th
831-624-8823
18th- & 19th-c. furniture, silver,
porcelain, paintings, accessories.

McKinley & Co. Antiques
Lincoln (betw. Ocean & 7th)
831-625-1200
www.mckinleycoantiques.com
19th-c. American & European
furniture, porcelain, art glass, silver,
Oriental furnishings & rugs.

Portico
Lincoln (betw. Ocean & 7th)
831-625-6800
www.porticocarmel.com
European furnishings, accessories.

Sabine Adamson Antiques
Dolores (betw. 5th & 6th)
831-626-7464
European furniture, decorative objects,
French textiles, lighting.

Vermilion Asian Arts
240 The Crossroads
831-620-1502
Japanese furniture, decorative arts.

Viau Estate Jewelry
Mission (betw. Ocean & 7th)
831-624-5991
European & Oriental furnishings,
decorative objects, fine art, jewelry.

Pacific Grove

Antique Clock Shop
489 Lighthouse Ave.
831-372-6435
Clocks & other items.

Hambrook's Auction Center
480 Lighthouse Ave.
831-373-2101
www.hambrooks-auction.com

Holman's Antique Plaza
542 Lighthouse Ave.
831-646-1677
50 dealers: varied furnishings.

Patrick's Consignment Store
105 Central Ave.
831-372-3995
Home furnishings.

Trotter's Antiques
183 Forest Ave.
831-373-3505
18th- & 19th-c. formal furniture, art
glass, porcelain, silver, bronzes.

Other

Cambridge Golf Antiquities
The Lodge at Pebble Beach
Pebble Beach
831-626-3334
www.cambridgegolfantiquities.com
Vintage clubs & other golfing items.

Cannery Row Antique Mall
471 Wave St.
Monterey
831-655-0264
150+ dealers: varied furnishings,
incl. architectural & garden.

San Francisco, California

Belvedere

Arthur Leeper Asian Art
208 San Rafael Ave.
415-435-6165
www.asianart.com/leeper
Over 2,000 year-old Chinese textiles
& lacquerware.

The Custom House
1550 Tiburon Blvd.
415-435-5350
18th- to 19th-c. English,
French, & Asian furniture, crystal,
jewelry, lamps.

Berkeley

**Carter West Antiques
& Estate Liquidation**
2373 San Pablo Ave.
510-848-8317
Furniture & collectible objects.

Craftsman Home
3048 Claremont
510-655-6503
www.craftsmanhome.com
Period Mission & Arts & Crafts
furniture, lighting, carpets, pottery.

De Sino Antiques
2216 San Pablo Ave.
510-843-1449
www.desinogallery.net
Garden Buddhas, stone statues,
Chinese furniture, political items.

Eastern Classics
1456 4th St.
510-526-1241
Early-19th-c. Oriental furniture.

Fenton MacLaren
1325 & 2575 San Pablo Ave.
510-526-5377; 510-848-7635
www.fentonmaclaren.com
American furniture, 1910-1930.

Louis A. Capellino Antiques
1987 Ashby Ave.
510-845-5590
1800-1910 American, Asian, & English
furniture, collectibles.

Nigel Imports
2940 7th St.
415-776-5490; 510-841-4868
Furniture, lamps & shades.

Prize Antiques
2361 Fenton Ave.
510-848-1168
Varied shabby chic & cottage
furnishings, lighting, art.

Trout Farm Antiques
2179 Bancroft Way
510-843-3565
Scandinavian & American mid-20th-c.
arts & crafts.

Von Hemert Antiques
1989 Ashby Ave.
510-548-1327
Furniture, collectibles, silver,
Asian artifacts.

Oakland

Art Deco Collections
546 Grand Ave.
510-465-1920
www.artdecocollections.com
Furniture, glassware, collectibles.

Legend Antiques
5427 Telegraph Ave., Ste. E3
510-658-9123
French furniture & lighting, 1840-1930.

Off Broadway Enterprises
316 38th St.
510-428-0895
Silver, jewelry, collectibles.

San Francisco

Ambiance Antiques
550 15th St.
415-626-0145
www.ambianceantiques.com
18th- & 19th-c. French furniture.

Antique and Art Exchange
151 Vermont St., #4
415-522-3580
www.antiqueandartexchange.com
35 dealers: 18th- & 19th-c. Chinese,
Continental, & American furniture,
decorative arts, silver, ceramics.

Argentum Antiques
472 Jackson St.
415-296-7757
www.argentum-theleopard.com
Late-17th- to mid-20th-c. silver.

Art de Asia
1235 Sutter St.
415-922-6688
Chinese & Japanese furniture,
1900 to present.

Bonhams & Butterfields Auctions
220 San Bruno Ave.
415-861-7500
www.butterfields.com

Candace Barnes Antiques
151 Vermont St., Ste. 7
415-431-1018
17th- to 20th-c. European furniture
& accessories.

Challiss House
463 Jackson St.
415-397-6999
www.challisshouse.com
18th- to 19th-c. Italian, Provincial
French, & Spanish furniture,
decorative arts.

Chappell McCullar
495 Jackson St.
415-693-0760; 415-693-0882
www.chappelmccullar.com
17th- to early-19th-c. English &
European furniture & accessories.

Charles Gaylord & Co.
419 10th St.
415-522-1682; 415-392-6085
www.charlesgaylord.com
French furniture, decorative arts,
European mantels, hearth
& garden items.

Colonial Arts
463 Union St.
415-505-0680
www.colonialarts.com
Spanish Colonial furniture, Mexican
religious & folk art, ceramics, textiles,
ethnographic arts.

Daniel Stein Antiques
458 Jackson St.
415-956-5620
www.danielsteinantiques.com
18th- & 19th-c. English & European
furniture & decorative arts, prints,
scientific instruments, sporting art.

Decorum
1400 Vallejo St.
415-474-6886
www.decorumsanfran.com
French & American Art Deco
furniture, collectibles.

Dragon House
455 Grant Ave.
415-781-2351; 415-421-3693
Chinese pottery, porcelain, carvings,
1000 BC to 1900 AD.

Drum & Co.
151 Vermont St., Ste. 8
415-551-1538
18th- &19th-c. French & Italian
painted furniture.

Fenton-Moscatelli
432 Jackson St.
415-398-3046
International folk art, sculpture from
SE Asia & India, tribal arts of Africa,
Indonesia, & SE Asia.

Folk Art International
140 Maiden Lane
415-392-9999
Asian & Oceanic art & artifacts,
1000 BC to the 15th c.

Foster-Gwin Antiques
38 Hotaling Pl.
415-397-4986
www.fostergwin.com
16th-, 17th-, & 18th-c. Continental
furniture, tapestries, art.

Golden Gate Antiques
1564 Market St.
415-626-3377
19th- & 20th-c.
furnishings, collectibles.

Habité
963 Harrison St.
415-543-3515
www.habite.com
Continental furniture & decorative
accessories, Louis XIII to Art Deco.

Holmes-Samsel Antiques
Corner, Kansas & 16th Sts.
415-864-7300
www.holmes-samsel.com
18th- to 20th-c. European furniture,
mirrors, lighting, paintings, statues.

**J. Edward Cook/Kuromatsu
Oriental Art**
722 Bay St.
415-474-4027
Early-20th-c. Japanese furniture,
Asian-Pacific items.

**James Blackmon Antique
Textile Gallery**
2140 Bush St., #1
415-922-1859
Central Asian, African, Andean, & Near
East carpets & textiles.

Kuraya
2425 California St.
415-885-3313
www.kurayaantiques.com
18th- & 19th-c. Japanese furnishings,
ceramics, lacquer, hibachis, etc.

Montgomery Gallery
406 Jackson St.
415-788-8300
www.montgomerygallery.com
19th- & 20th-c. European, American
& California art, incl. Old Masters.

Narumi Japanese Antiques
1902B Fillmore St.
415-346-8629
www.narumiantiques.com
Japanese tansu chests, ceramics, obi
& kimonos, scrolls, dolls, etc.

Nathan Hawley Antiques
3640 Sacramento St.
415-885-8545
www.sanfranciscoantiquedealers.com
European, American, Asian furniture,
decorative accessories.

Penelope Clark Antiques
2430 Polk St.
415-474-7775
Stained & leaded glass.

Peter Pap Oriental Rugs
470 Jackson St.
415-956-3300
www.peterpap.com
Oriental rugs, textiles, tribal weaves.

Quality First Estate Sales
415-931-1000
www.qfes.com

Rebuffel Antiques
963 Harrison St.
415-543-3515
www.rebuffelantiques.com
17th- to 19th-c. French furnishings,
objects, art, lighting, architecturals.

Richard Gervais Collection
1465 Custer Ave. (warehouse)
415-642-1056
965 Natoma St.
415-255-4579 (by appt.)
www.richardgervaiscollection.com
SE Asian furniture, religious
iconography, decorative arts, folk art,
ceramics, artifacts, baskets.

Robert Domergue and Co.
560 Jackson St.
415-781-4034
17th- to early-19th-c. Continental
furniture & decorative arts.

San Francisco Antique/Design Mall
701 Bayshore Blvd.
415-656-3530
www.sfantique.com
200 dealers: variety of furnishings,
from Americana to Art Deco.

Sandra Whitman
361 Oak St.
415-861-4477
www.sanfranciscoantiquesdealers.com
Rugs & textiles from China & East
Turkistan, 16th- to early 20th c.

Sarah Stocking
431 Jackson St.
415-984-0700
www.sarahstocking.com
American & European posters,
1880-1940.

The Antique Traders
4300 California St.
415-668-4444
www.theantiquetraders.com
Lighting, stained & art glass, Art
Nouveau items, 1880-1920.

The Lotus Collection
445 Jackson St.
415-398-8115
www.ktaylor-lotus.com
European, Asian, & ethnic textiles.

The North Point Gallery
407 Jackson St.
415-781-7550
19th-c. American paintings, early
California & Realist paintings.

Therien & Co.
411 Vermont St.
415-956-8850
Furniture & decorative accessories.

Thomas Livingston Antiques
550 Jackson St.
415-296-8150
www.thomaslivingstonantiques.com
Period American & English furniture;
English, Dutch, & French faience;
Chinese export ceramics.

Urban Chateau
3228 Sacramento St.
415-673-8026
www.urbanchateau.com
18th- to19th-c. French & Italian
furniture & furnishings.

Vintage Modern
576 Ortega St.
415-861-8162
Mid-20th-c. Moderne furnishings.

W. Graham Arader III Antiques
435 Jackson St.
415-788-5115
www.aradergalleries.com
Rare books, maps, paintings, prints,
incl. Audubon.

Other

Antiques by the Bay
2100 Ferry Point
Alameda
510-522-7500
www.antiquesbybay.com
800 vendors: 1st Sun., every month,
at the Naval Air Station.

Sonoma County, California

Healdsburg

Antique Harvest
225 Healdsburg Ave.
707-433-0223
20 dealers: eclectic selection of items
from furniture to fine art.

Healdsburg Classic Antiques
226 Healdsburg Ave.
707-433-4315
1720-1920 furniture & glassware.
1950s jewelry, silver.

Mill St. Antiques
44 Mill St.
707-433-8409
30+ dealers: furniture, collectibles, art,
architectural items.

Kenwood

Susan Gardner Estate Sales
707-579-5251 (by appt.)
susangardnerestatesales.com

William and Mary's Antiques-Silver
707-538-5285 (by appt.)
Silverware pattern matching a specialty.

Occidental

Revival Antiques
3692 Bohemian Hwy.
707-874-1359
1850-1950 vintage jewelry,
silver, collectibles.

Verdigris
72 Main St.
707-874-9018
Art lamps, home & garden furnishings.

Petaluma

Chelsea Antiques
148 Petaluma Blvd., N.
707-763-7686
40 dealers: 1700-1950 furniture
&decorative accessories.

Monarch Antiques
199 Petaluma Blvd.
707-769-3092
1800-present French, German, English
furniture, art, Oriental rugs.

Sienna Antiques
119 Petaluma Blvd., N.
707-763-6088.
European furniture, collectibles, toys
and tin from the 18th c.

Vintage Bank Antiques
101 Petaluma Blvd., N.
707-769-3097
32 dealers: paintings, jewelry,
decorative items, furniture.

Santa Rosa

Antique Junction
105 3rd St.
707-570-1494
Furniture, collectibles & glassware
from the early 19th c.

Harry's Second Hand Warehouse
820 Ripley
707-526-7713
18th-c. American furniture
& collectibles.

Treasure House
700 Wilson
707-523-1188
Glassware, figurines, jewelry,
collectibles, kitchenware.

Whistlestop Antiques
130 4th St.
707-542-9474
30 dealers: glass pottery, furniture,
other items.

Sebastopol

Antique Society
2661 Gravenstein Hwy.
707-829-1733
100 dealers: furniture, collectibles,
toys, glassware.

Chestnut St. Antiques
44 Sebastopol Rd.
707-579-8488 (by appt.)
1800 to 1960s lighting fixtures,
knick-knacks, pottery, furniture.

School Bell Antiques
3555 Gravenstein Hwy.
707-823-2878
1800-1900 furniture, china, glass,
books, Asian items.

Sebastopol Antique Mall
755 Petaluma Ave.
707-823-1936
35 dealers: variety of items.

Windmill Antiques
2830 Gravenstein Hwy., S.
707-823-7954
1950 to present high-end American,
Belgian, & country Western items.

Sonoma

A L'Ancienne
707-996-2550 (by appt.)
www.alaimports.com
French artifacts & building materials,
1500-1900.

Curry & I Antiques
17000 Hwy. 12
707-996-8226
19th-c. glass, silver, porcelain.

Richards Antiques
4358 Sonoma Hwy.
707-537-1891
1800s American furniture.

Sonoma County Antiques
23999 Arnold Dr.
707-938-8315
1800s to 1900 European furniture.

Portland & Aurora, Oregon

Aurora

Amish Workbench Furniture
14936 3rd St.
503-678-7799
19th-c. American country furniture,
restored & new items.

Antique Colony
21581 Main St., NE
503-678-1010
19th-c. European & American
furniture, glassware, collectibles.

Aurora Antiques & Décor
21418 Hwy. NE
503-678-1007
1850-1950 American & French
furniture, fine arts.

Aurora Depot Antiques
21651 Main St.
503-678-3060
19th- to mid-20th-c. English &
American lighting, incl. oil lamps.

Aurora Mills Architectural Salvage
34971 1st St.
503-678-6083
Lighting fixtures, statues, marble
pieces, stained glass.

Home Again Antiques
21631 Main St., NE
503-678-0227
Early-20th-c. American country
furniture, carvings, small items.

Portland

1874 House
8070 SE 13th Ave.
503-233-1874
Architectural lighting, doors, windows,
Victorian & later china.

Antique Alley
2000 NE 42nd Ave.
503-287-9848
70 dealers: variety of American items.

Antique Table Specialties
11223 SE 42nd Ave.
503-224-8640
Pool tables & accessories, 1845-1925.

Antiques and Oddities
1605 Everett St. NW
503-222-4246
Asian & European home furnishings.

Asia America
79 SE Taylor St.
503-230-9322
18th- to 19th-c. Chinese, Mongolian,
& Indian furniture.

**Bernadette Breu, Antiques and
Ornament**
1134 NW Everett St.
503-226-6565
Furniture, accessories, textiles,
architecturals, garden.

Cargo
380 NW 13th Ave.
503-209-8349
Old & new furniture, artifacts from
around the world.

Christiane Millinger Oriental Rugs
208 NW 13th Ave.
503-274-4440
Hand-made rugs & textiles.

Circa 1904 Antiques
8027 SE 13th Ave.
503-235-2638
10 dealers: furniture, pottery, Asian
artifacts, paintings.

Classic Antiques
1805 SE Martin Luther King Blvd.
503-231-8689
Furniture, collectibles, glassware,
decorative accessories.

Consignment Gallery
8133 SE 13th Ave.
503-234-6606
19th- & 20th-c. fine home furnishings
& accessories.

Cultured Pearl Antiques
532 NW 12th Ave.
503-226-4262
American & international furnishings
& accessories.

Farmhouse Antiques
8028 SE 13th Ave.
503-232-6757
8 dealers: glass, dishes, furniture.

Frederick E. Squire III Antiques
340 1st St.
503-675-9002
18th-c. European, English,
& French furniture.

Heirloom Carpets
923 NW 14th Ave.
503-227-7847
Persian rugs: Gabbeh, Tebriz, Bijar,
& others.

Lotus Antiques and Art
938 NW Everett St.
503-417-1888
Asian furniture & art.

Lumen Essence Antique Lighting
418 NW 8th Ave.
503-721-0939
American & European lighting.

Monticello Antique Marketplace
8600 SE Stark St.
503-256-8600
100+ dealers: furniture, glassware,
toys, collectibles.

Moreland House Antiques
826 NW 23rd St.
503-222-0197
18th-c. American furniture,
decorative accessories.

Multnomah Antique Gallery
7764 SW Capitol Hwy.
503-245-8283
6 dealers: 19th-c. American furniture,
furniture, glass, lighting, pottery,
china, silver.

Old Town Antique Market
32 NW 1st Ave.
503-228-3386
30 dealers: variety of items incl.
paintings, toys, furniture.

Pacific Orient Traders
221 NW 11th Ave.
503-241-9914
Asian furniture & decorative items.

Rejuvenation Hardware
1100 SE Grand Ave.
503-238-1900
Architecturals, hardware.

Retrospection
619 SW 10th Ave.
503-223-5538
17th- to 20th-c. Asian metalwork
& textiles.

Sellwood Antique Collective
8027 SE 13th Ave.
503-736-1399
12 dealers: furniture to glassware.

Sellwood Antique Mall
7875 SE 13th Ave.
503-232-3755
80 dealers: wide range of items.

Stars Antiques Mall
6717 & 7027 SE Milwaukee Ave.
503-235-9142; 503-235-5990
250+ dealers: variety of
furnishings, collectibles.

Washington's Puget Sound

Edmonds

Aurora Antique Pavilion
24111 Hwy. 99
425-744-0566
200+ dealers: American, French,
& English furniture, collectibles.

Waterfront Antique Mall
190 Sunset Ave., S.
425-670-0770
100+ dealers: books, tools, collectibles,
Victorian, Art Deco, & Mission
furniture. Auctions held.

Port Gamble

Best Friends Antiques
32239 Rainier Ave.
360-297-4848
Furniture, china, glassware,
textiles, collectibles.

Ms Bee Haven
32180 Rainier Ave., NE
360-297-1804
Vintage & earlier furnishings, quality
second-hand goods.

Olde Central Antique Mall
801 Bay St.
360-895-1902
40+ dealers: furnishings, collectibles.

Port Gamble Trading Co.
4719 Northeast State Hwy. 104
360-297-8114
40+ vendors: variety, incl. vintage
furnishings, Native American art.

Snohomish

Antique Gallery
117 Glen Ave.
360-568-7644
30 dealers: furnishings, pottery, glass,
collectibles, jewelry, quilts, dolls,
bottles, primitives.

Antique Station
1108 1st St.
360-568-4913
60 dealers: furniture, dishes, books,
tools, kitchenware, collectibles,
restoration hardware.

Black Cat Antiques
1234 1st St.
360-568-8144
Late-19th- & early-20th-c. furniture,
radios & phonographs, lighting,
collectible classic cars.

Collectors Showcase
829 2nd St.
360-568-1339
Fenton, Victorian, Carnival, Cameo,
& 20th-c. art glass.

Legends
905 1st St.
360-568-1820
Furniture, clocks, barometers, prints,
lamps, unusual items.

Pegasus Theatre Shops
1003 1st St.
360-568-8815
Nostalgia items, jukeboxes, gas
pumps, vintage ads, furniture, Fiesta,
collectibles, retro items.

Remember When Antique Mall
908 1st St.
360-568-0757
30+ dealers: pottery, glassware, china,
children's books, kitchen items,
furniture, vintage items.

Sharon's Antique Mall
111 Glen Ave.
360-568-9854
22 dealers; holiday items, tools,
lunchboxes, baseball, 1950's music
& TV-related collectibles, jewelry.

Star Center Antique Mall
829 2nd St.
360-568-2131
200 dealers: furnishings, lighting, art,
china, glass, collectibles.

Troybeck Antiques
923 1st St.
360-568-1031
30 dealers: pottery, glass, toys,
advertising, military & auto items.

Uppercase Books & Collectables
611 2nd St., Ste. L
360-568-5987
Used, out of print, & rare books,
miscellaneous collectibles.

The Magazine

ANTIQUES
Nationwide Calendar of Shows

This information was compiled by the staff of *The Magazine* ANTIQUES. Due to space constraints, this is only a selection of the numerous notable events around the country. Our apologies to the many wonderful shows we were unable to include.

Please note, listings include a sampling of items—if you're looking for a specific category, telephone or check the show website beforehand. Discounts on admission and lodging are often available. Admission fees frequently allow re-entry during the run of the show and may include a copy of the show catalogue. Higher-priced early-bird admission provides entry prior to the general public. Preview events are generally the evening before show openings, and many shows include lectures, tours, and other special events. All information is subject to change. Please check before you go.

For monthly information on shows, consult *The Magazine* ANTIQUES or its website (www.themagazineantiques.com).

MONTHLY

First Week
FL: WEST PALM BEACH ANTIQUE & COLLECTIBLES SHOW
S. Florida Fairgrounds. Fri.–Sat. $11. 400–1,200 dealers: furnishings, collectibles, decorative accessories. 561-640-3433.
www.dmgantiqueshows.com

NC: CHARLOTTE ANTIQUE & COLLECTIBLES SHOW
Metrolina Expo, 7100 N. Statesville Rd. Thurs.–Sat. 9–5, Sun. 10–5. $5. 500+ dealers. 1,500+ dealers in Apr. & Nov. 800-824-3770; 704-594-4643.
www.dmgantiqueshows.com

Second Week
IL: GRAYSLAKE ANTIQUE MARKET
Lake County Fairgrounds, Rt. 120. Sun. 8–4. $5. Pottery, furniture, jewelry, art glass, primitives, toys, linens. 715-526-9769.
www.zurkoantiquetours.com

Third Week
IL: WHEATON ANTIQUE MARKET
DuPage County Fairgrounds, Manchester Rd. Sat. 8–3. $5. 715-526-9769.
www.zurkoantiquetours.com

JANUARY

First Week
FL: FORT LAUDERDALE ANTIQUES WORLD
Conv. Cntr., 1950 Eisenhower Blvd. Fri. 12–8, Sat. 12–7, Sun. 12–5. $8. 100+ dealers: furniture & decorative accessories. 954-563-6747.
www.dolphinfairs.com

FL: PALM BEACH CONNOISSEUR FAIR
Kravis Cntr., 701 Okeechobee Blvd. West Palm Beach. Fri.–Sun. 11–7. $15. American & European fine art, 18th- 20th-c. furniture, jewelry, decorative items, textiles, silver, books, photographs, etc. 561-845-5453.
www.connoisseurfairs.com

VA: RICHMOND ANTIQUES SPECTACULAR & THE ANTIQUE TOOL SHOW
Showplace, 3000 Mechanicsville Tnpk. Sat. 10–6, Sun. 12–5. $5. 804-462-6190.
www.renaissancepromotions.com

DC: D.C. ANTIQUES SHOW
Omni Shoreham Hotel, 2500 Calvert St. NW. Thurs. 11–7, Fri. 11–9, Sat. 11–8, Sun. 11–4. $15. 45 dealers: furnishings & decorative arts, jewelry, ceramics, silver, etc. 413-436-7064.
www.washingtonantiques.org;
www.antiquescouncil.com

Second Week
FL: FORT LAUDERDALE ANTIQUES WORLD
Conv. Cntr., 1950 Eisenhower Blvd. Fri. 12–8, Sat. 12–7, Sun. 12–6. $8. 150 intl. dealers. 954-563-6747.
www.dolphinfairs.com

FL: MIAMI NATIONAL ANTIQUES SHOW & SALE
Sheraton Cntr., 777 NW 72nd Ave. Fri. 12–9, Sat. 12–8, Sun. 12–6. $10. 400+ intl. dealers: fine furniture, crystal, silver, Art Nouveau, Art Deco bronzes, porcelain, paintings, prints, jewelry, ceramics, Americana, folk art. 954-563-6747. www.dolphinfairs.com

FL: PALM BEACH WINTER ANTIQUES SHOW & SALE
Crowne Plaza, 1601 Belvedere Rd., West Palm Beach. Fri.–Sat. 11–6, Sun. 11–5. $15. 50 dealers: furniture, fine art, accessories. 561-483-4047.
www.zitawatersbell.com

MD: HISTORIC ANNAPOLIS ANTIQUES SHOW
Medford Armory, Hudson St. Fri.–Sat. 11–6, Sun. 12–5. $8. American & English furniture, fine & decorative arts, Oriental rugs, jewelry, silver, children's books, folk art, garden items. 410-961-5121. www.annapolis.org;
www.armacostantiquesshows.com

WA: SEATTLE PRINT FAIR
Seattle Cntr., Warren Ave. N. Sat. 10–6,
Sun. 11–5. Prints & works on paper,
from miniature bookplates to museum-
quality drawings. 212-674-6095.
www.seattleprintfair.com;
www.printdealers.com

Third Week

CA: PHOTO LA
Civic Auditorium, 1855 Main St., Santa
Monica. Fri.–Sat. 12–7, Sun. 12–6. $20.
70 intl. dealers: 19th-c. photography &
contemporary images. 323-937-4659.
www.artfairsinc.com

CA: SAN FRANCISCO PRINT FAIR
Fort Mason Cntr. Sat. 10–6, Sun. 11–5.
Free. 18 fine art dealers from U.S. &
Canada: prints, from old masters to
contemporary. 212-674-6095.
www.sanfrancisco-fineprintfair.com
www.printdealers.com

FL: MIAMI MODERNISM
James L. Knight Cntr., 400 SE 2nd Ave.
Sat. 10–8, Sun. 12–5. $10. 65+ intl.
decorative & fine arts dealers of
20th-c. design. 954-563-6747.
www.dolphinfairs.com

FL: ORIGINAL MIAMI BEACH
ANTIQUES SHOW
Conv. Cntr., 1901 Conv. Cntr. Dr.
Thurs.–Sun. $15. 1,000+ intl. dealers:
items for all levels of enthusiasts.
239-732-6642.
www.dmgantiqueshows.com

MA: GREATER BOSTON
ANTIQUES FESTIVAL
Shriner's Auditorium, 99 Fordham Rd.,
Wilmington. Sat. 9–5, Sun 10–4. $7.
162 dealers: furniture, Asian objects,
fine & folk art, quilts, rugs, silver,
jewelry, ceramics, collectibles, maps,
linens, tiles, etc. 781-862-4039.
www.neantiqueshows.com

NYC: AMERICAN ANTIQUES SHOW
Metropolitan Pavilion, 125 W. 18th St.
Thurs.–Sat. 12–7, Sun. 12–5. $15. 45
dealers: 18th–early 20th-c. folk art,
Americana. 212-977-7170, ext 319.
www.folkartmuseum.org

NYC: ANTIQUES AT THE ARMORY
& AMERICANA & ANTIQUES
AT THE PIERS
69th Reg. Armory, Lexington Ave. at
26th St. & Piers at Twelfth Ave.,
50–55th Sts. Fri.–Sat. 11–8, Sun. 11–5.
$20. 300 dealers at the piers & 100
dealers at the Armory: American,
English, & French furniture & decorative objects, fine & folk art, textiles, art
glass, designer fashions, porcelains,
silver, jewelry, prints, ceramics, etc.
212-255-0020. www.stellashows.com

NYC: NEW YORK CERAMICS FAIR
National Academy Museum & School
of Fine Arts, 1083 Fifth Ave. Wed.–Sat.
12–7, Sun. 12–6. $15. 40 dealers:
porcelain, pottery, glass, & enamels.
310-455-2886. www.caskeylees.com

NYC: WINTER ANTIQUES SHOW
7th Reg. Armory, Park Ave. at 67th St.
10 days: Fri.–following Sun.: 12–8,
except Sun. & Thurs. 12–6. $20.
74 prestigious dealers: American,
English, Asian, & European furniture,
fine & decorative arts. 718-292-7392.
www.winterantiquesshow.com

Fourth Week

CA: LOS ANGELES PRINT FAIR
L.A. County Museum of Art, 6067
Wilshire Blvd. Sat. 11–7, Sun. 11–5.
25 dealers: 16th–21st-c. works on
paper. 212-674-6095.
www.printdealers.com;
www.laprintfair.com

CA: LOS ANGELES ART SHOW
Barker Hanger, Santa Monica Air Ctr.,
Santa Monica. Thurs.–Sat. 12–7,
Sun. 12–5. $18. Historical, modern
& contemporary paintings, drawings,
prints, photographs, sculpture.
310-822-9145. www.laartshow.com

FL: SARASOTA WINTER
ANTIQUES SHOW & SALE
Municipal Auditorium, 801 N. Tamiami
Trail. Fri.–Sat. 10–6, Sun. 12–5. $5.
Furniture, paintings, jewelry, glass,
porcelain, etc. 954-563-6747.
www.dolphinfairs.com

NYC: OUTSIDER ART FAIR
Puck Building, Houston & Lafayette
Sts. Fri.–Sun. $15. 30+ dealers:
unconventional, non-mainstream art.
212-777-5218. www.sanfordsmith.com

FEBRUARY

First Week

CA: ARTS OF PACIFIC ASIA
Fort Mason Cntr., San Francisco.
Fri.–Sat. 11–7, Sun. 11–5. $15. Ancient
artifacts & antiques from Asia & the
Pacific. 310-455-2886.
www.caskeylees.com

CT: WINTER MARKET
ANTIQUES SHOW & SALE
Hyatt Regency, 1800 E. Putnam Ave.,
Old Greenwich. Sun. 10–5. $6.
American, English, & European
furniture, fine art, prints, decorative
objects, silver, glass, rugs, etc.
203-222-2259.

FL: WINTER ANTIQUES
SHOW AT NAPLES
Edison Comm. College, 7007 Lely
Cultural Pkwy. Fri. 5–8, Sat. 10–6, Sun.
12–5. $8. 35 intl. dealers: furniture,
fine art, antique jewelry, books, & decorative accessories. 954-563-6747.
www.dolphinfairs.com.

FL: PALM BEACH!
AMERICA'S INTERNATIONAL
FINE ART & ANTIQUE FAIR
County Conv. Cntr., 650 Okeechobee
Blvd., West Palm Beach. 10 days: daily
12–7, Sun. 12–6. 100 intl. dealers:
furniture, fine & decorative arts,
jewelry, etc., from classical antiquity to
the 1960s. 561-209-1338.
www.palmbeachfair.com

MI: VISIONS TO REMEMBER
Ford House, 1100 Lake Shore Rd.,
Grosse Pointe Shores. Sat.–Sun. $8.
30 dealers: furniture & decorative
pieces. 313-824-4710. www.eyeson.org

TN: ANTIQUES & GARDEN
SHOW OF NASHVILLE
Conv. Cntr., 601 Commerce St.
Thurs.–Sat. 10–7, Sun. 10–5. 150
dealers: horticultural & garden items.
800-891-8075.
www.antiquesandgardenshow.com

VA: RICHMOND ANTIQUES
SPECTACULAR & THE CIVIL
WAR SPECTACULAR
Showplace, 3000 Mechanicsville Tnpk.
Sat. 10–6, Sun. 10–5. $5.
804-462-6190.
www.renaissancepromotions.com

Second Week

CA: SAN FRANCISCO TRIBAL
& TEXTILE ARTS SHOW
Fort Mason Cntr. Fri.–Sat. 11–7, Sun.
11–5. $15. 80 intl. dealers: pre-1940s
tribal, textiles, folk objects, artifacts,
& art. 310-455-2886.
www.caskeylees.com

FL: DELRAY BEACH HISTORICAL
SOCIETY ANTIQUES SHOW & SALE
Comm. Cntr., 50 NW First Ave. Sat.
10-5:30, Sun. 11-5. $10. Furniture,
ceramics, jewelry, silver, garden items,
etc. 561-243-2577; 410-961-5121.
www.armacostantiquesshows.com

FL: SARASOTA WINTER
ANTIQUES FESTIVAL & SALE
Municipal Auditorium, 801 N. Tamiami
Trail. Fri.–Sat. 10–6, Sun. 12–5. $5. 60
dealers presenting furniture, porcelain,
silver, glass, estate jewelry, paintings,
bronzes, lamps, & pottery.
954-563-6747. www.dolphinfairs.com.

NYC:. AIPAD PHOTOGRAPHY SHOW
7th Reg. Armory, Park Ave at 67th St.
Thurs.–Sat. 12–7, Sun. 12–6. $20. 75
dealers: rare early works to images
by emerging artists. 914-698-3442.
www.aipad.com; www.wendyshows.com

NC: PRESERVATION FOUNDATION ANTIQUES SHOW & SALE
Riverfront Conv. Cntr., New Bern. Fri.–Sun. $5. 40 dealers: 19th–early 20th-c. furniture, decorative arts, jewelry, silver, prints, linens, etc. 252-633-6448. www.newbernpf.org

Third Week

FL: PALM BEACH JEWELRY & ANTIQUE SHOW
County Conv. Cntr., 650 Okeechobee Blvd., West Palm Beach. Sat.–Mon. 11–7, Tues. 11–6. $15. 200+ intl. dealers. 561-822-5440. www.palmbeachshow.com

TN: HEART OF COUNTRY ANTIQUES SHOW
Gaylord Opryland Hotel, 2800 Opryland Dr., Nashville. Fri. 10–8, Sat.–Sun. 10–7. 200+ dealers: Americana, country furniture, folk art, etc. 800-862-1090. www.heartofcountry.com

TX: HOUSTON ANTIQUES DEALERS ASSN. SPRING ANTIQUES SHOW
George R. Brown Conv. Cntr., 1001 Ave. de las Americas. Thurs. 11–8, Fri.–Sat. 10:30–7, Sun. 12–5. $10. 150+ dealers. www.hadaantiques.com.

VA: LEE DISTRICT WINTER ANTIQUES SHOW & SALE
Lee District Rec. Cntr., 6601 Telegraph Rd., Alexandria. Sat. 10–6, Sun. 11–5. $6. 75 dealers: American & Continental furniture, decorative accessories, art glass, bronzes, silver, folk art, ceramics, textiles, jewelry, etc. 301-933-9433. www.pappabello.com

Fourth Week

MD: HUNT VALLEY ANTIQUES SHOW
Holiday Inn Select, 2004 Greenspring Dr., Timonium. Fri.11–8, Sat.11–7, Sun. 11–5. $12. Dealers from 15 states: American, English, & Continental furniture, fine & decorative arts. 410-366-1980 ext. 253; 410-961-5121. www.armacostantiquesshows.com

NJ: MONTCLAIR HISTORICAL SOCIETY ANTIQUE SHOW
200 Cooper Ave. Sat. 11–8, Sun. 11–5. 973-744-1796. www.montclairhistorical.org

NYC: THE MODERN SHOW
69th Reg. Armory, Lexington Ave. at 26th St. Fri.–Sat. 11–7, Sun. 11–5. $12. 100 dealers: 20th-c. furniture, glass, ceramics, silver, jewelry, books, photography, etc. 212-255-0020. www.stellashows.com

PA: MID-WINTER CLASSIC ANTIQUE & COLLECTIBLES SHOW
Valley Forge Conv. Cntr., 1160 First Ave., King of Prussia. Sat. 8–6, Sun. 10–5. $6. 300+ dealers. 877-385-0104. www.renningers.com

TN: MEMPHIS ANTIQUES, GARDEN & GOURMET SHOW
Agricenter Intl., 7777 Walnut Grove Rd., Memphis. Fri.–Sat. 10–6, Sun. 11–5. $10. 85 dealers: furniture, decorative accessories, objets d'art, jewelry, garden furniture. 708-336-2710. www.dolphinfairs.com; www.madonnacircle.org

MARCH

First Week

GA: ANTIQUES SHOW & SALE
Madison-Morgan Cultural Cntr., Madison. Fri. 10–7, Sat. 10–5. $5. American furnishings. 877-233-0598. www.madisonmorgancultural.org

FL: SARASOTA SPRING ANTIQUES SHOW & SALE
Municipal Auditorium, 801 N. Tamiami Trail. Fri.–Sat. 10–6, Sun. 12–5. $5. 60 dealers: antique furniture, silver, porcelain, jewelry, bronzes, glass, pottery, paintings, prints, etc. 954-563-6747. www.dolphinfairs.com

IL: WINNETKA WOMAN'S CLUB ANTIQUES SHOW
485 Maple St. Fri. 10–8, Sat. 10–6, Sun. 11–5. $12. 40+ dealers: 18th- & 19th-c. antiques. 847-446-1830. www.winnetkawomansclub.org

NYC: GRAMERCY GARDEN ANTIQUE SHOW
69th Reg. Armory, Lexington Ave. at 26th St. Fri.–Sat. 11–7, Sun. 11–5. $12. 80 dealers: garden furniture, ornaments, planters, pots, fences, gazebos, & architectural elements. 212-255-0020. www.stellashows.com

NYC: WORKS ON PAPER
7th Reg. Armory, Park Ave. at 67th St. Thurs.–Fri. 12–8, Sat.–Sun. 12–7. 80+ intl. dealers: watercolors, fine prints, photography, drawings, posters, & illustrated books, from old masters to contemporary. 212-777-5218. www.sanfordsmith.com

PA: CHESTER COUNTY HISTORICAL SOCIETY ANTIQUES SHOW
QVC Studio Park, West Chester. Sat. 10–7, Sun. 11–5. $12. 49 dealers: 18th- & 19th-c. furniture, rare glass, prints, porcelain, folk art, quilts, silver, rugs, paintings, etc. 610-692-4800. www.chestercohistorical.org

VA: FLEUR-DE-LIS ANTIQUES & GARDEN SHOW
E. Rivanna Fire Hall, Rt. 250 E., Charlottesville. Sat. 10–5, Sun. 11–4. 434-846-7452.

DC: SPRING ANTIQUES FAIR
D.C. Armory, 2001 E. Capitol St. Fri.–Sat. 11–6, Sun. 11–5. $7. 100 dealers: American, Victorian, English, Asian & French furniture, Art Deco, etc. 301-933-9433. www.pappabello.com

Second Week

CT: CONNECTICUT SPRING ANTIQUES SHOW
Expo Cntr., 265 Rev. Moody Overpass, Hartford. Sat. 10–5, Sun. 10–4. 60+ dealers of pre-1840 American furniture & decorative arts. 860-345-2400. www.haddamhistory.org

FL: NAPLES ANTIQUES SHOW & SALE
Trinity-by-the-Cove Episcopal Church, 553 Galleon Dr. Thurs.–Sat. 11–5. $15. 410-961-5121; 239-262-0353. www.armacostantiquesshows.com

IN: INDIANAPOLIS ART & ANTIQUES SHOW & SALE
State Fairgrounds, 1202 E. 38th St. Fri. 11–8, Sat. 11–7, Sun. 11–5. $8. 100 dealers: American & European furniture, folk art, prints, bronzes, silver, early glass, linens, woodenware, Oriental carpets, jewelry, etc. 301-933-6994. www.shador.com

KY: LEXINGTON ANTIQUES & GARDEN SHOW
Keeneland Race Track. Fri.–Sat. 10–6, Sun. 11–4. 18th–20th-c. furniture, Oriental rugs, paintings, porcelains, garden & outdoor furnishings, jewelry. 859-253-0362. www.bluegrasstrust.org

NYC: NEW YORK DESIGN FAIR
7th Reg. Armory, Park Ave. at 67th St. Thurs.–Fri. 11–8, Sat. 11–7:30, Sun. 11–6. Antique through 21st -c. items. 914-698-3442. www.newyorkdesignfair.com

VA: ANTIQUES IN ALEXANDRIA SHOW
Episcopal H.S., 3900 W. Braddock Rd. Fri. 11–8, Sat. 11–7, Sun. 11–5. $14. 60 dealers. 703-548-7469. www.antiquesinalexandria.com

Third Week

CT: HISTORICAL SOCIETY ANTIQUES SHOW
Wilton H.S. Field House, Rt. 7, Wilton. Sat. 10–5, Sun. 11–5. $10. Fine furniture, Americana, folk art, ceramics, textiles, etc. 203-762-7257. www.wiltonhistorical.org

NYC: TRIPLE PIER ANTIQUES SHOW
Piers 88, 90 & 92, Twelfth Ave.,
48–55th Sts. Sat. 9–6, Sun. 11–6. $15.
600 dealers: early American furniture,
porcelains, silver, ceramics, paintings,
prints, lighting, timepieces, Asian
objects, bronzes, folk art, rugs, quilts,
tribal arts, garden & architectural
items, toys, etc. 212-255-0020.
www.stellashows.com

PA: OAKMONT ANTIQUES SHOW
Oakmont Country Club. Sat. 10–5, Sun.
11–4. $8. 18th–19th-c. furniture,
porcelain, paintings, rugs, silver, etc.
412-826-9295. www.kerrmuseum.com

SC: CHARLESTON INTERNATIONAL
ANTIQUES SHOW
40 E. Bay St. Fri.–Sat. 10–6, Sun. 11–5.
$15. 33 dealers: American & European
furnishings, fine & decorative arts.
843-722-3405.
www.historiccharleston.org

Fourth Week

NJ: ATLANTIQUE CITY
Conv. Cntr., 1 Miss America Way,
Atlantic City. Sat. 10–7, Sun. 10–5. $10.
1,000+ booths: glass, ceramics, silver,
fine arts, furniture, collectibles.
800-526-2724. www.atlantiquecity.com

NY: BEDFORD SPRING
ANTIQUES SHOW
Rippowam Cisqua School, Rt. 22. Sat.
10–5, Sun. 11–5. $10. 914-234-9636.
www.stmatthewsbedford.org

APRIL

First week

IL: SPRING ANTIQUES SHOW & SALE
Arlington Park Racecourse, 2200 W.
Euclid Ave., Arlington Heights. Sat.
10–7, Sun. 11–5. $8. 200+ dealers:
furniture, silver, porcelain, bronzes,
glass, pottery, rugs, jewelry, textiles,
paintings, posters, maps, prints,
watches, etc. 954-563-6747.
www.dolphinfairs.com

MA: BOYS & GIRLS CLUBS DECORA-
TIVE ARTS & ANTIQUES SHOW
Castle at Park Plaza Hotel, 130
Columbus Ave., Boston. Fri. 11–8,
Sat. 11–7, Sun. 11–5. $10. 40 American
& English dealers: 18th–19th-c.
American & Continental furniture &
accessories. Preview Thurs.
914-698-3442; 617-462-2000.
www.wendyshows.com

NYC: ARTS OF PACIFIC ASIA SHOW
69th Reg. Armory, Lexington Ave. at
26th St. Thurs.–Sat. 11–7, Sun. 12–6.
$15. 70 dealers: Asian decorative &
fine arts. 310-455-2886.
www.caskeylees.com

NYC: INTERNATIONAL
ASIAN ART FAIR
7th Reg. Armory, Park Ave. at 67th St.
Fri.–Sat. 11–7:30, Sun. 11–6. $18.
50+ dealers from U.S., Europe, Asia:
furniture, sculpture, bronzes, art,
ceramics, carpets, textiles, jewelry.
212-642-8572. www.haughton.com

PA: WOMEN'S COMMITTEE
ANTIQUES, ART & DESIGN
SHOW & SALE
Carnegie Museum of Art, 4400 Forbes
Ave., Pittsburgh. Fri.–Sun. $10. 40+
dealers. 914-698-3442; 412-622-3325.
www.cmoa.org; www.wendyshows.com

VA: RICHMOND ANTIQUES
SPECTACULAR & THE GARDEN
ANTIQUES SHOW
Showcase, 3000 Mechanicsville Tnpk.
Sat. 10–6, Sun. 12–5. $5.
804-462-6190.
www.renaissancepromotions.com

Second Week

IL: CHICAGO MODERNISM
SHOW & SALE
1418 N. Kingsbury. Sat. 10–7, Sun.
12–5. $10. 75 dealers: 20th-c. objects.
708-366-2710.
www.chicagomodernism.net

PA: ANTIQUES AT
PHILADELPHIA'S NAVY PIER
Cruise Terminal at Pier One,
5100 S. Broad St. Fri. 10–5, Sat.10–6,
Sun. 10–4. $15 Fri., $10 Sat. & Sun. 70
dealers: American & English antiques.
703-914-1268. www.b4rtime.com

PA: ORIGINAL 23RD STREET
ARMORY ANTIQUES SHOW
22nd–23rd Sts., bet. Market &
Chestnut, Philadelphia. Fri. 12–6,
Sat. 10–7, Sun. 10–5. $10+. 40
Americana dealers. 845-876-0616.
www.barnstar.com

PA: PHILADELPHIA ANTIQUES SHOW
33rd St. Armory at Arch St. Sat. 11–8,
Sun. 11–6, Mon 11–4:30, Tues. 11–8.
$15. 60 leading dealers of Americana.
215-387-3500. www.philaantiques.com

Third Week

CO. DENVER ANTIQUES
SHOW & SALE
Wings over the Rockies Air & Space
Museum, 7711 E. Academy Blvd.
Fri.–Sat. 11–6, Sun. 11–5. $10. 30
dealers: furniture, paintings, majolica,
prints, silver, jewelry, rugs, garden
items. 303-292-6500.
www.denverantiquesshow.com;
www.armacostantiquesshows.com

IL: CHICAGO BOTANIC
GARDEN ANTIQUES & GARDEN FAIR
1000 Lake Cook Rd., Glencoe. Fri.–Sat.
10–7, Sun. 10–5. $18. 100+ dealers
from the U.S. & Europe: fine garden
furniture, statuary, ornaments,
fountains, gazebos, etc. 212-255-0020.
www.stellashows.com;
www.chicagobotanic.org/antiques

NYC: NEW YORK ANTIQUARIAN
BOOK FAIR
7th Reg. Armory, Park Ave. at 67th St.
Fri. 12–8, Sat. 12–7, Sun. 12–5. $15.
180 intl. dealers: nation's oldest book
fair; diverse titles. 212-777-5218.
www.sanfordsmith.com

Fourth Week

CA: LOS ANGELES ANTIQUES SHOW
Barker Hangar, Santa Monica Airport
Cntr., Santa Monica. Fri.–Sat. 11–8,
Sun. 11–5. $15. 65 dealers: American
& European furniture & paintings,
Asian art, silver, ceramics, jewelry,
prints, books, maps, manuscripts,
carpets, textiles, toys, folk art, etc.
310-455-2886. www.caskeylees.com;
www.losangelesantiqueshow.com

IL: CHICAGO ANTIQUES FAIR
Merchandise Mart. Fri. 11–8, Sat. 11–6,
Sun. 11–5, Mon. 11–3. $15.
100 dealers: 20th-c. design, Asian art
& antiquities, ceramics, decorative
arts, folk art, furniture, glass, jewelry,
posters, prints, rare books & maps,
sculpture, silver, textiles, tribal art.
800-677-6278.
www.merchandisemart.com/
chicagoantiques

IL: PHEASANT RUN SPRING
ANTIQUE SHOW & SALE
DuPage Expo, Rt. 64, St. Charles.
Sat. 10–7, Sun. 10–5. $7. Furniture,
decorative & fine arts, ceramics,
jewelry, bronzes, textiles, etc.
715-526-9769.
www.zurkoantiquetours.com

MD: ANTIQUES SHOW & SALE
40 S. Harrison St., Easton. Sat. 10–5,
Sun. 11–5. $6. 18th–19th-c. furnish-
ings, silver, jewelry, garden items.
410-822-0444. www.talbotcounty.org

NY: ANTIQUE GARDEN
FURNITURE SHOW & SALE
New York Botanical Garden, Bronx
River Pkwy./Fordham Rd., Bronx.
Fri. 11–8, Sat.–Sun. 11–5. 30 dealers:
garden furnishings, ornaments
& accessories incl. botanical prints.
718-817-8700. www.nybg.org

NYC: THE SPRING INTERNATIONAL ART & ANTIQUES SHOW
7th Reg. Armory, Park Ave. at 67th St. Fri.–Sat., Mon.–Tues. 11–8, Sun. & Wed., 11–7. $15. 50 dealers: 17th–20th-c. European, American, & Asian furniture, Oriental rugs, tapestries, rare books & autographs, boxes, clocks, silver, jewelry, etc. 914-698-3442. www.wendyshows.com; www.nyinternationalantiquesshow.com

MAY

First Week

CA: LOS ANGELES MODERNISM SHOW
Civic Auditorium, 1855 Main St., Santa Monica. Sat. 11–7, Sun. 11–5. $15. Decorative, functional, fine, & applied arts, 1900–2001. 818-244-1126. www.lamodernism.com

MA: EPHEMERA CITY
Topsfield Fairgrounds, Rt. 1N., Topsfield. Sat. 9–3. 978-535-4811. www.bornsteinshows.com

OH: COLUMBUS ACADEMY ANTIQUES SHOW
4300 Cherry Bottom Rd., Gahanna. Sat. 10:30–6, Sun. 12–5. $10. 60 dealers. 614-509-2293. www.columbusacademy-antiquesshow. org

PA: PENNSYLVANIA SPRING ANTIQUES SHOW
York Expo Cntr., 334 Carlisle Ave., York. Fri. 11–7, Sat. 10–5. $10. 80+ dealers. 845-876-0616. www.barnstar.com

PA: YORK COUNTY CLASSIC ANTIQUES SHOW
York Expo Cntr., 334 Carlisle Ave., York. Fri. 8–5, Sat. 10–4. $10. 70+ dealers: American & English country & formal furniture, folk art, accessories. 703-914-1268. www.b4rtime.com

VA: SPRING SHENANDOAH ANTIQUES EXPO
Augusta Expoland, I-64/Exit 91, Fishersville. Sat. 9–5, Sun. 10–4. $5. 400 dealers. www.crossroadsshenvalley.org; www.augustaexpo.com

Second Week

MA: BRIMFIELD ANTIQUES & COLLECTIBLES SHOW
Rt. 20. Tues.–Sun. starting at daybreak. 4,000+ dealers. www.brimfieldshow.com

MI: GREENFIELD VILLAGE ANTIQUES SHOW & SALE
Henry Ford Museum, Dearborn. Sat.–Sun. $8. 40+ dealers: 18th–19th-c. furniture, textiles, jewelry, decorative arts. 313-982-6001. www.hfmgv.org

NYC: INTERNATIONAL FINE ART FAIR
7th Reg. Armory, Park Ave. at 67th St. Fri.–Sat. 11–7:30, Sun. 11–6. 40 dealers: 15th–20th-c. paintings, drawings, sculpture by European & American artists. 212-642-8572. www.haughton.com

Third Week

CA: BEVERLY HILLS CLASSIC ANTIQUES, FINE ART, & JEWELRY SHOW
Peterson Automotive Museum, 6060 Wilshire Blvd. $18. 80+ dealers: paintings, sculpture, vintage jewelry, home furnishings, lighting, garden items. www.lpmevents.com

NJ: WATERLOO ANTIQUES FAIR
Waterloo Concert Field, Stanhope. Sat.–Sun. 10–5. $6. 200 dealers: furniture, textiles, quilts, toys, fishing & sporting collectibles, postcards, maps, pottery, folk art, books, prints, glass, jewelry. 212-255-0020. www.stellashows.com

NYC: NEW YORK INTERNATIONAL TRIBAL & TEXTILE ARTS SHOW
69th Reg. Armory, Lexington Ave. at 26th St. Sat.–Mon. 11–8, Tues. 11–6. $15. 70 dealers: fine arts, artifacts, objects, carpets, & textiles of the Americas, Oceania, Asia, & Africa. 310-455-2886. www.caskeylees.com

RI: SPRING FAIR AT BLITHEWOLD: GARDEN ANTIQUES & SPECIALTY PLANT SALE
101 Ferry Rd., Bristol. Sat. 10–4. $15. 30 dealers: American, English, & Continental garden furniture, ornaments, gates, statuary, urns, botanical prints. 401-253-2707. www.blithewold.org

VA: TOWN & COUNTRY ANTIQUES SHOW & SALE
Rose Benté Lee Cntr., Marymount Univ., 2807 N. Glebe Rd., Arlington. Fri.–Sat. 11–7, Sun. 11–5. $12. 18th–19th-c. American, English, French, & Chinese formal & country furniture, accessories. 703-780-9200.

Fourth Week

PA: BRANDYWINE RIVER MUSEUM ANTIQUES SHOW
Rt. 1, Chadds Ford. Sat.–Mon. 10–5. $10. 32 dealers from 13 states: 17th–19th-c. American & English country & formal furniture, folk art, accessories. 610-388-2700; 410-961-5121. www.armacostantiquesshows.com

JUNE

First Week

CA: SANTA BARBARA ANTIQUES & FINE ARTS SHOW
City College of Santa Barbara Sports Pavilion, 721 Cliff Dr. Fri.–Sat. 11–6, Sun. 12–5. 505-753-2553. www.antiquities-shows.com

KY: PLEASANT HILL ANTIQUES SHOW & SALE
3501 Lexington Rd., Harrodsburg. $12. 75 dealers from 18 states. 800-734-5611. www.shakervillageky.org

NJ: TWO RIVERS ANTIQUES SHOW
Red Bank Armory & Ice Complex, Red Bank. Sat.–Sun. $10. 732-923-6886.

NY: HAMPTON'S SPRING GARDEN ANTIQUES SHOW & SALE
Bridgehampton Comm. House, Montauk Hwy., Bridgehampton. Fri.–Sat. 10–6, Sun. 10–5. 631-537-0333. www.hamptonsantiques.com

Second Week

CT: FARMINGTON ANTIQUES WEEKEND
Polo Grounds, Town Farm Rd. Sat. 8–5, Sun. 10–5. $10. 600 dealers: fine & rustic furniture, garden ornaments, architectural items, silver, jewelry, nautical items, linens etc. 317-598-0012. www.farmington-antiques.com

Third Week

CT: LITCHFIELD COUNTY ANTIQUES SHOW
Kent School, Kent. Sat.–Sun. 10–5. 40 dealers. 860-567-0300. www.antiquescouncil.com

PA: ANTIQUES IN THE VALLEY
Oley Valley H.S., Rt. 73, Oley. Fri. 11–7, Sat. 10–4. $6. 55 dealers: 18th–early 20th-c. furniture, folk art, accessories. 610-987-3312; 610-779-0705.

Fourth Week

CT: WILTON OUTDOOR
ANTIQUES SHOW
Wilton H.S., Rt. 7. Sat.–Sun. 10–5.
$10. 150 dealers of 18th–20th-c.
American, English, European, & Asian
furniture, decorative arts, jewelry,
architectural & garden items, etc.
203-762-3525. www.wiltonkiwanis.org

NY: ANTIQUES & DESIGN
IN THE HAMPTONS
Corwith House Museum, 2368
Montauk Hwy., Bridgehampton. Sat.
10–6, Sun. 11–5. $8. 50 dealers:
furniture, garden items, Art Deco,
silver, ceramics, rugs, textiles, folk art,
jewelry, etc. 212-255-0020.
www.stellashows.com

JULY

First Week

NY: HAMPTON'S MODERNISM
& ART SHOW
Bridgehampton Comm. House,
Montauk Hwy., Bridgehampton.
Fri.–Sat. 10–6, Sun. 10–5.
631-537-0333.
www.hamptonsantiques.com

Second Week

CT: MADISON ANTIQUES SHOW
Green, Boston Post Rd. Sat. 9–4.
www.northmadisoncongregational
church .org

MA: BRIMFIELD ANTIQUES &
COLLECTIBLES SHOW
Rt. 20. Tues.–Sun. starting at daybreak.
4,000+ dealers.
www.brimfieldshow.com

NY: HAMPTON'S ANTIQUES
AT AMAGANSETT
First Presbyterian Church, 350
Montauk Hwy. Sat. 10–5, Sun. 11–5. $6.
631-261-4590.
www.flamingoshows.com

NY: HAMPTON'S ANTIQUES
& GARDEN SHOW
Bridgehampton Comm. House,
Montauk Hwy., Bridgehampton.
Fri.–Sat. 10–6, Sun. 10–5.
631-537-0333.
www.hamptonsantiques.com

VT: ANTIQUES AT HILDENE
River Rd. off Rt. 7A, Manchester
Village. Sat. 207-767-3967.
www.forbesandturner.com

Third Week

ME: ROCKPORT ANTIQUES
& ART SHOW
MRC Ice Arena, Rt. 90, W. Rockport.
Sat. 10–4. $6. 56 dealers.
207-563-1013.
www.pauldavisshows.com

VT: BIENNIAL DORSET
ANTIQUES SHOW
Downtown Dorset.
Sat. 10–4. $7.
www.forbesandturner.com

Fourth Week

ME: BAR HARBOR ANTIQUES
SHOW & SALE
MDI H.S., Eagle Lake Rd. Sat. 10–4. $6.
50 dealers. 207-563-1013.
www.pauldavisshows.com

MA: ANTIQUES AT ELM
BANK ESTATE
MA Horticultural Society, 900
Washington St./Rt. 16, Wellesley.
Sat.–Sun. 150 dealers. 781-862-4039.
www.neantiqueshows.com

NY: ANTIQUES & DESIGN
IN THE HAMPTONS
Corwith House Museum, 2368
Montauk Hwy., Bridgehampton. Sat.
10–6, Sun. 11–5. $8. 50 dealers: furni-
ture, Art Deco, silver, ceramics, rugs &
textiles, folk art, garden items, jewelry,
etc. 212-255-0020.
www.stellashows.com

AUGUST

First Week

ME: ACADEMY ANTIQUES SHOW
George Stevens Academy, Union
St./Rt.177, Blue Hill. Thurs.–Fri. 10–6,
Sat. 10–5. $7. 207-359-2151.

MA: NANTUCKET HISTORICAL
ASSN. ANTIQUES SHOW
New School, 15 Nobadeer Farm Rd.
Fri.–Sat. 10–5, Sun. 10–4.
508-228-1894. www.nha.org;
www.antiquescouncil.org

Second Week

NH: MIDWEEK IN MANCHESTER
Quality Inn & Wayfarer Conf. Cntr., 121
S. River Rd., Bedford. Wed. 9–7, Thurs.
11–4. $10. 110 dealers: Americana.
845-876-0616.
www.barnstar.com

NH: BEDFORD PICKERS' MARKET
ANTIQUES SHOW
Quality Inn & Wayfarer Conf. Cntr.,
121 S. River Rd. Fri. 11–4. $8.
111 dealers: 18th–20th-c. items.
845-876-0616. www.barnstar.com

NH: AMERICANA CELEBRATION
ANTIQUE SHOW & SALE
Deerfield Fairgrounds, Rt. 43,
Deerfield. Tues. 10–4. $6. 100 dealers:
American furnishings. 207-625-3577.

NH: NEW HAMPSHIRE ANTIQUES
DEALERS ASSN. SHOW
Radisson Hotel, 700 Elm St.,
Manchester. Thurs.–Fri. 10–7, Sat.
10–4. $10. 65 dealers: fine formal
& country American furniture & decorative arts. 603-585-9199.
www.nhada.org

NH: RIVERSIDE ANTIQUES SHOW
Best Western Executive Ct., 13500 S.
Willow St., Manchester. Tues. 5–9,
Wed. 12–6, Thurs. 12–4. $10. 18th–
19th-c. country & formal furniture &
decorative accessories. 207-767-3967.
www.forbesandturner.com

NJ: ANTIQUES SHOW & ART SALE
St. Paul's United Methodist Church,
Bridge & W. Lake Aves., Bay Head.
Tues. 10–7, Wed. 10–5. $5. 20 dealers:
furniture, glass, jewelry, & linens.
732-892-5926. www.bayhead.org

VA: VIRGINIA BEACH
ANTIQUES SHOW
Conv. Cntr., 1000 19th St. Fri.–Sat.
10–6, Sun. 12–5. $7. 125+ dealers:
American, European, & Asian
furniture, decorative & fine arts,
silver, ceramics. 757-417-7771.
www.emgshows.com

Third Week

NM: HISTORIC INDIAN
& WORLD TRIBAL ARTS SHOW
Shellaberger Tennis Cntr., College of
Santa Fe, 1600 St. Michael's Dr., Santa
Fe. Fri.–Sat. 10–5, Sun. 10–4. $12.
95 dealers: Native American antiques,
ethnographic arts, textiles, pottery,
rugs, Western Americana, folk art, etc.
703-914-6144.
www.tribalantiqueshow.com

Fourth Week

CT: FARMINGTON ANTIQUES
WEEKEND
Polo Grounds, Town Farm Rd. Sat. 8–5,
Sun. 10–5. $10. 600 dealers: fine &
rustic furniture, garden ornaments,
architectural, silver, jewelry, nautical
items, linens, etc. 317-598-0012.
www.farmington-antiques.com

IL: CHICAGO O'HARE SUMMER
ANTIQUES, GARDEN & VINTAGE
CLOTHING SHOW & SALE
Donald E. Stephens Conv. Cntr., 5555
N. River Rd., Rosemont. Fri. 12–8,
Sat. 12–7, Sun. 12–5. $10. 350 dealers:
fine furniture, garden statuary, vintage
clothing, silver, ceramics, folk art,
quilts, lighting, rugs, advertising,
jewelry, dolls, etc. 954-563-6747.
www.dolphinfairs.com

ME: MAINE ANTIQUES DEALERS ASSN. COASTAL MAINE ANTIQUES SHOW
Round Top Cntr. for the Arts, Business Rt. 1, Damariscotta. Wed. 9:30–4. $7. 110+ dealers. www.maineantiques.org

MA: NEWBURYPORT ANTIQUES SHOW
Historic downtown waterfront. Sat. 10–7:30, Sun. 11–5. $9. 40 East Coast dealers: fine & country furniture, folk art, books, ceramics, silver, brass, rugs, textiles, fine art. 978-462-2681. www.newburyhist.com

NY: HAMPTON'S SUMMER ANTIQUE FESTIVAL & SALE
Bridgehampton Comm. House, Montauk Hwy., Bridgehampton. Fri.–Sat. 10–6, Sun. 10–5. 631-537-0333. www.hamptonsantiques.com

SEPTEMBER

First Week

MD: BALTIMORE SUMMER ANTIQUES FAIR
Inner Harbor Conv. Cntr., W. Pratt St. Fri. 12–9, Sat. 11–7, Sun. 11–5. $12. 450 dealers: fine art, furniture, silver, porcelain, jewelry, bronzes, prints, Asian art, books, etc. 301-933-6994. www.shador.com

MA: BOSTON CONNOISSEUR
Castle at Park Plaza, 64 Arlington St. Fri.–Sun. 11–7. $15. American & European fine & decorative arts, 18th–20th-c. furniture, jewelry, textiles, silver, paintings, drawings, prints, books, manuscripts, photographs, etc. 561-845-5453. www.connoisseurfairs.com

Second Week

CT: DAUGHTERS OF THE AMERICAN REVOLUTION ANTIQUES SHOW
Wilton H.S. Field House, Rt. 7, Wilton. Sun. 10–5. $9. 18th– 20th-c. American, English, & Continental furniture, decorative accessories, folk & fine art. 203-762-3525.

MD: CHEVY CHASE ANTIQUES SHOW
Woman's Club, 7931 Connecticut Ave. Fri. 11–7, Sat. 11–6, Sun. 12–5. $10. American & English furniture & accessories, clocks, glass, ceramics, silver, jewelry, fine art, classical antiquities, Oriental rugs, folk art, etc. 410-961-5121; 301-229-0730. www.armacostantiquesshows.com

ME: MAINE ANTIQUE DEALERS' ANNUAL ANTIQUES SHOW
Racquet & Fitness Cntr., 2445 Congress St., Portland. Sat.–Sun. $8. www.maineantiques.org

MA: BRIMFIELD ANTIQUES & COLLECTIBLES SHOW
Rt. 20. Tues.–Sun. starting at daybreak. 4,000+ dealers. www.brimfieldshow.com

Third Week

CA: LOS ANGELES ASIAN & TRIBAL ARTS SHOW
Civic Auditorium, Main St., Santa Monica. Fri.–Sat. 11–7, Sun. 12–5. $10. 60+ dealers: furniture, folk art, costumes, sculpture, bronzes, pottery, textiles, rugs, ceremonial objects, jewelry, from Asia, Indonesia, the Philippines, Oceanic Islands, Africa, & the Americas. 310-455-2886. www.caskeylees.com

NE: LAURITZEN GARDENS ANTIQUE & GARDEN SHOWS
Omaha Botanical Gardens, 100 Bancroft St., Omaha. Fri. 9–5, Sat. 9–7, Sun. 9–5. $10. 402-346-4002. American & English dealers: furniture, silver, art, jewelry, ceramics, garden items. www.omahabotanicalgardens.org

PA: SEWICKLEY VALLEY ANTIQUE SHOW
Edgeworth Club, Sewickley. Sat. 10–5, Sun. 11–4. $9. 18th–19th-c. furniture, porcelain, rugs, paintings, silver, etc. 724-458-0450.

TX: HOUSTON ANTIQUES DEALERS ASSN. FALL ANTIQUES SHOW
George R. Brown Conv. Cntr. 1001 Ave. de las Americas. Thurs. 11–8, Fri.–Sat. 10:30–7, Sun. 12–5. $10. 150+ dealers. www.hadaantiques.com

TX: HEART OF COUNTRY ANTIQUES SHOW
Gaylord Texan Resort, Grapevine. 100+ dealers: Americana, country furniture, folk art, etc. 800-862-1090. www.heartofcountry.com

TX: THETA CHARITY ANTIQUES SHOW
George R. Brown Conv. Cntr., Houston. Thurs. 10:30–7, Fri.–Sat. 10:30–7, Sun. 12–5. $10. 50+ American & European dealers: 17th–20th-c. furnishings. 713-622-3560. www.thetaantiquesshow.com

VT: VERMONT ANTIQUES DEALERS ASSN. SHOW
Hunter Park, Rt. 7, Manchester. Sat. 10–5, Sun. 10–4. $7. 76 dealers from the eastern U.S.: fine formal & country furniture, decorative arts, folk art. www.vermontada.com

VT: ANTIQUES SHOW
Weston Playhouse, Village Green, Weston. Fri.–Sat. 10–5, Sun. 11–4. $7. 40 dealers: American & English furniture, Americana, folk art, ceramics, prints, silver, Oriental rugs, samplers, jewelry, etc. 802-824-5307.

OCTOBER

First Week

NYC: THE WENDY FALL FAIR
7th Reg. Armory, Park Ave. at 67th St. Wed. 4–8, Thurs.–Fri. 11–8, Sat. 11–7:30, Sun. 11–6. $15. 80 intl. dealers of 17th–21st-c. furniture, paintings, pottery, silver, jewelry, carpets, prints, rare books, etc. 914-698-3442. www.wendyshows.com

VA: HAMPTON ANTIQUES SHOW
Conv. Cntr. Fri.–Sat. 10–6, Sun. 11–5. $7. 80+ dealers: 18th–early 20th-c. American, Asian, & European furniture & decorative arts, fine art, silver, ceramics, & textiles. 757-417-7771. www.emgshows.com

Second Week

OH: CINCINNATI ANTIQUES FESTIVAL
Conv. Cntr., 11355 Chester Rd., Sharonville. Fri. 11–6, Sat. 11–9, Sun. 11–5. $10. 44 dealers: English & Continental furniture, silver, porcelain, fine art, & decorative accessories. 513-561-0950. www.cincinnatiantiquesfestival.org

MA: ANTIQUE DEALERS ASSN. OF AMERICA / HISTORIC DEERFIELD ANTIQUES SHOW
Deerfield Academy. Sat. 11–6, Sun. 11–5. $12. Early Americana, furniture, decorative arts, folk art, fine paintings, textiles, samplers, pewter, pottery, etc. 413-775-7214. www.adadealers.com

NJ: ATLANTIQUE CITY
Atlantic City Conv. Cntr., 1 Miss America Way, Atlantic City. Sat. 10–7, Sun. 10–5. $10. 1,000+ booths: ceramics, glass, silver, fine art, furniture, & collectibles. 800-526-2724. www.atlantiquecity.com

NYC: INTERNATIONAL ART & DESIGN FAIR 1900-2005
7th Reg. Armory, Park Ave. at 67th St. Fri.–Tues. $18. 50 intl. dealers: 20th-c. fine art & decorative arts. 212 642-8572. www.haughton.com

NYC: THE MODERN SHOW
69th Reg. Armory, Lexington Ave. at 26th St. Fri.–Sat. 11–7, Sun. 11–5. $12. 100 intl. dealers: furniture, art, jewelry, lighting, rugs, books, photography, ceramics, glass, posters, silver, etc., Art Nouveau & Art Deco through the 1950s & '60s. 212-255-0020. www.stellashows.com

PA: HISTORIC YELLOW SPRINGS ANTIQUES SHOW
1685 Art School Rd., Chester Springs. Sat. 10–5, Sun. 11–4. $10. 18th–19th-c. country & formal furniture, accessories, folk art, toys, jewelry, metalwork, textiles, ceramics, etc. 610-827-7414.
www.yellowsprings.org

SC: COUNTY MUSEUM OF ART ANTIQUES SHOW
420 College St., Greenville. Fri.–Sat. 11–6, Sun. 1–5. $8. 20+ dealers: formal & country furniture, Oriental rugs, porcelain, folk art, silver, paintings, etc. 864-271-7570.
www.greenvillemuseum.org

VA: FALL SHENANDOAH ANTIQUES EXPO
Augusta Expoland, I-64/Exit 91, Fishersville. Sat. 9–5, Sun. 10–4. $5. 400 dealers.
www.crossroadsshenvalley.org; www.augustaexpo.com

Third Week

CT: FALL HARTFORD ANTIQUES SHOW
Expo Cntr., 265 Reverend Moody Overpass. Sat. 10–5, Sun. 11–4. American furniture, textiles, folk art, ironware, porcelains, nautical items, hearth implements, etc. 207-767-3967. www.forbesandturner.com

FL: MIAMI ANTIQUE JEWELRY, WATCH & FINE SILVER SHOW
Miami Beach Conv. Cntr., 1901 Conv. Cntr. Dr. Fri.–Sat. 11–7, Sun. 11–6. $12. 100s of dealers. 239-732-6642.
www.dmgantiqueshows.com

IL: ARLINGTON PARK FALL ANTIQUES SHOW & FAIR
Arlington Park Racecourse, 2200 W. Euclid Ave., Arlington Heights. Sat. 10–7, Sun. 11–5. $8. 150+ U.S. & Canadian dealers: furniture, silver, porcelain, bronzes, glass, pottery, rugs, jewelry, textiles, paintings, posters, maps, prints, etc. 954-563-6747; 708-366-2710. www.dolphinfairs.com

NYC: GRAMERCY PARK ANTIQUES SHOW
69th Reg. Armory, Lexington Ave. at 26th St. Fri.–Sat. 11–7, Sun. 11–5. $12. 100 intl. dealers: formal, country, & modern French, English, American, & Asian furniture, prints, paintings, folk art, textiles, lighting, outsider art, mirrors, architectural & garden items, jewelry, ceramics, etc. 212-255-0020. www.stellashows.com

NYC: INTERNATIONAL FINE ART & ANTIQUE DEALERS SHOW
7th Reg. Armory, Park Ave. at 67th St. Fri.–Tues. 11–7, Sun. 11–6. $18. 50 intl. dealers: fine art, furniture, glass, rugs, ceramics, jewelry, watches, textiles, metalwork, books, photographs, Asian art, ethnographica. 212 642-8572. www.haughton.com

PA: US ARTISTS: AMERICAN FINE ART SHOW
33rd St. Armory, bet. Market & Arch Sts., Philadelphia. Fri.–Sat. 11–8, Sun. 11–5. $15. 50+ dealers of 18th–21st-c. American works, classic to contemporary, by new & established artists. 800-455-8312. www.usartists.org

Fourth Week

CA: SAN FRANCISCO FALL ANTIQUES SHOW
Fort Mason Cntr. Thurs.–Sat. 10–7, Sun. 12–6. $15. 70+ top intl. dealers: fine furniture & decorative arts, porcelain, silver, rugs, glass, fine art, all styles & periods, incl. American, Asian, English, & Continental. 415-989-9019. www.sffas.org

---

NOVEMBER

First Week

IL: PHEASANT RUN FALL ANTIQUE SHOW & SALE
DuPage Expo, Rt. 64, St. Charles. Sat. 10–7, Sun. 10–5. $7. Furniture, decorative & fine arts, ceramics, jewelry, bronzes, textiles, etc. 715-526-9769. www.zurkoantiquetours.com

IL: MODERNISM: EXPOSITION & SALE OF 20TH CENTURY DESIGN
Comm. House, 620 Lincoln Ave., Winnetka. $12. Sat. 10–6, Sun. 11–5. 55 dealers: furniture, paintings, photography, jewelry, pottery, textiles, clothing, & other decorative arts. 847-446-0537.
www.winnetkacommunityhouse.org

MA ELLIS ANTIQUES SHOW
Boston Park Plaza Hotel, 158 Columbus Ave., Boston. Thurs. 11–5, Fri.–Sat. 11–8, Sun. 11–5. $15. 37 dealers: American, European, & Asian art, formal & country furniture, porcelain, glass, silver, paintings, rugs, folk art, jewelry, etc. 617-248-8571. www.ellisantiques.com

NJ: MORRISTOWN ANTIQUES SHOW
National Guard Armory, 430 Western Ave. Fri.–Sat. 11–7, Sun. 11–5. 75 U.S. & European dealers: 18th–19th-c. furniture & accessories, jewelry, silver, prints, glass, paintings, rugs, books. 914-698-3442. www.wendyshows.com

NY: WHITE PLAINS ANTIQUES SHOW
198 Central Ave. Fri.–Sat. 11–7, Sun. 11–6. 40 dealers: American, English, & Continental furniture & accessories. 914-698-3442. www.wendyantiquesshows.com

NYC: INTERNATIONAL FINE PRINT DEALERS ASSN. ANNUAL PRINT FAIR
7th Reg. Armory, Park Ave. at 67th St. Thurs.–Sat. 12–7, Sun. 12–6. Free. 25+ dealers present 16th–21st-c. works on paper. 212-674-6095.
www.printdealers.com

NYC: TRIPLE PIER ANTIQUES SHOW
Twelfth Ave., 48th–52nd Sts. Two weekends: Sat. 9–6, Sun. 11–6. $15. 600 dealers: classical antiques, formal furniture, silver, ceramics, timepieces, paintings, Art Deco, Arts & Crafts, '40s, '50s, '60s furniture & furnishings, vintage fashion, appliances, textiles, folk art, Americana, garden & architectural artifacts, rugs, tribal arts, sporting, toys, books, etc. 212-255-0020. www.stellashows.com

PA: PENNSYLVANIA FALL ANTIQUES SHOW
York Expo Cntr., 334 Carlisle Ave., York. Fri. 10–7, Sat. 10–5. $10. 100 dealers: American furniture & accessories. 845-876-0616. www.barnstar.com

PA: YORK COUNTY CLASSIC ANTIQUES SHOW
York Expo Cntr., 334 Carlisle Ave., York. Fri. 8–5, Sat. 10–4. $10. 95+ dealers: American & English country & formal furniture, folk art, accessories. 703-914-1268. www.b4rtime.com

Second Week

DE: DELAWARE ANTIQUES SHOW
Bank One Cntr. on the Riverfront, Wilmington. Fri. 11–8, Sat. 11–6, Sun. 11–5. $15. 60 dealers: 17th–20th-c. American furniture, fine & decorative arts. 800-448-3883; 302-888-4600. www.winterthur.org

GA: ATLANTA INTERNATIONAL
ANTIQUES FAIR
Cobb Galleria Cntr. Fri. 12–8, Sat. 10–8,
Sun. 12–5. $10+ 200+ intl. dealers:
18th–20th-c. furniture, fine art,
jewelry, decorative accessories.
561-209-1335.
www.dmgantiqueshows.com

NYC: MODERNISM:
A CENTURY OF ART & DESIGN
7th Reg. Armory, Park Ave. at 67th St.
Thurs.–Fri. 12–8, Sat. 11–7, Sun. 12–6.
70 intl. dealers: late 19th–20th-c.
design movements: Art Deco, Art
Nouveau, Arts & Crafts, Bauhaus,
Memphis, Wiener Werkstätte.
212-777-5218. www.sanfordsmith.com

Third Week

CA: LOS ANGELES INTERIOR
DESIGN & ANTIQUES SHOW
Civic Auditorium, Main St., Santa
Monica. Sat. 11–7, Sun. 11–5. $10.
18th–21st-c. furniture & decorative
arts, lighting, vintage posters,
sculpture, Americana & folk art, outsider art, art glass & pottery, Persian
& tribal carpets, jewelry, Asian art &
antiques, American Indian artifacts,
silver, & porcelain. 310-455-2886.
www.caskeylees.com

CT: WETHERSFIELD ANTIQUE SHOW
Pitkin Comm. Cntr., 30 Greenfield St.
Sat. 10–4. $6. 48 dealers.
860-529-7656.

FL: SARASOTA FALL ANTIQUES
SHOW & SALE
Municipal Auditorium, 801 N. Tamiami
Trail. Fri.–Sat. 10–6, Sun. 12–5. $5.
60 dealers: furniture, silver, porcelain,
antique & estate jewelry, bronzes,
glass, pottery, paintings, prints, Asian
items, etc. 954-563-6747;
708-366-2710. www.dolphinfairs.com

MA: GREATER BOSTON
ANTIQUES FESTIVAL
Shriner's Auditorium, 99 Fordham Rd.,
Wilmington. Sat. 9–5, Sun 10–4. $7.
162 dealers: furniture, fine art, Asian
objects, fine & folk art, quilts, rugs,
silver, estate jewelry, linens, ceramics,
maps, Victorian collectibles, vintage
tiles. 781-862-4039.
www.neantiqueshows.com

NYC: CONNOISSEUR'S
ANTIQUES FAIR
69th Reg. Armory, Lexington Ave. at
26th St. Thurs.–Fri 11–8, Sat. 11–7,
Sun. 11–5. $15. 50 dealers: furniture,
decorative & fine arts from around the
world. 310-455-2886.
www.caskeylees.com

VA: HISTORIC ALEXANDRIA
ANTIQUES SHOW
Holiday Inn, 625 First St. Fri. 11–8,
Sat. 11–7, Sun. 12–5. $12. 44 dealers:
17th–19th-c. furniture & decorative
accessories, fine & folk art, ceramics,
jewelry, silver, Shaker objects, garden
furnishings, etc.
703-549-5811; 410-961-5121.
www.armacostantiquesshows.com

VA: RICHMOND ANTIQUES
SPECTACULAR & THE
ANTIQUARIAN BOOK FAIR
Showcase, 3000 Mechanicsville Tnpk.
Sat. 10–6, Sun. 12–5. $5.
804-462-6190.
www.renaissancepromotions.com

Fourth Week

MA: PEABODY ESSEX MUSEUM
ANNUAL ANTIQUES SHOW
Salem. Sat.–Sun. 10–5. $13. 30+
dealers: furniture, paintings, porcelain,
jewelry, decorative accessories.
978-745-9500. www.pem.org

DC: TOWN & COUNTRY
ANTIQUES SHOW
Lab School of Washington, 4759
Reservoir Rd. NW. Fri. 11–7, Sat. 11–6,
Sun. 11–5. $12. Fine furniture,
decorative accessories, clocks, silver,
paintings, music boxes, bronzes,
linens, American art, jewelry, carpets,
ceramics, walking sticks, etc.
703-780-9200.

DECEMBER

First Week

CT: ANTIQUARIUS ANTIQUES SHOW
Greenwich Civic Cntr., 90 Harding Rd.,
Old Greenwich. Fri.–Sat. 11–6,
Sun. 11–5. $10. 203-869-6899.
www.hstg.org

CT: HOLIDAY ANTIQUES SHOW
Wilton H.S. Field House, Rt. 7, Wilton.
Sun. 10–5. 120 dealers: fine furniture,
decorative arts, folk art, vintage
holiday items. 203-762-3525.

DC: WINTER ANTIQUES
& JEWELRY SHOW
D.C. Armory, 2001 E. Capitol St.
Fri. 12–7, Sat. 11–6, Sun. 11–5. $8.
100 dealers. 301-933-9433.
www.pappabello.com

Second Week

CT: ANTIQUE STOCKING
STUFFERS SHOW & SALE
Civic Cntr., 90 Harding Rd., Old
Greenwich. Sun. 10–5. $6. Porcelain,
glass, jewelry, sterling, picture frames,
spoons, toys, dresser sets.
914-273-4667. www.cordshows.com

NYC: ANTIQUES & FINE ART
AT THE ARMORY
7th Reg. Armory, Park Ave. at 67th St.
Thurs. & Mon. 11–5, Fri. 11–8, Sat.
11–7:30, Sun. 11–6. 55 intl. dealers:
17th–21st-c. furnishings, decorative
arts, jewelry, etc. 914-698-3442.
www.wendyshows.com

Fourth Week

FL: ANNUAL HOLIDAY
ANTIQUE SHOW
War Memorial Auditorium, 800 N.
Federal Hwy./U.S. 1, Ft. Lauderdale.
Tues. 11–7, Wed. 11–5. $5. 75 dealers.
954-563-6747. www.dolphinfairs.com

FL: SARASOTA HOLIDAY ANTIQUES
SHOW & SALE
Municipal Auditorium, 801 N. Tamiami
Trail. Fri.–Sat. 10–6, Sun. 12–5. $5.
60 dealers: furniture, silver, porcelain,
jewelry, bronzes, glass, pottery,
paintings, prints, etc. 954-563-6747.
www.dolphinfairs.com

NM: SANTA FE WINTER
ANTIQUITIES SHOW
El Museo Cultural De Santa Fe, 1615
Paseo De Peralta. Thurs.–Fri. 11–5,
Sat. 11–4. $10. 50+ dealers: folk & fine
art from Asia, Europe, Africa, & the
Americas. 505-753-9889.
www.antiquities-shows.com

Acknowledgments

❋

In the 20 years that I've been writing about historic buildings and furnishings, I've been especially fortunate to work with Mimi Handler, former editor of *Early American Life,* and with David Larkin, who introduced me to Rizzoli.

At Rizzoli, I am grateful to Charles Miers, Ellen Nidy, Anet Sirna Bruder, and Jane Newman. Editor Sandy Gilbert helped turn an abundance of information from dross into gold, and made our collaboration a total pleasure. Thanks to the talented Victoria Pohlmann for her design, to copy editor John Morrone, and to Michael Itkoff, Trish McElroy, and Lynn Scrabis for their assistance.

The Magazine ANTIQUES compiled the nationwide calendar of antiques shows appearing herein, for which thanks are due to publisher Sandra Brant, editor Allison Eckardt Ledes, and to Eleanor H. Gustafson, Jennifer Norton, and Katryna Glettler.

This book benefited from suggestions by antiquing experts and enthusiasts, notably Michael Connors, H. Parrott Bacot, David and Sabra Larkin, David and Linda Cook, Mimi Handler, Martin Murphy, Fred Dirck, Chris Ohrstrom, Jean Cresnick, John Fulop, Mark Jipp, Molly Maginnis, John Schaffner, Jane Morrison, David Schorsch, Ruth Van Tassel, and Don Weise.

Helpful information was sourced from *Antiques and the Arts Weekly, Maine Antique Digest,* regional antiquing publications, state and city antiques dealers associations, Antiques Council listings, show catalogs, and antiquing websites. *Sloan's Green Guides, Leggett's Antiquing Atlases,* and antiquing books specific to New York, Vermont, and Texas were also useful. RandMcNally.com was an excellent tool for calculating mileage and routes.

No shop, show, or lodging paid to appear in this book, and no complimentary travel was involved. But inn owners, PR professionals, antiques dealers, show managers, and CVB staffs contributed much to it, and their assistance is much appreciated. I thank editor Patty Poore of *Old House Interiors* for my travel to Charleston for the magazine, and Michael Haga and others at the College of Charleston for being wonderful hosts while I was there.

The background for this book evolved over time—in fact over many happy hours—spent antiquing with my mother, and with my friends, particularly Linda Miller, Mimi Zaugg, John Young, Clay Jones, David and Sherrill Sanger, Steve and Rose Butler, Francesca Becker, Paul and Lynn Weaver, Diane Halpern, Don Carpentier, Peggy Flavin, and "the buds" Roger Pheulpin and Hollis Brodrick.

To my friend Marc, a heartfelt thank you for his presence while I was working on this project. Finally—and foremost—I thank my daughter Lily for her patience during our visits to shops and shows, for fixing our Internet connection when all other technical assistance failed, and for being the most luminous person I know.

❋

Gladys Montgomery is a writer who specializes in travel and in historic architecture, period interiors, and antiques. Her work appears regularly in national and regional magazines. Her previous books include *Mountain & High Desert Hideaways* and *E. Masferré: Peoples of the Philippine Cordillera, Photographs 1934-1956,* which won a Philippine National Book Award. She lives in West Stockbridge, Massachusetts.